THE MAPS
OF FIRST BULL RUN

*An Atlas of the First Bull Run
(Manassas) Campaign, Including the Battle of
Ball's Bluff, June - October 1861*

*To David Hofstadter,

With Warmest regards to a fellow
Civil War enthusiast.

Bradley M. Gottfried

July 12, 2011*

Bradley M. Gottfried

SB

Savas Beatie

New York and California

Cataloging-in-Publication Data is available from the Library of Congress.

ISBN-13: 978-1-932714-60-9

10 9 8 7 6 5 4 3 2
First Edition, First Printing

SB
Published by
Savas Beatie LLC
521 Fifth Avenue, Suite 3400
New York, NY 10175

Editorial Offices:

Savas Beatie LLC
P.O. Box 4527
El Dorado Hills, CA 95762
Phone: 916-941-6896
(E-mail) editorial@savasbeatie.com

Savas Beatie titles are available at special discounts for bulk purchases in the United States by corporations, institutions, and other organizations. For more details, please contact Special Sales, P.O. Box 4527, El Dorado Hills, CA 95762. You may also e-mail us at sales@savasbeatie.com, or click over for a visit to our website at www.savasbeatie.com for additional information.

For Bryan

Contents

Contents

Matthews Hill Fight

Henry Hill Fight

Contents

Chinn Ridge

Blackburn's Ford

The Federal Retreat

Part 2: August—September 1861

Contents

Part 3: Ball's Bluff

Introduction

The Civil War in general (and Gettysburg in particular) has long been the subject of deep interest and study for me. Over the years I have researched and written several books on the Gettysburg campaign, including *The Roads to Gettysburg, The Brigades of Gettysburg,* and *The Artillery of Gettysburg.* The completion of *The Maps of Gettysburg* (2006)—the first book in what would become the bedrock of the Savas Beatie Military Atlas Series—left me at something of a crossroads: do I continue my Gettysburg studies or strike out in a new direction? Based upon the heavy feedback I have received, I decided to strike out on the latter course.

According to many readers of *The Maps of Gettysburg,* that book's unique approach helped them gain a better understanding of campaign and battle than had more traditional approaches—even though they had studied it for many years and visited the field. "Your book," my publisher and I often heard, "helped unlock all the other Gettysburg titles I had in my library, and now I use your *Maps* book when I read the others." Comments like that are both humbling and deeply appreciated. From my own experience, I can understand how original maps placed opposite the text describing them can be helpful. Like nearly everyone who reads military history, even the most basic troop movements are difficult to follow and visualize without a good map.

Based upon the positive feedback and success of *The Maps of Gettysburg,* I decided to put aside my Gettysburg explorations for a more ambitious journey that will, with a little luck and a lot of work, document the campaigns of the Civil War's Eastern Theater. The volume you now hold in your hands is the result of that decision. Although I do not intend to put the volumes out in chronological order, my goal is to eventually complete the series with books spanning from First Bull Run/Manassas to Appomattox. Having produced two books for the series, I am keenly aware that this process will take me many, many years to complete. While the task is daunting, meaningful journeys begin one step at a time, or in this case, one map at a time.

The Maps of First Bull Run: An Atlas of the First Bull Run (Manassas) Campaign, including the Battle of Ball's Bluff, June – October 1861 takes a different approach on two levels. First, its neutral coverage includes the entire campaign from both points of view. The text and maps travel with the armies from the opening steps of the campaign in the weeks before the actual fighting to the battlefield on the plains of Manassas in north-central Virginia. Coverage continues through the skirmishing at Blackburn's Ford, the day-long fighting on July 21, and the collapse and retreat of the Federal army, and Confederate pursuit. My purpose is to offer a broad and full understanding of the complete First Bull Run/Manassas campaign, rather than a micro-history of one aspect of the campaign or one sector of the battle.

Second, *The Maps of First Bull Run* dissects the actions within each sector of the battlefield for a deeper and hopefully more meaningful experience. Each section of this book includes a number of text and map combinations. Every left-hand page includes descriptive text corresponding with a facing right-hand page original map. An added advantage of this arrangement is that it eliminates the need to flip through the book to try to find a map to match the text. Wherever possible, I utilized relevant firsthand accounts to personalize the otherwise straightforward text.

To my knowledge, no single source until now has pulled together the movements and events of the war's first major campaign and offered them in a cartographic form side-by-side with reasonably detailed text complete with end notes. I hope readers find this method of presentation useful. Newcomers to First Bull Run/Manassas should find the plentiful maps and sectioned coverage easy to follow and understand. The various map sections may also trigger a special interest and so pry open avenues for additional study. I am optimistic that readers who approach the subject with a higher level of expertise will find the maps and text not only interesting to study and read, but helpful. If someone, somewhere, places this book within reach to refer to it now and again as a reference guide, the long hours invested in this project will have been worthwhile.

The Maps of First Bull Run is not the last word or definitive treatment of this campaign, the main battle of July 21, or any part thereof—and I did not intend it to be so. Given space and time considerations, I decided to cover the major events of the campaign and battle, the retreat, pursuit, and reorganization of the Federal army, and follow that up with operations that fall, including the skirmish at Lewinsville (September 11, 1861) and the mini-campaign of Ball's Bluff (mid-October 1861). Original research was kept to a minimum. My primary reliance was upon firsthand accounts, battle reports, various other official records, and quality secondary scholarship. I am also very familiar with the entire battlefield, having walked it many times. Therefore, you should not expect to find any groundbreaking revelations within these pages (although you find a few new theories or twists on various movements, personalities, and reasons why the battle unfolded as it did).

Whenever a book uses short chapters or sections, as this one does, there will inevitably be some narrative redundancy. As far as possible, I have endeavored to minimize those occurrences. I am also keenly aware that the Civil War is a very hot topic of debate in many circles, and even relatively bland observations can spark rancorous discourse. And of course, the sources themselves can and usually do conflict on many points, including numbers engaged and casualties. I have tried to follow a generally accepted interpretation of the campaign and battle, and (I hope with some success) portray the information accurately and with an even hand.

Inevitably, a study like this makes it likely that mistakes of one variety or another have slipped into the text (or on a map) despite endless hours of proofreading. I apologize in advance for any errors and assume full responsibility for them.

Acknowledgments

Many people contributed to this volume. First and foremost is my editor and friend Theodore P. Savas. You will rarely meet a person who is more fun, diligent, and supportive than Ted and his staff at Savas Beatie. Marketing Director Sarah Keeney works hard to garner publicity and I deeply appreciate her ongoing efforts. I was blessed to work with three experts: James Burgess, Museum Specialist at the Manassas National Military Park, James Morgan, author of *A Little Short of Boats: The Fights at Ball's Bluff and Edwards Ferry*, and Harry Smeltzer, whose website "Bull Runnings" contains a wealth of information on everything related to First Bull Run. If you have not visited it, I highly recommend you do so: www.bullrunnings.wordpress.com/. Each reviewed the manuscript for accuracy and provided many useful suggestions, corrected embarrassing mistakes, and pondered a host of questions raised by the sources. Any errors that remain are mine and mine alone.

R. L. Murray generously provided me with copies of his many books. They are a gold mine of information and I deeply appreciate his support. Mr. Murray has published two books on New Yorkers at First Bull Run and they were very helpful in gaining a better understanding of their role in the battle.

Linda Nieman, who helped me learn and perfect my map making skills, was a constant source of inspiration. I deeply appreciate her support.

Now, on to the Maryland Campaign!

Bradley M. Gottfried
La Plata, Maryland

THE MAPS
OF FIRST BULL RUN

An Atlas of the First Bull Run
(Manassas) Campaign, Including the Battle of
Ball's Bluff, June – October 1861

Map 1: The Armies Face Off Near Washington (June, 1861)

On May 26, Maj. Gen. George McClellan launched a campaign into western Virginia (now West Virginia) to protect the Baltimore & Ohio Railroad and aid pro-Union sympathizers there. Federal troops occupied Newport News, and gunboats attacked the Confederate batteries on Aquia Creek. On May 28, Brig. Gen. Irvin McDowell assumed command of the Department of Northeastern Virginia. Three days later, Brig. Gen. P. G. T. Beauregard was put in charge of the "Alexandria Line," which effectively placed all Confederate troops in northern Virginia under his command.

A mini-war had broken out along the Potomac River and Chesapeake Bay. Elements of McDowell's Federal Army of Northeastern Virginia and Beauregard's Confederate Army of the Potomac skirmished outside Washington, D.C. A small Federal cavalry force left the defenses around Washington on the last day of May and advanced through Fairfax Court House, skirmishing with Confederate infantry and cavalry the following day before falling back. On June 10, some 3,000 Federals ventured out from Fortress Monroe to attack a smaller detachment of some 1,200 Confederates stationed at Little and Big Bethel, Virginia. After a confused hour-long engagement, mostly fought at Big Bethel Church, the Federals retired.[1]

The flow of troops from Washington to McDowell's army was initially slow, possibly because of the ill-will between McDowell and Lt. Gen. Winfield Scott, commander-in-chief of the Federal armies. The mass of regiments camped in and around Arlington and Alexandria began to jell into something resembling an army with the formation of brigades in June and July. On June 26, Gen. McDowell counted nearly 14,000 men present for duty in five brigades. That number doubled in the next few weeks, with McDowell now able to organize his brigades into five divisions. The First Division, composed of brigades led by Robert Schenck, William Sherman, and Israel Richardson, was given to Brig. Gen. Daniel Tyler. Col. David Hunter took command of the Second division, composed of Andrew Porter's and Ambrose Burnside's brigades. Col. Samuel Heintzelman assumed command of the Third division, composed of the brigades of William Franklin, Orlando Willcox, and Oliver Howard. The Fourth division was composed of New Jersey militia and volunteers commanded by Brig. Gen. Theodore Runyon. Louis Blenker's and Thomas Davies' brigades comprised the Fifth Division under Col. Dixon Miles' command.[2]

With almost 15,000 men at his disposal, Gen. Beauregard organized his Confederate Army of the Potomac into six brigades. The First was led by Brig. Gen. Milledge Bonham; the Second by Brig. Gen. Richard Ewell; the Third by Brig. Gen. David R. Jones; the Fourth by Col. George Terrett; the Fifth by Col. P. St. George Cocke; and the Sixth by Col. Jubal Early. Terrett would hold his command a mere two weeks before being replaced by Brig. Gen. James Longstreet. Beauregard did not organize these brigades into divisions.[3]

As events heated up along the Potomac, Gen. Joseph Johnston was training and organizing his 8,000-man Confederate army in the Shenandoah Valley. His force was composed of a hodge-podge of troops from Virginia, Mississippi, Alabama, Maryland, and even Kentucky. Like the commanders of the other armies, Johnston spent much of each day trying to transform civilians into soldiers. His job was made more difficult by the scarcity of equipment.

Maj. Gen. Robert Patterson, a former Regular Army officer with close ties to Gen. Scott, was given command of the Department of Pennsylvania in late April. A month later, the immediate threat to Washington having subsided, Patterson was ordered to transfer his headquarters and troops to Chambersburg, Pennsylvania. Ultimately, Patterson would leave the friendly confines of the Keystone State to march into Maryland to capture Frederick, Hagerstown, and Cumberland. His next move was against the logistical center at Harpers Ferry, which would put his army in direct contact with Joe Johnston's Confederates.[4]

Patterson's army was an unusual one. It was composed of almost entirely Pennsylvania militia regiments, and there were no West Point-trained officers at the regimental level. A high percentage of his officers had fought in the Mexican War.[5]

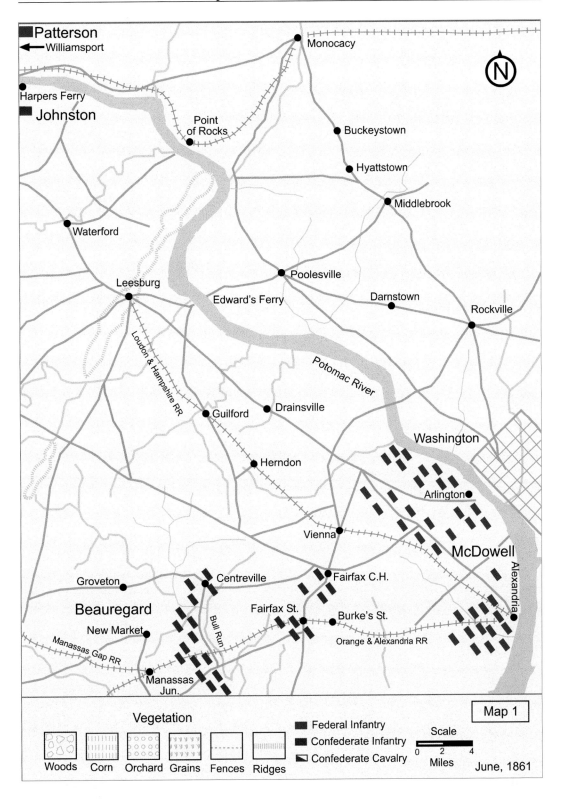

Patterson
← Williamsport
Monocacy
N

Harpers Ferry
Johnston
Point of Rocks
Buckeystown
Hyattstown
Middlebrook

Waterford
Poolesville
Darnstown
Leesburg
Edward's Ferry
Rockville

Loudon & Hampshire RR

Potomac River

Guilford
Drainsville
Washington
Herndon
Arlington

Vienna
McDowell

Groveton
Centreville
Fairfax C.H.
Beauregard
Fairfax St.
Burke's St.
New Market
Bull Run
Orange & Alexandria RR
Manassas Gap RR
Manassas Jun.
Alexandria

Vegetation

Woods   Corn   Orchard   Grains   Fences   Ridges

Federal Infantry
Confederate Infantry
Confederate Cavalry

Scale
0   2   4
Miles

Map 1

June, 1861

Map 2: The Armies Grow in Size (June & July, 1861)

The first major campaign was driven by the theory that the war would be won if the opposing capital could be captured. With the growing host of Federal troops descending on Washington, it appeared that the South would, by necessity, be thrown into a defensive mode. Beauregard, however, proposed an ambitious offensive to Confederate President Jefferson Davis. His plan called for combining his army with Gen. Johnston's near Harpers Ferry and attacking Patterson's smaller command. With Patterson's army defeated, the Confederates would then move east and fall upon McDowell, whose defeat would leave Washington exposed to capture. Davis rejected the idea. With Beauregard forced on the defensive, the initiative fell to McDowell as to when and where he would launch his growing army against the Confederates in northern Virginia. In order to do so, however, McDowell would need Gen. Patterson to hold Johnston's Confederate army in the Shenandoah Valley.

Beauregard spent considerable time examining the terrain south of Centreville. His engineering background helped him quickly discern that this area, bisected by a creek called Bull Run, offered outstanding defensive positions. The deep waterway was largely impassible except at a handful of fords, behind which Beauregard could concentrate his men. By the end of June , Beauregard had three of his five brigades aligned behind Bull Run. The other two brigades, Bonham's at Fairfax Court House and Ewell's at Fairfax Station, occupied advanced positions on the east side of the creek.[1]

Skirmishes between the two opposing armies grew in frequency with each passing week. In an effort to test Confederate strength and repair and guard the railroad, McDowell on June 17 sent about 700 men from the 1st Ohio (Schenck's brigade) toward Vienna on the Loudoun & Hampshire Railroad. Elements from Bonham's Brigade quickly put an end to the excursion.[2]

Once he left Pennsylvania, Patterson intended to sweep through Maryland during the first week of June, cross the Potomac River at Williamsport, and capture Harpers Ferry. He did not finish organizing his army until June 11, however, and it was not until June 15 that his campaign actually began. An old officer with some experience leading men in battle in Mexico, Patterson overestimated the size of his adversary's army and claimed that he lacked the wagons and horses to mount an expeditious advance. Patterson waved off frequent rumors that Johnston had (or was about to) evacuate Harpers Ferry. To his way of thinking, Johnston would never give up the town without a fight. The rumors, however, were true. Johnston knew he did not have enough men to defend the heights ringing the town. When he learned of Patterson's pending advance, he moved his wagons and supplies south toward Winchester on June 13, with his men following two days later. Patterson occupied Harpers Ferry without incident on June 16.[3]

Gens. McDowell and Scott met with President Lincoln (the primary mover behind the operation) and his cabinet on June 29 to discuss plans for an advance against Manassas Junction. The operation would involve some 30,000 Federals, with another 10,000 held in reserve. The plan called for Tyler's large division, on McDowell's right flank, to march south by way of Vienna and cut between Centreville and Fairfax Court House, where it would join the middle column under Col. Hunter on the Little River Turnpike. This movement would cut off Bonham's Brigade at Fairfax Court House. McDowell's left column comprised of Heintzelman's division, meanwhile, would march along the Orange and Alexandria Railroad and eventually meet the other two Federal columns somewhere north of Bull Run. The overall objective of these movements was to turn Beauregard's right flank, and so avoid assaulting the heavily defended fords along Bull Run. The details still needed to be worked out, but the basic strategy was sound. No one raised serious doubts about the plan, but Gen. Charles Sandford was pessimistic about Patterson's ability to hold Johnston in the Shenandoah Valley. The campaign was slated to begin on July 8, but McDowell's army was not ready by that day. The men moved out about 2:00 p.m. on July 16.[4]

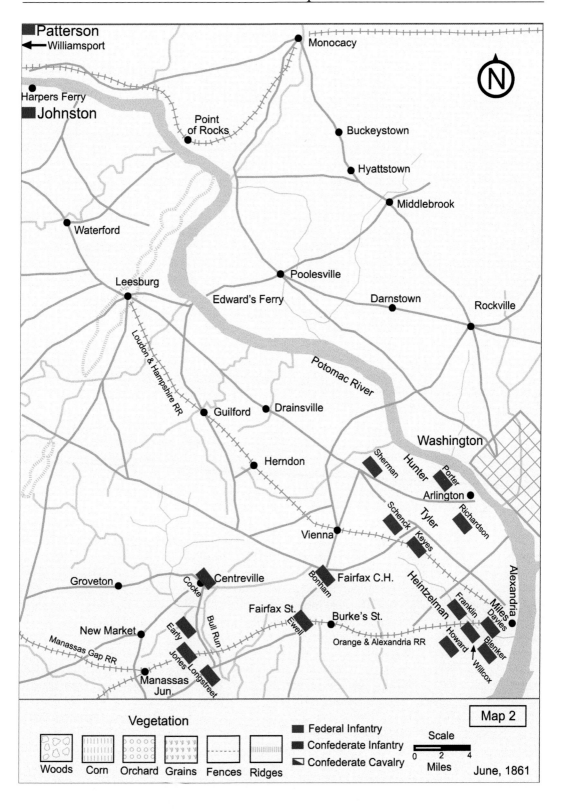

Patterson

← Williamsport

Monocacy

N

Harpers Ferry

Johnston

Point of Rocks

Buckeystown

Hyattstown

Middlebrook

Waterford

Leesburg

Poolesville

Edward's Ferry

Darnstown

Rockville

Loudon & Hampshire RR

Potomac River

Guilford   Drainsville

Washington

Herndon

Sherman   Hunter

Porter

Arlington

Schenck   Tyler   Richardson

Vienna   Keyes

Groveton   Cocke   Centreville   Bonham   Fairfax C.H.   Heintzelman   Alexandria

Fairfax St.   Franklin   Miles
Davies

New Market   Early   Bull Run   Ewell   Burke's St.   Howard   Blenker

Manassas Gap RR   Jones   Longstreet   Orange & Alexandria RR   Willcox

Manassas Jun.

Vegetation

Woods   Corn   Orchard   Grains   Fences   Ridges

■ Federal Infantry
■ Confederate Infantry
◣ Confederate Cavalry

Map 2

Scale

0   2   4
Miles

June, 1861

Map 3: Patterson's Army Crosses the Potomac (June 18-July 3)

When George Cadwalader's division crossed the Potomac River on June 16 at Williamsport, Maryland, north of Harpers Ferry without opposition, Gen. Patterson finally accepted the fact that Johnston had abandoned the place. Patterson began planning his next move, but his slow pace did not sit well with his superiors. Sitting in his office in Washington, Gen. Scott made a fateful decision: if Patterson did not move at once against Johnston, he would have to consider a command change. Scott fired off a dispatch ordering Patterson to send his Regular Army units (mostly artillery) to McDowell, along with a Rhode Island regiment under Col. Ambrose Burnside. Patterson vigorously protested, to no avail. Scott ended the discussion with a telegram: "We are pressed here. Send the troops that I have twice called for without delay." Patterson complied. Scott was now convinced the major thrust against the Confederacy in Virginia must be delivered by McDowell.

The following day, Patterson received word that Johnston was approaching Harpers Ferry with an army that far exceeded his own. While untrue, the loss of his Regulars made Patterson even more hesitant and indecisive than usual. Without consulting Scott—whom he now considered unsympathetic to his army's needs—Patterson on June 18 withdrew his command to the opposite side of the Potomac River at Williamsport. The withdrawal angered Scott, who immediately ordered Patterson back across the river. In another duel of wills, Patterson declined. He refused a second time on June 20. At one point during the exchange Patterson wired Scott that Johnston's army numbered more than 25,000 men. Patterson's adamant insistence that he was heavily outnumbered had the desired effect, and on June 25 Scott ordered Patterson to stay put.[1]

On June 28, Patterson's army numbered about 14,000 men. It was organized into five brigades divided among two divisions, one under Maj. Gen. George Cadwalader and the other under Maj. Gen. William H. Keim. Gen. Johnston's smaller Confederate army fielded fewer than 11,000 men in four brigades commanded by Brig. Gens. Barnard Bee, Thomas Jackson, and Kirby Smith, and Col. Arnold Elzey. Johnston was fortunate to have Col. James Ewell Brown (Jeb) Stuart and his 1st Virginia Cavalry. An additional infantry brigade of Georgians under Col. Francis Bartow would be added later.[2]

Jackson's Brigade was detached from Johnston's army on June 19 and sent to Martinsburg to destroy a large supply of railroad equipment stored there. Jackson had his command on the road at 5:00 p.m. and the men marched through half the night. After a few hours of rest they were back in column at dawn. When they reached this staunchly Unionist town Jackson reported that there was time to move the equipment, but Johnston insisted on its destruction. Overruled, Jackson fired the equipment. This was but one of a growing number of incidents between the cautious Johnston and the more aggressive Jackson. The Virginians set to work, destroying 56 locomotives and tenders and 305 coal cars, firing round houses and machine shops, and ripping up miles of track.[3]

Gathering his forces, Patterson decided on June 30 to once again cross the Potomac at Williamsport the following day. The move did not begin until 4:00 a.m. on July 2. When he learned of the attempt, Jackson pondered Johnston's orders to retire if the enemy approached his front in force. He decided instead to send a regiment and a battery of artillery to Falling Waters to reconnoiter and possibly resist the movement. Although he managed to slow the crossing for a short time, the overwhelming size of the Federal army, coupled with Johnston's clear orders, resulted in Jackson's slow withdrawal.

Demonstrating glimpses of the aggressiveness that would be evident on future fields, Jackson called up two more regiments and, together with Stuart's cavalry, tried to cut off a column of Federal troops. When three Federal regiments were found in his front and an enemy brigade began to creep around his flank, however, Jackson wisely withdrew to Darksville on the road to Winchester, where he combined with the rest of Johnston's army about dawn on July 3.[4]

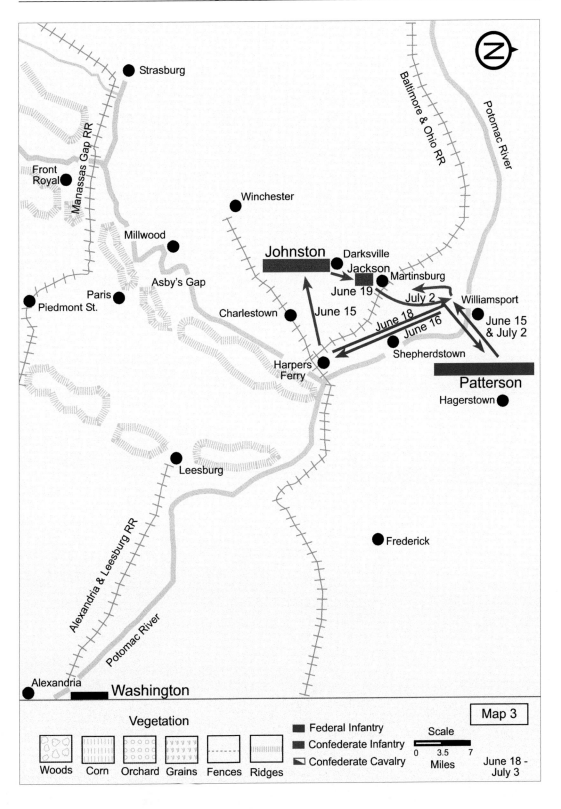

Strasburg

Baltimore & Ohio RR

Potomac River

Manassas Gap RR

Front Royal

Winchester

Millwood

Johnston   Darksville

Jackson

Martinsburg

Asby's Gap

June 19   July 2   Williamsport

Paris
Piedmont St.

Charlestown   June 15   June 18   June 15 & July 2

June 16

Shepherdstown

Harpers Ferry

Patterson

Hagerstown

Leesburg

Alexandria & Leesburg RR

Frederick

Potomac River

Alexandria   Washington

Vegetation

Woods   Corn   Orchard   Grains   Fences   Ridges

■ Federal Infantry
■ Confederate Infantry
◩ Confederate Cavalry

Scale
0   3.5   7
Miles

Map 3

June 18 -
July 3

Map 4: Johnston's Army Leaves Shenandoah Valley (July 7-19)

With Patterson's army advancing up (south) the Shenandoah Valley, Johnston developed plans to interfere with the move. Patterson proved uncooperative, however, when he decided to hole up at Martinsburg awaiting supplies before moving farther south. After waiting several days for Patterson to advance, Johnston gave up and pulled back to Winchester on July 7. Johnston did not think he had the strength to mount an attack against Patterson at Martinsburg, whose army he believed numbered in excess of 18,000 men. In fact it was much smaller (around 14,000).

Patterson was ready to launch his campaign against Johnston on July 8, but not before receiving a number of regiments from a variety of states to replace those units whose terms of enlistment were about to expire. Among the new officers were West Pointers, including George Thomas and John Abercrombie. Patterson's initial euphoria about his chances to hold Johnston's Confederates in the Valley while McDowell moved against Beauregard quickly evaporated, and his former cautious attitude returned when subordinates voiced concerns about moving against Johnston.

Patterson's temperament did not improve when he convinced himself that Johnston's army numbered more than 40,000 of all arms, when in reality it was about one-quarter that number. Patterson began moving south on July 15, but he made it only as far as Bunker Hill, a bit more than five miles from Martinsburg. A reconnaissance party launched the next day met up with Stuart's cavalry and obstructions across the road, and no further action or move south was undertaken. Believing that he had done enough to convince Johnston that he was planning to launch an attack, Patterson halted his advance.[1]

Patterson's officers once again counseled caution. In conjunction with their urging, the commanding Gen. decided to move east toward Charlestown, where the army could either attack Johnston or move toward Washington. The march got underway on July 17. When Gen. Scott protested the move, Patterson drafted orders to advance toward Winchester. Before moving, he consulted with his Pennsylvania troops, whose terms of enlistment were set to expire on the morning of July 18. To his dismay, most of the units refused to remain with the army—despite the fact that a major battle that might decide the fate of the nation was rapidly approaching. Patterson called off the movement to Winchester.[2]

Meanwhile, McDowell's move toward Manassas Junction spurred the Confederate high command in Richmond into action. Johnston received a wire at 1:00 a.m. on July 18 ordering him to unite with Beauregard's army aligned behind Bull Run creek. Before issuing orders, Johnston pondered what to do about Patterson's Federals. When word reached him that Patterson's men were still in their camps as of 9:00 a.m. that morning, Johnston moved to act upon his orders. The men in the ranks were unaware of where they were headed or why. When orders were received to pack up their gear and break camp, they expected a march north toward Patterson's army. When they marched southeast toward the Blue Ridge Mountains, rumors about their ultimate destination spread like wildfire through the ranks. Jackson's Brigade led the army and its commander set a blistering pace. After a brisk march of ninety minutes, he stopped his men so a communication from Johnston could be read: "Gen. Beauregard is being attacked by overwhelming forces. . . . Every moment now is precious, and the Gen. hopes that his soldiers will step out and keep closed, for this march is a forced march to save the country." The men responded with cheers, for they were anxious to engage the enemy. Many worried they would not have an opportunity to fight before the war came to a close.[3]

Jackson marched to Millwood near the Shenandoah River. His men waded the river after lunch and continued through Ashby's Gap to the hamlet of Paris, which they reached at 2:00 a.m. on July 19. Jackson halted here and allowed the men to sleep for a few hours while he personally stood guard over them. Johnston's other brigades—Bartow's, Bee's, Smith's, and Elzey's—followed Jackson in that order. The head of Jackson's column reached Piedmont Station on the Manassas Gap Railroad line about 6:00 a.m. on July 19. Not yet hardened by war and hard marching, the exhausted men devoured breakfast while their officers rounded up rail cars to haul them to Manassas Junction.[4]

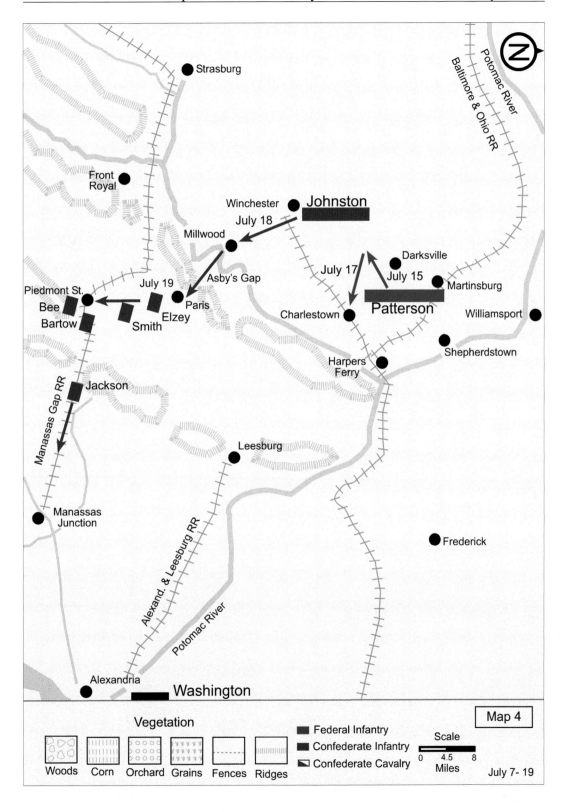

Map 4

Vegetation

Woods   Corn   Orchard   Grains   Fences   Ridges

■ Federal Infantry
■ Confederate Infantry
◤ Confederate Cavalry

Scale

0   4.5   8
Miles

July 7- 19

Map 5: McDowell's Army Begins Marching to Bull Run (July 17-18)

After much planning and debate, Gen. McDowell's march toward Confederate-held Manassas Junction got underway on July 16. The first day's march by the green troops was fairly easy, a short five-mile hike beginning at 2:00 p.m. One modern historian called the marching orders "as explicit as any this war would see." Gen. Tyler's division, on McDowell's right, marched the short distance to Vienna. Col. Hunter led his division in the center of the army along Columbia Pike to Little River Turnpike, just south east of Annandale. The left division under Gen. Heintzelman had the longest march. It would tramp along Old Fairfax Road, cross Accotink Creek, and camp just across Pohick Run. Col. Miles' division, tapped as the army's reserve, marched along Little River Turnpike and camped at Annandale. The march was unopposed except for some light firing by retreating Confederate vedettes who had thrown up obstructions across the roads.[1]

July 17 witnessed the first day of real marching. In addition to continuing the march toward Centreville, trapping and destroying Gen. Bonham's Confederate brigade at Fairfax Court House was another goal. Tyler moved his division south from Vienna toward Germantown. His soldiers frequently scurried out off the road to forage, despite their officers' efforts to prevent it. It took seven hours to march seven miles to Germantown. Trapping Bonham was easier sketched on a map than achieved in the flesh. The Confederate had orders to vacate Fairfax Court House if he was approached by a superior Federal force, so when Tyler approached Bonham pulled his men back toward Gen. Beaurgard's main army. First, however, his men fired several buildings. When Tyler entered Germantown, he found many houses there ablaze; his own men had continued the earlier efforts of the enemy. The other two forward Confederate brigades under Col. Cocke and Gen. Ewell also fell back. Tyler's slow march continued, halting for the night midway between Germantown and Centreville.[2]

Hunter's division in the middle of McDowell's advancing line also moved slowly on July 17 along the Little River Turnpike and entered Fairfax Court House, where some of its soldiers also contributed to the arson begun by Bonham's men. Miles' division, formerly situated behind Hunter's division, initially made better time by marching south along Braddock Road. However, it quickly encountered obstructions that impeded its progress. The march ended about one-half mile south of Fairfax Court House.[3]

Heintzelman's division began its march on July 17 on the west bank of Pohick Run. Willcox's and Howard's brigades pushed on to Sangster's Station on the Alexandria and Orange Railroad, while Franklin's brigade moved north toward Fairfax Court House to try and round up some fleeing Confederates, and then south, spending the night at Fairfax Station.[4]

The large scale advance of McDowell's Army of Northeastern Virginia was plagued by the inexperience of the troops, the hot dry conditions, and the lack of effective cavalry to scout in front of the army. The embarrassment of Gen. Robert Schenck and his men in "the Vienna affair" one month earlier on June 17 may or may not have been on McDowell's mind, but he must have been cognizant that marching southward on four separate roads carried inherent risk. The army commander instructed Tyler to attack Centreville at first light on July 18. Unable to get precise information on Heintzelman's position that morning, McDowell undertook his own reconnaissance (his chief engineer George Barnard declined to accompany him!) and rode along the road to Sangster's Station. McDowell soon realized that "the roads were too narrow and crooked for so large a body to move over." This convinced him to change his plans. He would now concentrate his army and turn the Confederate left instead of the right. McDowell returned to his headquarters around midday and issued orders to his division commanders. Their destination was now Centreville. Heintzelman's division would march northeast from Sangster's Station to where Little Rocky Run crossed the Warrenton Turnpike. This would put the division about one mile south of Centreville. Hunter would continue his westward march, halting as close to Centreville as he could. The same was true of Miles, marching on Braddock Road. Tyler, meanwhile, would take the town and march beyond it toward Gainesville.[5]

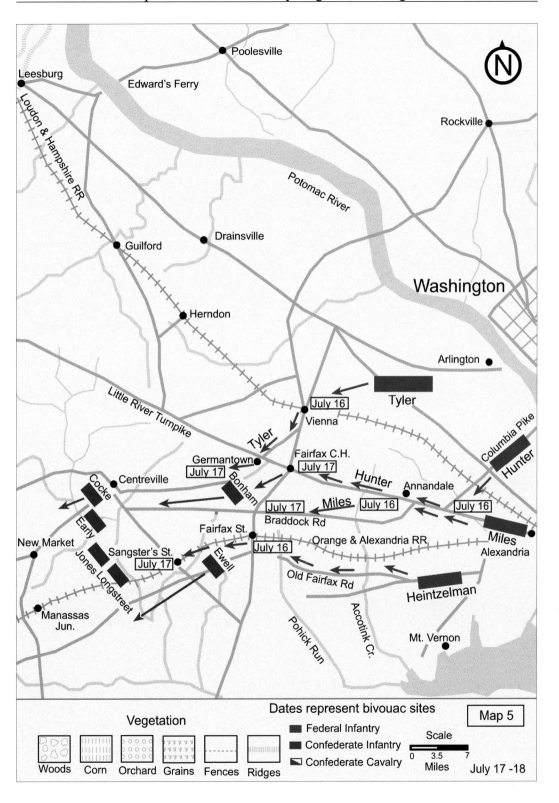

Poolesville

Leesburg

Edward's Ferry

Loudon & Hampshire RR

Rockville

Potomac River

Drainsville

Guilford

Washington

Herndon

Arlington

Little River Turnpike

Tyler

July 16

Tyler

Vienna

Columbia Pike

Hunter

Germantown

Fairfax C.H.

July 17

Centreville

July 17

Bonham

Hunter

Annandale

Cocke

July 17

Miles

July 16

July 16

Braddock Rd

Early

New Market

Fairfax St.

Orange & Alexandria RR

Miles

Jones Longstreet

Sangster's St.

July 17

Ewell

July 16

Alexandria

Old Fairfax Rd

Manassas
Jun.

Heintzelman

Accotink Cr.

Mt. Vernon

Pohick Run

Vegetation

Woods   Corn   Orchard   Grains   Fences   Ridges

Dates represent bivouac sites

■ Federal Infantry
■ Confederate Infantry
◨ Confederate Cavalry

Map 5

Scale

0   3.5   7
Miles

July 17 -18

Map 6: The Confederate Positions Behind Bull Run (July 16-20)

The increasing aggressiveness of the Federal troops in front of Washington, coupled (perhaps) with information from Mrs. Rose Greenhow, a Southern sympathizer living in the capital, suggested to Gen. Beauregard that a full-scale advance was in the offing. Believing that Gen. McDowell's move would begin on July 16, Beauregard pulled his advanced troops back behind Bull Run. Gen. Ewell slipped back to Union Mills Ford after burning the bridge over the nearby Orange and Alexandria Railroad. Col. Cocke left Centreville and retired behind Bull Run, where he was well positioned to defend Ball, Island, and Lewis fords. Gen. Bonham's Brigade had orders to remain at Fairfax Court House until the enemy approached; it fell back on July 17. By the morning of July 18, Beauregard's army was behind Bull Run. It occupied a six-mile front stretching from Union Mills Ford on the right to the Stone Bridge across Warrenton Turnpike on the left.[1]

Believing that McDowell would take the tactical offensive and strike his right flank at Mitchell's Ford, Beauregard strengthened that part of his line by ordering Bonham's Brigade to take up a position to defend the crossing. Gen. James Longstreet's Brigade straddled a large northward bulge in Bull Run near Blackburn's Ford, about one-half mile to the right of Bonham's position. Beauregard's orders were imprecise and subject to subjective interpretation. When he heard gunfire signaling the arrival of the Federal troops, Longstreet was to cross the creek to reunite his brigade and attack the advancing Federal left flank as it moved against Bonham. Gen. Jones' Brigade, camped along the Orange and Alexandria Railroad between Manassas Junction and Bull Run, would march quickly to McLean's Ford, southeast of Blackburn's Ford, cross the creek, and fall upon the Federal flank and rear on the road to Centreville. Ewell and Cocke, meanwhile, would leave their positions and advance to Centreville to strike the Federal rear. Jubal Early's Brigade, meanwhile, would function as a mobile reserve, occupying the area between McLean's and Blackburn's fords. As a

recent historian put it, "like all of Beauregard's plans, it was hastily concocted and an ill-conceived notion that depended entirely upon McDowell doing exactly as the Confederates expected him to do."[2]

Knowing that he was outnumbered, Beauregard continued to request reinforcements. Brigadier Gen. Theophilus Holmes had orders to march with his small 1,300-man brigade to Manassas Junction should Beauregard request him. When the latter did just that on the afternoon of July 18, the 2nd Tennessee, 1st Arkansas, and Walker's battery marched quickly to Beauregard's aid, reaching their destination on the morning of July 20. The Creole Gen. positioned the troops in reserve near Ewell's Brigade on the right side of the Confederate line. The 5th North Carolina and 13th Mississippi were also sent forward. The former was added to Longstreet's Brigade, and the latter to Early's. Hampton's Legion, organized and supplied by wealthy South Carolina plantation owner Wade Hampton, also moved forward. Its infantry rode the train from Richmond, while its cavalry and artillery traveled by road.[3]

While these troops helped bolster Beauregard's attenuated line, his primary concern rested with the timely arrival of Joe Johnston's small army from the Shenandoah Valley. His roughly 10,000 men could make the difference between victory and defeat, and both generals knew it. If they were going to have an impact, however, they would have to move soon. A telegram to Johnston arrived at his headquarters at 1:00 a.m. on July 18 summoning him to join Beauregard's army. When he confirmed that Gen. Robert Patterson's army had not budged from Charlestown, Johnston put his own army in motion toward Piedmont Station on the Manassas Gap Railroad. Gen. Thomas Jackson had his brigade on the road first and marched it relentlessly. Gen. Bartow's Brigade followed, with Gen. Bee's behind it. Johnston's remaining pair of brigades under Kirby Smith and Arnold Elzey were delayed; only the latter would arrive in time for the upcoming battle. Reaching Piedmont Station ahead of his men, Johnston began rounding up trains for the last leg of the trip to Manassas Junction.[4]

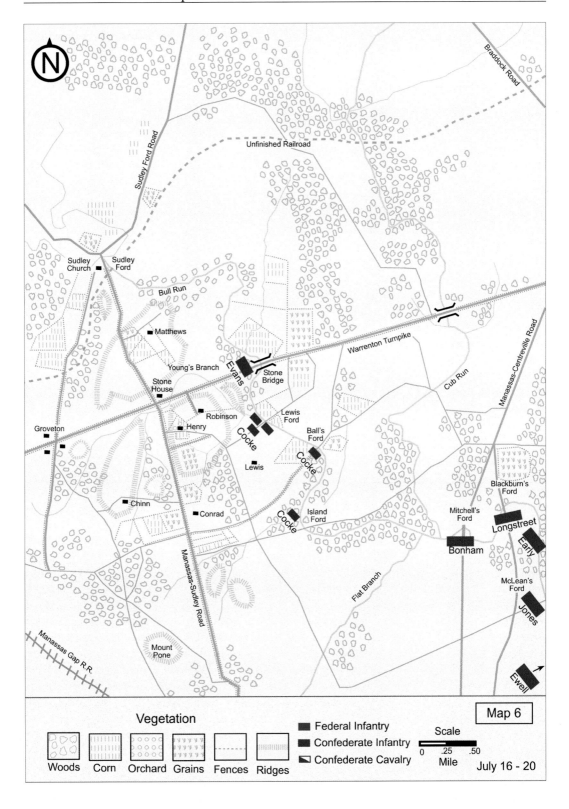

Braddock Road

N

Sudley Ford Road

Unfinished Railroad

Sudley
Church

Sudley
Ford

Bull Run

Matthews

Warrenton Turnpike

Cub Run

Manassas-Centreville Road

Young's Branch

Evans

Stone
Bridge

Stone
House

Robinson

Lewis
Ford

Cocke

Groveton

Henry

Ball's
Ford

Cocke

Lewis

Blackburn's
Ford

Chinn

Conrad

Cocke

Island
Ford

Mitchell's
Ford

Longstreet

Early

Bonham

Flat Branch

McLean's
Ford

Manassas-Sudley Road

Jones

Manassas Gap R.R.

Mount
Pone

Ewell

Vegetation

Woods   Corn   Orchard   Grains   Fences   Ridges

Federal Infantry
Confederate Infantry
Confederate Cavalry

Scale

0   .25   .50

Mile

Map 6

July 16 - 20

Skirmish at Blackburn's Ford

Map 7: The Federals Approach Blackburn's Ford (Noon, July 18)

Gen. Tyler ordered his Federal division forward to occupy Centerville shortly after 7:00 a.m. on July 18. Col. Richardson's brigade led the column. Tyler prudently threw out pickets to prevent an ambush, followed by a light infantry battalion under Captain Robert Brethschneider composed of forty men from each of Richardson's four regiments. The captain's command marched about one-half mile in front of the main column, supported by Lt. Benjamin's section (a pair of twenty-pounder rifled guns) of Lt. John Edwards' Battery G, 1st U.S. Richardson's men entered Centreville about 9:00 a.m. to find the town deserted: Cocke's rebels had hastily retreated the night before.[1]

Once he reached Centreville, Tyler was to watch the roads running to Bull Run and Warrenton and not bring on an engagement. However, when he learned from local residents that the enemy could not have gone far, Tyler continued marching south in direct violation of McDowell's orders. His men halted about one mile south of Centreville to fill their canteens. While they rested, Tyler suggested that Richardson accompany him on a reconnaissance toward Mitchell's Ford some two miles distant. The generals took Captain Brethschneider's men and three companies of the 1st Massachusetts with them, along with a squad of cavalry. The column moved south along the Manassas-Centreville Road. The Federals moved close enough to see that the ford was defended by what was estimated to be a brigade-strength command (Bonham's). Tyler shifted his march left (southeast) along an inconsequential farm lane leading to Blackburn's Ford. To the "astonished" Tyler, no enemy was visible defending the high ground behind the ford.[2]

In fact, the Confederates were there in strength: James Longstreet's Brigade was resting amongst the trees on the opposite side of the ford, with a well hidden skirmish line covering his front. Six companies of the 1st Virginia guarded the farm lane that crossed the creek at the ford, with the other four regiments waiting in reserve in the rear. The 17th Virginia was on the left of the 1st Virginia, with the 11th Virginia extending the line south by southwest along the curving creek. All told, these regiments totaled perhaps 1,200 men. A pair of guns from the Washington Artillery unlimbered behind and to the right of the 1st Virginia, but Longstreet did not have much confidence in the small six-pounders. Several other brigades in that sector were available for support, including Bonham's at Mitchell's Ford, Jones' at McLean's Ford, and Ewell's at Union Mills Ford farther to the right. The most readily accessible reserve was Jubal Early's Brigade, in position near the McLean house.[3]

While pondering his next move, an aide from McDowell's staff arrived to remind Tyler not to trigger a battle. The Gen. waved off the warning and ordered Benjamin's guns (long range twenty-pounders) to open fire about noon from near the Butler house. The guns fired down the road at Captain Delaware Kemper's Alexandria Artillery battery (outdated and short-range six-pounder pieces) situated north of Mitchell's Ford. Kemper's guns responded with six rounds, but all fell far short of Benjamin's guns. Kemper wisely ordered his Virginia battery back across the stream. Benjamin shifted his attention to the two small guns defending Blackburn's Ford. To Tyler's dismay, the artillery fire did not stir the Confederates enough to reveal themselves. Determined to press ahead, Tyler ordered Brethschneider's light battalion to force the issue (No. 1 on the map). A fresh battery under Captain Romeyn Ayres (Battery E, 3rd U.S., or Sherman's Battery, named after Thomas Sherman) arrived and dropped trail next to Benjamin's section near the Butler house. A second McDowell aide arrived to counsel caution, but Tyler ignored him as well. When Brethschneider's men tumbled back from the woods lining the creek, Tyler advanced three companies of the gray-clothed 1st Massachusetts (No. 2 on map). Some of Longstreet's men fell back, believing the Massachusetts men numbered in the thousands. It took a mounted Longstreet with an unsheathed sword to get the green soldiers back into line. As the Federals approached Blackburn's Ford, the hidden Confederate infantry opened fire, killing and wounding many of the attackers. The Bay Staters held their ground and returned the fire.[4]

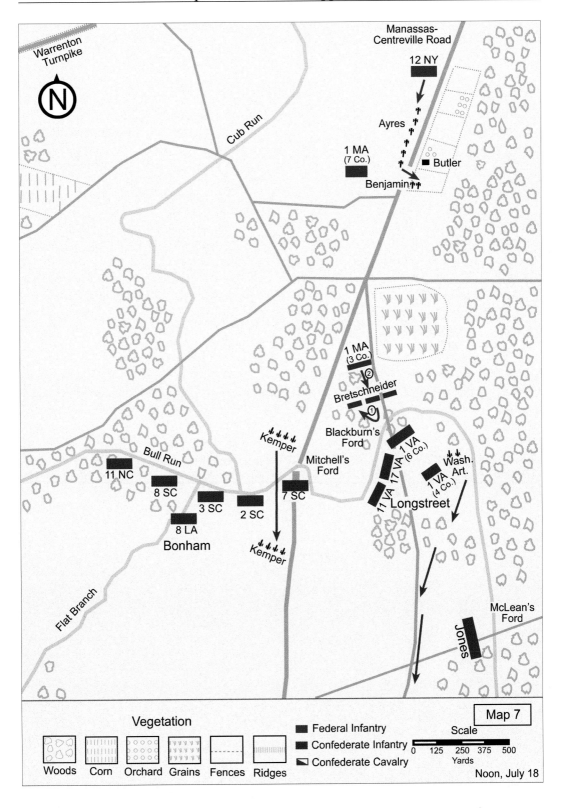

Manassas-
Centreville Road

12 NY

Ayres

1 MA
(7 Co.)

Butler

Benjamin

Warrenton
Turnpike

N

Cub Run

1 MA
(3 Co.)

Bretschneider

Blackburn's
Ford

Kemper

Mitchell's
Ford

1 VA
1 VA
(6 Co.)

17 VA

Wash.
Art.

Bull Run

11 NC

8 SC

3 SC

2 SC

7 SC

11 VA

1 VA
(4 Co.)

Longstreet

8 LA

Bonham

Kemper

Flat Branch

McLean's
Ford

Jones

Vegetation

Woods   Corn   Orchard   Grains   Fences   Ridges

■ Federal Infantry
■ Confederate Infantry
◥ Confederate Cavalry

Map 7

Scale
0   125   250   375   500
Yards

Noon, July 18

16

Map 8: The Fight is Joined (12:30 – 2:00 p.m.)

The three advancing companies of the 1st Massachusetts, clothed entirely in gray uniforms, exchanged rounds with Gen. Longstreet's men in a tactical stalemate that lasted for about one hour (No. 1 on map). Frustrated by his inability to clear the Rebels away from the ford, Col. Richardson asked Gen. Tyler if he could bring up his entire brigade. To the dismay of Gen. McDowell's aides, Tyler consented. Richardson quickly prepared his men for action.

While Richardson gathered his remaining regiments, Tyler ordered two of Captain Ayres' howitzers forward to a position 500 yards from the ford to throw canister into the unseen enemy lurking beyond the creek (No. 2 on map). This was a perfect distance for these smoothbore guns, which Tyler hoped would develop the enemy's strength. The guns galloped into place, unlimbered, and opened fire. If the preliminary artillery fire was bad, close-in canister was almost unbearable to the inexperienced Rebels. Longstreet's men threw themselves to the ground or hid behind trees in an effort to find protection from the shotgun-like explosions.[1]

Ayres' artillery was still firing when Richardson sent the balance of his brigade forward (No. 3 on map). Richardson guided his mount to the 12th New York on the left of his line and ordered it to prepare to attack the unseen enemy across Blackburn Ford. Richardson next rode to his right to ensure that the rest of the 1st Massachusetts, 2nd Michigan, and 3rd Michigan, in that order, were in position and ready to provide support when needed. It took about thirty minutes for the green New Yorkers to get into position, and when they finally stepped off, an array of sights and sounds bombarded their senses as they swept toward the creek. Ahead, they could see the three gray-clad companies of the 1st Massachusetts. Thinking they were the enemy, the New Yorkers raised their muskets, but cooler heads convinced the men to hold their fire. As the New Yorkers stepped forward, the devastation that had been wreaked on Ayres' pair of guns became obvious. The nearness of Ayres' pieces to the enemy exposed them to a heavy and accurate gunfire.

Every horse from one of the guns was down, as were a few of his men. Unable to hold his position, Captain Ayres ordered his remaining movable piece back to the relative safety of the Butler house. Another team of horses was dispatched to retrieve the abandoned gun.[2]

The pummeling of Ayres, coupled with the confused advance toward Blackburn Ford and stout Confederate defense, convinced Tyler it was time to pull back. When he rode to Col. Richardson, however, he learned to his dismay that the New Yorkers had already begun their advance and there was no viable way to recall them. Tyler's options at this point were limited: leave the New Yorkers to their fate, or advance the rest of his brigade into supporting distance and hope for the best. He decided upon the latter course.

Immature pine trees and intermittent brush broke up the New Yorkers' finely dressed lines until their view opened and the men saw not only Bull Run, but masses of Confederate infantrymen waiting to meet them. When the New Yorkers stepped out into the open, the Southern soldiers leveled their weapons and opened fire. According to a Federal soldier, "their first volley was the most murderous to us." With a potential disaster looming, the New Yorkers were ordered by their officers to lie down and open fire. Few if any had ever practiced loading their muskets in a prone position, however, so the rate of fire and accuracy was substantially reduced, and at least one man shot himself in the face.[3]

With a growing host of enemy soldiers gathering in front of him, Gen. Longstreet ordered up the four reserve companies of the 1st Virginia. He also called for additional reinforcements in the form of Gen. Jubal Early's Brigade and guns from the Washington Artillery located near the McLean house about one mile to the south. The two guns of the Washington Artillery that had retired from the ford when the Federal artillery opened fire also responded to the call for reinforcements. Early initially put his entire brigade on the road, but after a short distance an order arrived from Beauregard to send just two regiments. Early tapped the 7th Louisiana and 7th Virginia for the task and sent them at a quick pace toward Blackburn Ford.[4]

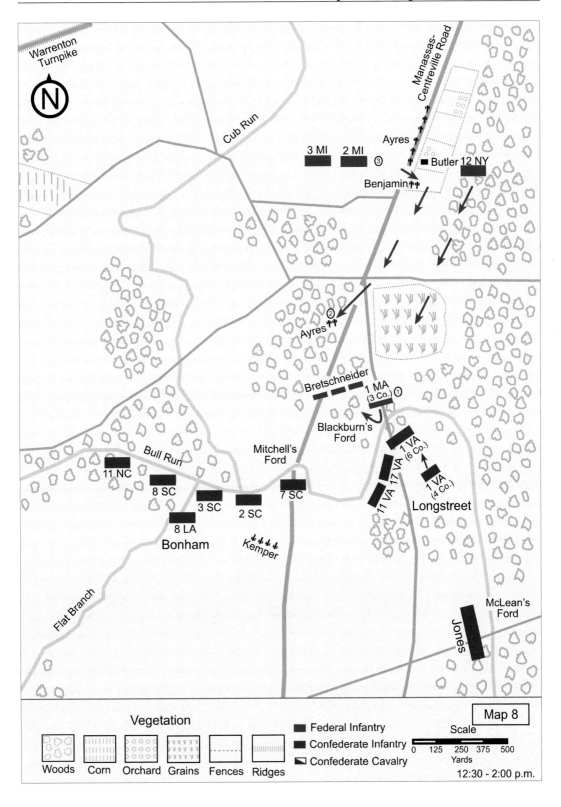

Warrenton Turnpike

Manassas-Centreville Road

Cub Run

N

3 MI   2 MI   ③

Ayres

Butler 12 NY

Benjamin

Ayres ②

Bretschneider

1 MA (3 Co.) ①

Blackburn's Ford

1 VA (6 Co.)

1 VA 17 VA

Mitchell's Ford

11 NC

Bull Run

8 SC

3 SC   2 SC   7 SC

11 VA

1 VA (4 Co.)

Longstreet

8 LA

Bonham   Kemper

Flat Branch

McLean's Ford

Jones

Vegetation

Woods   Corn   Orchard   Grains   Fences   Ridges

■ Federal Infantry
■ Confederate Infantry
◣ Confederate Cavalry

Map 8

Scale

0   125   250   375   500
Yards

12:30 - 2:00 p.m.

Map 9: Federal Defeat (2:00 – 3:00 p.m.)

Like the other two Federal advances against Longstreet's position, the thrust of the 12th New York quickly bogged down. Caught north of Blackburn's Ford, the regiment battled the mostly unseen Confederates for at least thirty minutes. Help was on the way for the New Yorkers in the form of the rest of Richardson's brigade, which moved up to provide support.

As the 1st Massachusetts prepared to enter the fighting in support of the New Yorkers, the 12th New York began heading for the rear. Some of the men claimed the regimental commander ordered a withdrawal; others said the order originated from company commanders. Either way, all but two companies of the 12th New York left the field. Their retreat exposed the left flank of the 1st Massachusetts (No. 1 on map). An alarmed Col. Richardson rode over to staunch the rearward flow, yelling, "What are you running for . . . there is no enemy here; I cannot see anybody at all!" Some of the fleeing men yelled back that the regiment had been destroyed. Troops from the 2nd and 3rd Michigan regiments, moving into battle on the right of the 1st Massachusetts, may not have known what was transpiring a few hundred yards to the left. Many thought they were so safe they broke ranks to pick ripe blackberries. Their naive and brief interlude abruptly ended when a smattering of small arms fire hissed through their ranks from the direction of Blackburn's Ford.[1]

Seeing the confusion within the enemy's ranks, Gen. Longstreet ordered his men across the creek in a counter-attack to drive Richardson's men away from the ford (No. 2 on map). The move did not go as smoothly as planned for all the regiments involved, with many units bunching up behind the ford. "The Fourth Brigade, in their drills . . . had not progressed as far as the passage of defiles," was how Longstreet explained it. Four companies of the 1st Virginia and some of the 17th Virginia managed to cross and engage Richardson's men, scooping up prisoners and outflanking the 1st Massachusetts. Jubal Early's 7th Virginia received a brisk fire from its left as it approached Bull Run. The Virginians returned fire, not knowing or perhaps not caring that many of Longstreet's men were in their front. Longstreet stopped the firing, but not before some of his men were hit. Worried about another Federal attack, another anxious volley from Early's rattled troops, and the exhausted condition of his men, Longstreet broke off the counterattack and ordered the men back across the creek.[2]

Longstreet was moving ahead with his counterattack when a distraught Richardson sent word to Tyler about the New Yorkers' shameful withdrawal. When Tyler arrived, Richardson asked for permission to rally the 12th New York and charge the ford with his three remaining regiments (1st Massachusetts, 2nd and 3rd Michigan). He also hoped that Col. William Sherman's brigade would arrive soon to provide weight to the renewed attack. Tyler, knowing that he had exceeded his orders, studied the creek and ford and proclaimed the fight over. He ordered Richardson to pull his men back to the Butler house and reform them behind the artillery. As for the 12th New York, Tyler added, "Let them go," for he knew the New Yorkers would eventually reform themselves. The visibly angry and upset Richardson turned to his regiments and "in a scornful sort of manner," told them to withdraw.[3]

Col. Sherman's brigade arrived a short time later and formed next to Richardson's men near the Butler house. This was about the same time Early's Brigade advanced to relieve Longstreet's men at the ford. The 7th Virginia replaced the 1st Virginia on the right side of the line, while the 7th Louisiana replaced the 17th Virginia (No. 3 on map). Six companies of the 24th Virginia arrived and formed on the left of the 7th Louisiana. Longstreet's 11th Virginia remained in its original position. The action at Blackburn's Ford ended when five Washington Artillery guns took up a position that triggered an artillery duel, which fitfully tapered into silence about 4:15 p.m. Tyler withdrew to Centreville after darkness settled on the battlefield.[4]

By later standards, the action at Blackburn's Ford was nothing more than a light skirmish. The early-war action, however, may have had a profound influence on the leaders and men in both armies. Casualties were light: Richardson lost eighty-three men from all causes, and the Confederates seventy.[5]

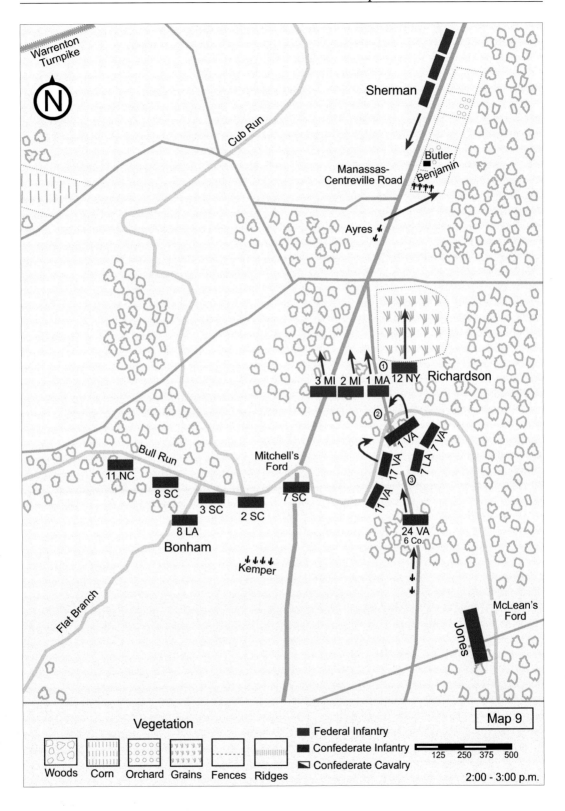

Warrenton Turnpike

N

Cub Run

Sherman

Manassas-
Centreville Road

Butler
Benjamin

Ayres

3 MI 2 MI 1 MA 12 NY ① Richardson

②

Bull Run

Mitchell's
Ford

11 NC

1 VA 7 VA

8 SC

17 VA 7 LA 7 VA

3 SC

2 SC 7 SC

③

11 VA

8 LA

Bonham

24 VA
6 Co.

Kemper

Flat Branch

McLean's
Ford

Jones

Vegetation

Federal Infantry

Confederate Infantry

Confederate Cavalry

Woods Corn Orchard Grains Fences Ridges

Map 9

125 250 375 500

2:00 - 3:00 p.m.

Map 10: McDowell Plans While Beauregard Prepares (July 19 – 20)

As Col. Richardson's brigade battled Gen. Longstreet's Confederates at Blackburn's Ford, Gen. Joseph E. Johnston's Shenandoah Valley command was on the march to Piedmont Station and the Manassas Gap Railroad. Gen. Thomas Jackson's men arrived first before 8:00 a.m. on July 19. Since no cars or engines were there to carry them, the men broke ranks to rest. When they finally hopped into the cars the Southerners found the rickety ride painfully slow; it took almost eight hours to cover the thirty miles. Everyone was bone tired by the time the train arrived at Manassas Station late that afternoon. Col. Bartow's men reached Manassas station at 8:00 a.m. on July 20, with Gen. Bee's jumping from the cars about noon that day. The three Southern brigades marched to the right of the Confederate defensive line behind Bull Run, where they formed a strong reserve. Believing that a major battle was about to be fought, and determined not to miss it, Col. Jeb Stuart rode thirty-six hours with the First Virginia Cavalry to reach the field on the evening of July 20. His exhausted riders fell to the ground behind Bonham's and Cocke's brigades.[1]

By the time the bulk of Johnston's army arrived, the numbers of the opposing forces equalized considerably, with McDowell fielding 37,000 men to Beauregard's/Johnston's 31,000. Johnston's movement to Manassas, however, frustrated Gen. Beauregard because it was not in keeping with his grand plan. Beauregard wanted Johnston to march against Gen. McDowell's right flank and savagely attack it, while Beauregard assaulted the Federals in front. Not only did Beauregard's grand plan fail to materialize, but he officially lost command of the Confederate forces in and around Manassas because Joe Johnston outranked him.[2]

McDowell had considered moving farther east at Union Mills Ford to turn the Confederate right, but the roads and terrain there made the move impracticable. (Whether the affair at Blackburn's Ford influenced his thinking is unclear.) McDowell thus shifted his attention to turning the Confederate left flank. The army's chief engineer, George Barnard, had spent the last two days systematically reviewing the possible Bull Run crossings while McDowell waited for supplies. The best crossing point was over a stone bridge on the macadamized Warrenton Turnpike, but he believed that the sector of the enemy line was heavily defended (it was not) and possibly mined (also untrue). Another good crossing point was a few miles northwest of the bridge at a place called Sudley Ford. According to the latest intelligence, Barnard believed the ford was defended by only a handful of infantry companies and that the crossing would support wheeled vehicles. Confederate patrols may have kept Barnard from even seeing the ford, and two subsequent reconnaissance attempts thrown out for that purpose by McDowell were also turned back.[3]

McDowell had another vexing problem. The longer he waited to give battle, the smaller his army would become, for the terms of enlistments of his three-month regiments were expiring. He begged the men of the 4th Pennsylvania not to leave just yet, but they remained unconvinced: a deal was a deal, and ninety days was all they bargained for.[4]

After hearing Barnard's report about Sudley's Ford about noon of July 20, McDowell decided he had enough information to formulate a plan to defeat the Confederates. It was an audacious operation. He would leave about one-half of his army to demonstrate in front of Beauregard while the other half marched around the Confederate left flank to fall upon its rear, forcing it to either flee the field completely or fight in the open at a disadvantage. McDowell expected that Gen. Patterson would keep Johnston's army in the Shenandoah Valley. What McDowell did not know was that the van of Johnston's army was already close at hand.[5]

Predicting that McDowell would move to strike the weakly held left side of his line, Beauregard decided that a good offense was the best defense. He convinced Johnston to attack the left side of the Federal line with most of his army. Beauregard made a few modifications, however, including the dispatch of the brigades under Bee and Bartow, together with the Hampton Legion, to the left of his line to reinforce Nathan "Shanks" Evans' small brigade defending the Stone Bridge.[6]

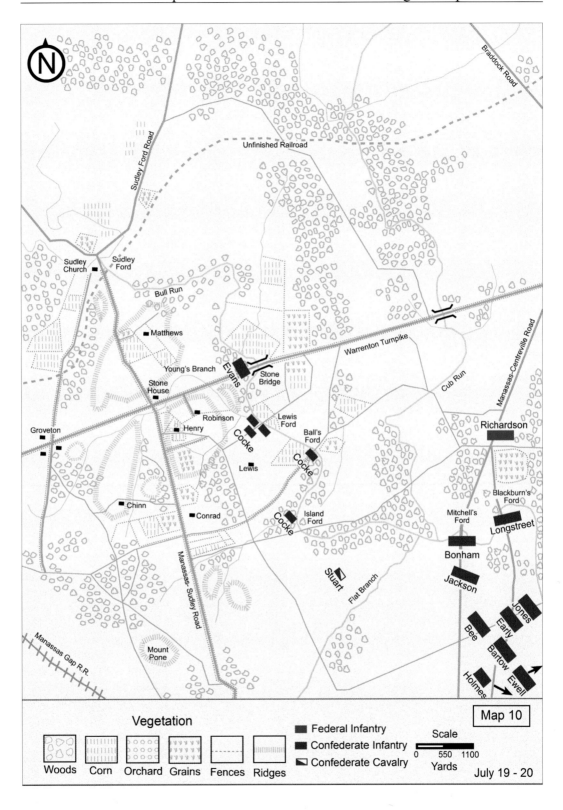

N

Braddock Road

Sudley Ford Road

Unfinished Railroad

Sudley Church

Sudley Ford

Bull Run

Matthews

Warrenton Turnpike

Young's Branch

Evans

Stone Bridge

Cub Run

Stone House

Manassas-Centreville Road

Robinson

Lewis Ford

Groveton

Henry

Cocke

Ball's Ford

Richardson

Cocke

Lewis

Blackburn's Ford

Chinn

Conrad

Cocke

Island Ford

Mitchell's Ford

Longstreet

Stuart

Bonham

Flat Branch

Jackson

Manassas-Sudley Road

Jones

Early

Bee

Bartow

Ewell

Manassas Gap R.R.

Mount Pone

Holmes

Vegetation

Map 10

Woods   Corn   Orchard   Grains   Fences   Ridges

■ Federal Infantry
■ Confederate Infantry
◣ Confederate Cavalry

Scale

0   550   1100

Yards

July 19 - 20

Map 11: The Federal Flanking Movement (a.m., July 21)

McDowell outlined his plan to his brigade and division commanders at 8:00 p.m. on July 20. While Richardson's brigade, with Gen. Thomas Davies' brigade of Dixon Miles' division, demonstrated in front of Blackburn's and Mitchell's fords to freeze the enemy in place, the rest of Tyler's division would march along Warrenton Turnpike to demonstrate against Confederates defending the Stone Bridge. The balance of Miles' division would remain in reserve near Centreville. Some 13,000 troops and five batteries of artillery from David Hunter's and Samuel Heintzelman's divisions, meanwhile, would march to Sudley Ford, cross it, and fall upon the enemy flank and rear behind Bull Run.

The marching order was complex for this early in the war. The plan was for the flanking troops to initially follow Tyler's division along the Warrenton Turnpike until they reached a secondary road, when they would head north and west to the Sudley Ford Road, which turned south directly for the Sudley crossing. Heintzelman had orders to halt near Poplar Ford, about midway between Sudley Ford and the Stone Bridge, while Hunter (in the lead) marched to the Sudley crossing. He would slip across and strike south along the creek, drawing defenders away from the Stone Bridge. Heintzelman would then cross the stream at Poplar Ford and form his brigades on Hunter's advancing left flank. Both divisions would then drive into the enemy rear. Tyler's orders were to begin marching at 2:30 a.m. on July 21; Hunter's men were expected to cross Sudley Ford by 7:00 a.m. after their ten-mile trek. The risky strategy was worthy of Napoleon, and depended upon close coordination—something that could not be reasonably expected by green troops and their equally inexperienced commanders.[1]

Tyler's men were on the road at 2:30 a.m. Robert Schenck's brigade led the march, followed by Sherman. These brigades had spent the night between Centreville and Cub Run. Erasmus Keyes' brigade, farther east at Centreville, began its march at 2:00 a.m., but fell behind the rest of the division. The night was very dark. Without cavalry to scout the route and

towing a large 30-lb. cannon, progress was excruciatingly slow. The narrow old suspension bridge over Cub Run stacked up Hunter's and Heintzelman's divisions and prevented them from initiating their flanking movement at the appointed hour. The rear of Tyler's division did not clear Cub Run until 5:30 a.m. Several hundred yards from Cub Run, Hunter's division (led by Ambrose Burnside's brigade, followed by Andrew Porter's and Captain Charles Griffin's battery), made a right turn onto a road leading to the Sudley Ford Road. The secondary road (little more than a narrow cart path) was marked by Mrs. Spindle's house. The pace of the march slowed as men wielding axes cleared out brush. Heintzelman's division brought up the rear.[2]

Tyler continued marching along Warrenton Turnpike to the Stone Bridge, where he arrived about 6:00 a.m. About dawn, Tyler deployed Schenck's and Sherman's brigades astride the turnpike and ordered up his artillery. Although he did not know it, on the far side of the bridge was Col. Nathan Evans' small brigade of two regiments and a pair of guns under Lt. Davidson deployed behind Van Pelt Hill. Evans learned of the Federal move as early as 3:30 a.m., when his pickets heard muffled commands.

Tyler opened the fighting with an artillery barrage of three shots from his 30-lb. rifled gun. Four other pieces joined in, but the firing failed to elicit an enemy response. The situation was reminiscent of the Blackburn's Ford action two days before. Federal skirmishers moved ahead to engage Evans' skirmishers, two companies of the 4th South Carolina (six more companies were on the hill and another two behind it) and one from the 1st Special Louisiana Battalion. The light pattering of fire lasted for about one hour. When he heard the large Federal gun opposite the Stone Bridge, Richardson responded to the signal by opening fire with his artillery at Blackburn's Ford on the left side of McDowell's line before sending forward his own skirmish line.[3]

As these events were transpiring, Johnston ordered Bee's and Bartow's Brigades, with the Hampton Legion, toward the Confederate left about 7:00 a.m. Thomas Jackson's Brigade was in reserve southeast of Flat Branch roughly one mile southwest of Mitchell's Ford. From there, he could support Cocke's Brigade behind Lewis' Ford or Bonham's Brigade at Mitchell's Ford.[4]

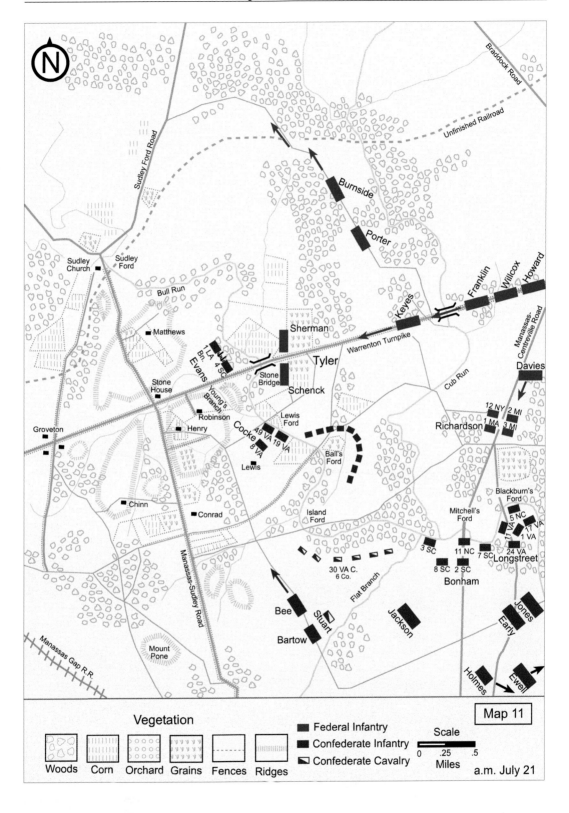

Map 11

Vegetation

Woods   Corn   Orchard   Grains   Fences   Ridges

■ Federal Infantry
■ Confederate Infantry
◤ Confederate Cavalry

Scale
0   .25   .5
Miles

a.m. July 21

Map 12: Hunter's Division Arrives on the Confederate Flank (9:30 – 10:15 a.m.)

Believing that a good defense was an offensive thrust, Gen. Beauregard ordered his brigades on the center and right—Bonham's, Longstreet's, Jones' and Ewell's—to cross Bull Run and drive against the weakened Federal troops there, veer left, and try to take the flank of McDowell's attacking force. In other words, while McDowell was moving a heavy column to attack Beauregard's left, Beauregard was trying to put in motion a plan to strike McDowell's left.

The initial Confederate thrust was fitfully delivered. Longstreet's men splashed across the creek at Blackburn's Ford and were hit with artillery fire. Longstreet halted to await Jones' arrival, who crossed at McLean's Ford to the southeast. Jones, in turn, marked time waiting for Ewell's men to arrive (see Map 35).[1]

On the other side of the long Bull Run line, Col. Hunter's attack was at least two hours behind schedule. The general was confused by the terrain and a local guide who insisted that engineer Barnard's route (which Hunter was trying to follow) would expose the column's left flank. He offered a different route that turned out to be twelve miles instead of six miles. Compounding the problem was the fact that the road to Poplar Ford could not be found. Gen. Heintzelman followed Col. Hunter, the men marching steadily to keep up. When Confederate signalman E. Porter Alexander caught a glimpse of the early-morning sun glinting on the moving flanking column, he fired off a message to Col. Evans, "Look out for your left, you are turned." Evans, who may have already suspected the move, responded decisively. He informed Col. Cocke on his right defending Lewis' Ford that he was taking most of his men from his left flank and moving them north to confront the approaching enemy. Evans left four 4th South Carolina companies at the Stone Bridge to keep an eye on Tyler's three stationary brigades (Schenck, Sherman, and Keyes) and rushed the rest of the regiment and Maj. Chatham Wheat's 1st Special Louisiana Infantry Battalion, about 900 men, north along a farm lane to face 15,000 Federals approaching the Confederate left.

Evans also had two six-pounder guns from Capt. H. G. Latham's Lynchburg Artillery. Evans apparently believed the Federal flanking column would turn onto the farm lane his men occupied in an effort to flank the Stone Bridge. He seems not to have fully comprehended the wide strategic envelopment McDowell was attempting to achieve.[2]

The Federals in the flanking column experienced quite an adventure. A chance to find glory in battle was approaching, and that was what most of them were seeking. Many soldiers left the ranks to snatch blackberries that grew wild along their route of march. As one New Yorker described it after the war, "[T]here we were, 'going it blind,' with the vain confidence of fools."[3]

Evans realized his error when a skirmisher informed him that the left was being outflanked by Federals marching south along the Manassas-Sudley Road. The South Carolinian double-quicked his men about one mile southwest from the vicinity of the Stone Bridge to Matthews Hill, where he formed them on the southern slope about 250 yards below its crest. The Louisianians arrived first, followed by the South Carolinians. One historian called Evans' position "an odd one." Although the reverse slope of Matthews Hill did not offer Evans a position of strength, it did offer the potential to surprise the approaching enemy. Latham's two guns (under Davidson) were widely separated and deployed about 300 yards behind the infantry.[4]

Hunter's men reached Sudley Ford about 9:30 a.m. and promptly began to cross Bull Run. Col. Ambrose Burnside's brigade led the way. There was great hope within the Federal ranks that the long seven-and-a-half hour trek would earn them the all-important element of surprise. That hope faded quickly when Evans' skirmishers leveled their rifles and fired a volley of gunfire at Burnside's men. Many of the surprised men at the front of the march fell to the ground and the bullets flew harmlessly over their heads.

Burnside threw out five companies of the 2nd Rhode Island into a skirmish line while the rest of the brigade rested for about thirty minutes. The loss of surprise dampened the desire for speed. Gen. McDowell reached Sudley Ford around this time only to find his plan had been discovered. He dispatched an order to Gen. Tyler to force his way across the Stone Bridge.[5]

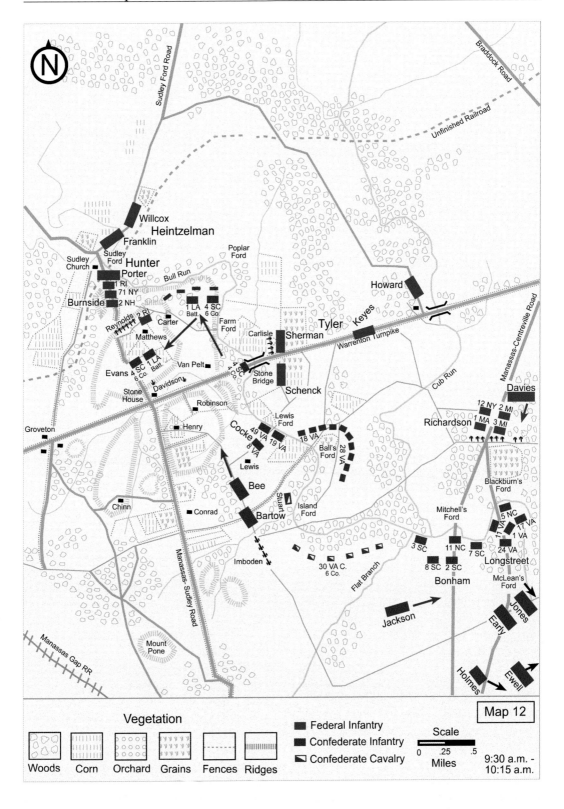

Vegetation

Woods   Corn   Orchard   Grains   Fences   Ridges

Federal Infantry
Confederate Infantry
Confederate Cavalry

Scale

0   .25   .5
Miles

Map 12

9:30 a.m. -
10:15 a.m.

Map 13: Evans' Brigade Battles Burnside (10:15 – 10:45 a.m.)

Once Col. Evans' skirmish line opened fire on the 2nd Rhode Islanders from their positions near the Matthews house, the two sides settled down to a steady exchange of musket fire. As the Rhode Island men steadily pushed back the Confederate skirmish line, Burnside brought up the rest of the regiment and ordered it forward on the left side of the road. When the men crested the hill, Confederates hidden on the far side opened fire with 900 muskets and a pair of guns. The Rhode Island regiment's commander, Col. John Slocum, boldly exposed himself atop a fence to observe the Rebel positions, was hit three times, with one of the balls striking his head and carving a grove in his scalp from front to back. Captain William H. Reynolds' battery galloped into position off to the side of the road and unlimbered, adding the weight of six guns to a spreading fight around Matthews Hill that would last for about ninety minutes, suck in sixteen regiments, and result in 1,054 casualties.[1]

Anxious to engage in combat, one company of Louisiana troops from Wheat's Battalion (the Tiger Rifles) rushed to face the Rhode Islanders only to realize that some of the bullets zipping through their ranks were coming from the rear. In the smoke and spreading confusion of their first battle, the men of the 4th South Carolina moved behind the Louisianians to take up a position on their left. Sometime during the process some of the men fired into the backs of the Tigers, wounding at least two. The Louisianians were so angry they returned the favor. Reason soon prevailed, however, and the Southerners turned their weapons on the enemy.[2]

The Confederates were not the only ones confused by the meeting engagement. Realizing that he needed to reinforce the 2nd Rhode Island, Col. Hunter ordered up Col. Andrew Porter's brigade, leaving the rest of Burnside's unemployed brigade to squander precious minutes standing idly by the side of the road. Assuming he would follow Burnside's brigade into the fight, Porter deployed behind his bewhiskered comrade's reserve regiments. This confused deployment wasted thirty minutes while the Rhode Island regiment suffered serious losses confronting Evans' 900 Southerners. Before the pair of Union brigades got into the fight, Hunter fell with a serious neck wound and quit the field, turning his command over to Burnside.

Burnside ordered his brigade forward. Unfortunately for the Federals, he did so in piecemeal fashion (a methodology both sides would use all day). The 2nd New Hampshire advanced on the right of the road, where it did nothing to provide assistance to the embattled 2nd Rhode Island. The 71st New York took too long to get ready, which prompted Burnside to bring up the 1st Rhode Island and send it forward into the fight. The 2nd Rhode Island shifted to its left, leaving a space between it and Reynolds' battery for its sister regiment to occupy (No. 1 on map). Earlier, while Burnside's men were resting along the road, they spotted a dust cloud in the southern distance. Although inexperienced, they had kicked up their own dust clouds that morning, and so knew well what this one portended: more Southern troops were approaching.[3]

The Confederate reinforcements kicking up dust on Henry Hill south of the Warrenton Turnpike were the brigades of Gen. Bee and Col. Bartow. Both deployed about 150 yards north of the Henry House (No. 2 on map). The men did not need much encouragement to speed their march to this sector, recalled one soldier, for they were anxious to get a "chance to get a dab at the Yankees." Bartow's Brigade was posted on the left (7th and then 8th Georgia) and the 2nd Mississippi and the 4th Alabama of Bee's Brigade extended the line to the right. Once in line, the men were ordered to load their muskets and await further orders. Bee brought up Captain John Imboden's four-gun battery. The guns dropped trail in front of and between the two brigades as Bee exclaimed, "Here is the battlefield, and we are in for it." The excitement felt by the green Southern soldiers waned a bit when Reynolds' Federal guns opened fire on them from beyond Matthews Hill. Some of the men had climbed trees to get at Mrs. Henry's unripe apples, and they quickly slid to the ground when the shells began exploding around them. One Georgia soldier recalled thinking, "This is so unfair . . . I didn't come out here to fight this way; I wish the earth would crack open and let me drop in."[4]

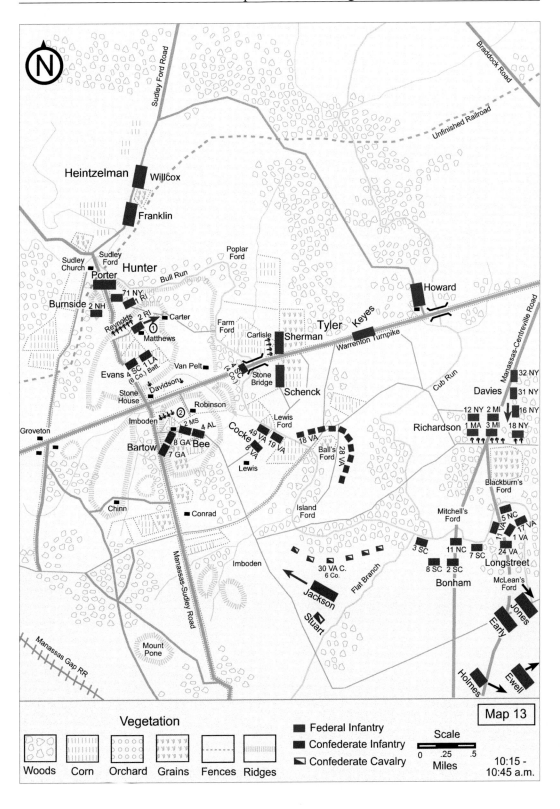

Map 13

Vegetation

Woods Corn Orchard Grains Fences Ridges

Federal Infantry
Confederate Infantry
Confederate Cavalry

Scale

0   .25   .5
Miles

10:15 -
10:45 a.m.

Map 14: Confederates Aggressively Confront Burnside's Thrust (10:45 – 11:00 a.m.)

The head of Col. Hunter's column and Col. Nathan Evans' Confederates continued their firefight around Matthews Hill along a front about 300 yards wide. Col. Burnside probably felt some relief when the 1st Rhode Island finally slid into position next to its sister regiment. Whether the words Hunter spoke after his wound forced him to relinquish his command—"Burnside, I leave the matter in your hands"—offered the same sensation is unknown.[1]

Given his desperate situation, no relief washed over Shanks Evans. He was heavily outnumbered and needed help if he was to maintain his position. About this point he discerned a weakness in the Federal line, possibly brought about by gap created when the 2nd Rhode Island sidled to the left to make room for the newly arriving 1st Rhode Island. Evans decided on a bold action. The colonel turned to Maj. Wheat and ordered him to assault Reynolds' Federal battery with his Louisianians. It was about 10:45 a.m. (No. 1 on map).

The Louisianians charged with a yell and opened a fire that knocked down several artillerymen and horses. The attack was launched at a vulnerable time for the Federals, for only the 2nd Rhode Island was ready to repel it. Many of the men, however, had either run out of ammunition and were scrounging the dead and wounded for additional cartridges, or their guns were so fouled by the heat of firing that they had to bang their ramrods against rocks or fence posts to seat their charges. The net result dramatically reduced the regiment's effective defensive fire. One soldier in the 2nd Rhode Island remembered it as "the most terrible moment of this terrific contest." Wheat's men reached a point just twenty yards from the battery when a concentrated fire from the 1st Rhode Island, which had finally arrived at the front, rocked their ranks. The two regiments within firing range "gave a most hideous scream" and fired volley after volley into the stunned Louisiana troops. Unable to fall back to their original position on the right side of the 4th

South Carolina, the Louisianians retreated east across the Manassas-Sudley Road. Though unsuccessful, Wheat's charge slowed the Federal advance along the Manassas-Sudley Road.[2]

Wheat's precipitous withdrawal dramatically reduced the length of Evans' right flank, making it vulnerable to a Federal flanking movement. The Federals already overlapped his left flank with Reynolds' battery. Evans had earlier sent an urgent message to Gen. Bee to bring up reinforcements. Bee, however, did not like the position Evans had selected to make a stand, and suggested Evans fall back to Bee's position on Henry Hill (No. 2 on map). When Evans refused, a reluctant Bee moved to reinforce him. Riding over to the 4th Alabama, he called out, "Up Alabamians!" and led them forward. Down Henry Hill they ran, and then up the steep slope of Buck Hill, all the while under fire by Reynolds' battery. When they spotted the long line of Alabamians approaching, Evans' men cheered their approval. Bee deployed the Alabamians in the woods formerly occupied by Wheat's men on the right side of the 4th South Carolina. To their front was a cornfield, and beyond it was the smoke pouring from the muskets of the Federals deployed on the summit of Matthews Hill. The commander of the 4th Alabama, Col. Egbert Jones, ordered his men to lie down and protect themselves as much as possible.[3]

Realizing that the Alabamians were insufficient to stem the Federal advance, Bee ordered up the remainder of his command. Some of the officers gave short remarks to calm their inexperienced men. The 8th Georgia and 2nd Mississippi, together with two additional companies of the 11th Mississippi, moved down the hill toward the Warrenton Turnpike. The 7th Georgia did not advance to Matthews Hill, instead occupying a reserve position in the turnpike in front of the Robinson house. Federal guns opened fire on the exposed troops, creating havoc in the ranks until they reached the road and moved up Buck Hill toward Matthews Hill. In all, Bee had with him perhaps 2,500 men and with Evans' remaining men, the defenders of Matthews Hill now numbered some 3,300 strong.[4]

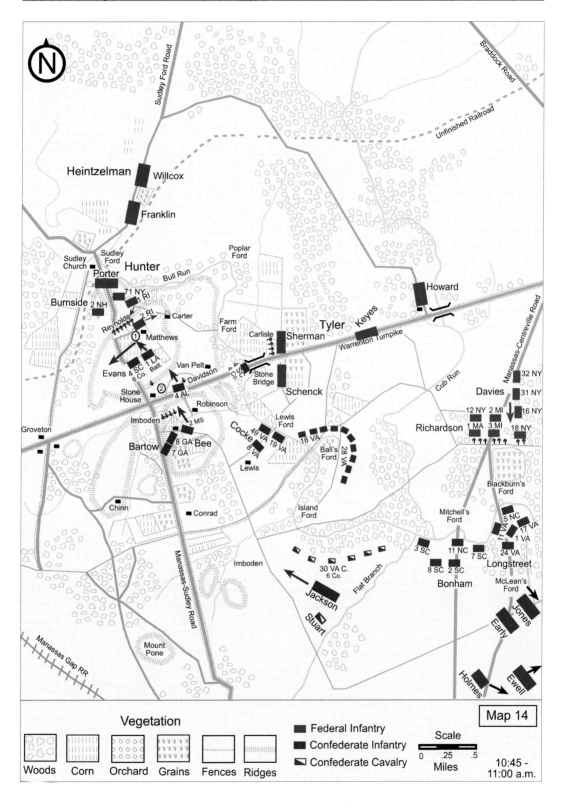

Map 15: Bee's and Bartow's Brigades Reinforce Evans (11:00 – 11:15 a.m.)

The men of Bee's and Bartow's brigades were hot and thirsty by the time they found themselves rushing toward Matthews Hill about 11:00 a.m. Many of the inexperienced soldiers had neglected to fill their canteens that morning; some drank standing water out of mud holes. The brown water "was not fit for a dog to drink, but it was the only chance," recalled one of the men. Many wondered if the dash toward Matthews Hill was better than lying near the Henry House under the angry fire of the Federal artillery pieces. "The projectiles sung and whizzed and exploded over us, around us, and a very few among us," noted John Reed of the 8th Georgia, part of Bartow's Brigade. It did not get much better as the men approached Matthews Hill. According to Reed, "I could hear the bullets zipping and zeeing among us like angry bees, and I knew that our men were falling fast." Some may have recalled Col. Bartow's remarks to them the night before—that the two armies would soon meet in combat. "But remember boys, that battle and fighting mean death," explained the colonel, "and probably before sunrise some of us will be dead."[1]

As Bee's regiments arrived on Matthews Hill, he slotted them into position to the right of Evans' embattled brigade. The 2nd Mississippi (along with two companies of the 11th Mississippi) slipped into the space between the six companies of the 4th South Carolina on the left and the 4th Alabama on the right. The 8th Georgia of Bartow's Brigade came next, forming at a slight angle running to the northeast. This deployment allowed Bartow's Georgians to throw an enfilade fire into the flank of the 2nd Rhode Island which, together with the 1st Rhode Island, fought in the front yard of the Matthews house. Because of a pine thicket, the 8th Georgia was forced to squeeze into a space only 110 yards in length (rather than the customary 200 or so yards) and the right side of the line was in the thicket. Many men recalled that they were ordered to lie down after reaching their position.[2]

Seeing the growing strength of enemy soldiers, Burnside countered by reinforcing his own lines. He quickly brought up his entire brigade to Matthews Hill, but not before the men shed their valued knapsacks and blankets. The two Rhode Island regiments (1st and 2nd) sidled to their left to allow room for the 71st New York while the 2nd New Hampshire formed in reserve behind Reynolds' artillery. As Burnside's soldiers formed a strong line on the left (eastern) side of Manassas-Sudley Road, Col. Andrew Porter prepared his men for battle on the right side of the road. Griffin's battery also galloped up and prepared to open fire on the enemy. This movement caused considerable confusion when the battery intermingled with the New Yorkers. Because he outranked Burnside, Porter assumed command of the division.[3]

Gen. Heintzelman's division, meanwhile, continued its march toward Sudley Ford. As he drew near the ford he spun off two regiments, the 1st Minnesota and the 11th Massachusetts, and sent them trotting toward the sound of the firing. Capt. James Ricketts' battery joined the move toward Matthews Hill. The Minnesota regiment marched through woods and fields to the east of the road, while the Bay Staters marched down the road. Following in their wake Heintzelman ordered the 1st Michigan and Arnold's battery to form as a reserve. Arnold moved his guns east of the creek; it is unclear where the Michiganders took up their position.[4]

For a while it looked as though Bee and Bartow would hold their own on Matthews Hill. The right flank, Bartow's 8th Georgia, extended beyond the left flank of the 2nd Rhode Island. Burnside tried to correct the problem by spreading the 2nd Rhode Island farther east in the direction of Bull Run. This thinned the line without any appreciable relief. The two sides fired away at one another along the quarter of a mile front. After the battle, a member of the 1st Rhode Island remembered that "shells were exploding and [the] cannon roaring made such a noise that the cry of the wounded could not be heard."[5]

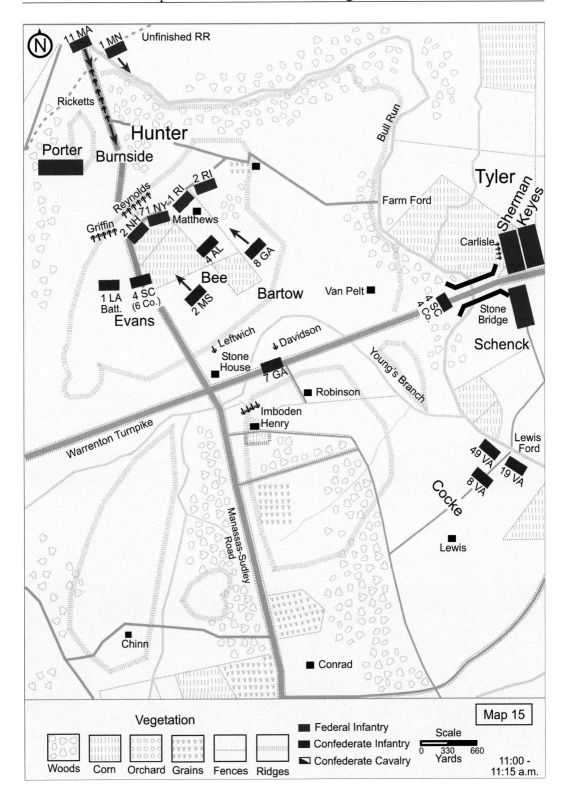

Vegetation

Woods Corn Orchard Grains Fences Ridges

■ Federal Infantry
■ Confederate Infantry
◣ Confederate Cavalry

Scale
0   330   660
Yards

Map 15

11:00 -
11:15 a.m.

Map 16: Bee and Bartow Enter the Fight (11:15 – 11:30 a.m.)

The fighting on Matthews Hill continued unabated with no clear advantage to either combatant. Federal soldiers occupied the Matthews farm buildings. "They were in the shrubbery in the front yard, down through the horse lot, behind the stables and barns and haystacks," recalled Pvt. Berrien Zettler of the 8th Georgia. "Seemingly a thousand rifles were flashing and the air was alive with whistling bullets. Men were dropping at my right and left. . . . I could hear the balls striking our boys, and I saw many of them fall forward, some groaning in agony, others dropping dead without a word." Despite these horrible sights and sounds, Zettler held his position with his comrades and "fired as rapidly as I could."[1]

After perhaps twenty minutes of stand-up fighting, Burnside grew increasingly alarmed as the right side of the Confederate line (the 8th Georgia) extended in a northeasterly direction beyond the flank of his own 2nd Rhode Island. He had just already committed his last reserves into the firing line.

On the other side of the line, Gen. Bee grimly watched as Porter's Federal brigade marched southward along the Manassas-Sudley Road and deployed opposite his vulnerable left flank. Only Evans' two small units (Wheat's battalion of five companies—the Tiger Rifles was one of the five—and six companies of the 4th South Carolina) blocked Porter's advance. Bee would not be able to hold his position much longer. He wanted a fight that day and that was exactly what he got. What he did not want, however, was a fight on Matthews Hill.

Burnside spurred his horse to the right to find Col. Porter and desperately needed reinforcements. "Porter, for God's sake let me have the Regulars. My men are all being cut to pieces!" he beseeched. In an army whose ranks were populated by green volunteers, Maj. George Sykes' battalion of Regular army infantry was a valued resource. When Porter refused to give away these troops so easily, Burnside convinced him that the Rhode Islanders' left flank was about to be turned and that the army would tumble back in defeat without more experienced soldiers stabilizing the front. Porter reluctantly agreed, and the Regulars marched to their left behind Burnside's line. The troops manning the firing line cheered as Sykes' Regulars tramped past. The movement was too slow for Burnside's liking, but he knew encouragement was exactly what was required. He galloped up to the column on his foaming horse and yelled to the unit's commander, "Good God! Major Sykes, you regulars are just what we want."

Sykes' men formed into line of battle immediately upon reaching the left flank of the 2nd Rhode Island. Their first volley was visibly disappointing—a ragged and poorly aimed affair unbefitting these storied Regular troops. "Our men fired badly. They were excited, and some of the recruits fired at the stars," wrote one member of the unit. Another man agreed. "I did my level best to fire as fast and often as possible," he explained, "but it does disconcert one's aim to be under the direct fire of cannon and musketry." The enemy fire may have been disconcerting, but at least one Georgia officer believed even the early rounds were deadly. Their first shots were "a trifle too high," he wrote, "but its effect was deadly enough. The blow was staggering and much confusion ensued."[2]

The Regulars quickly settled down and began pouring an effective fire into the front and flank of the Georgians. Within a short time the steady hail of small arms fire began to unravel the Georgia line, cutting through the pine thicket with deadly intensity. Gen. Bee watched as his men, individually and in small groups, began quitting the firing line and heading for the rear. He did his best to stop them and was sometimes successful in convincing men to return to their original positions. Those who visited the thicket after the battle were impressed by the sheer number of trees that had been hit by the gunfire.[3]

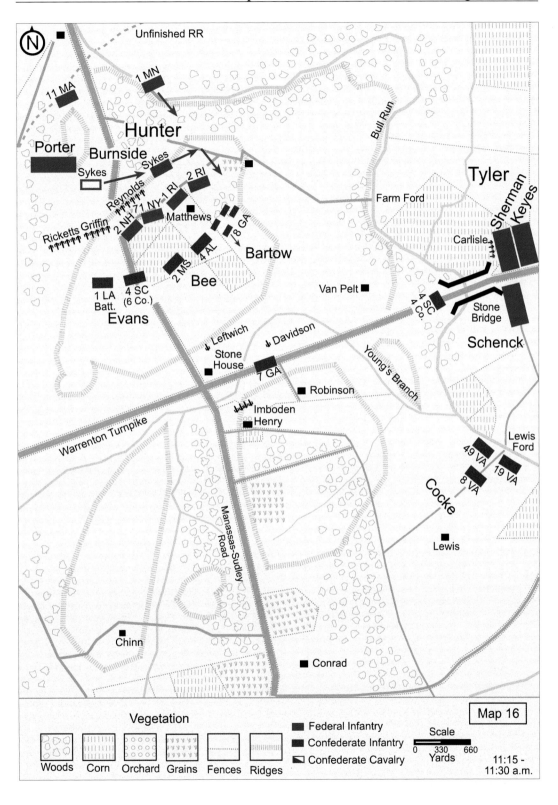

Unfinished RR

11 MA

1 MN

Hunter

Porter

Burnside

Sykes Sykes

Reynolds

2 NH 71 NY 1 RI

Ricketts Griffin

Matthews

2 RI

8 GA

Bartow

4 AL

2 MS

Bee

1 LA Batt.

4 SC (6 Co.)

Evans

Leftwich

Stone House

Davidson

7 GA

Robinson

Imboden

Henry

Warrenton Turnpike

Manassas-Sudley Road

Chinn

Conrad

Bull Run

Farm Ford

Tyler

Sherman

Keyes

Carlisle

4 SC 4 Co.

Stone Bridge

Schenck

Van Pelt

Young's Branch

Lewis Ford

49 VA

19 VA

8 VA

Cocke

Lewis

Vegetation

Woods Corn Orchard Grains Fences Ridges

Federal Infantry
Confederate Infantry
Confederate Cavalry

Scale

0   330   660
Yards

Map 16

11:15 -
11:30 a.m.

Map 17: Defeat on Matthews Hill (11:30 – 11:45 a.m.)

By virtue of seniority, Gen. Bee assumed command of the Confederates struggling to hold their position against Burnside's reinforced line. On Bee's left front, across Manassas-Sudley Road, Col. Porter's brigade and Griffin's battery deployed on Dogan's Ridge and opened fire on Imboden's pieces unlimbered and firing from Henry Hill. A battalion of Marines took up a position on Griffin's right, with the 27th New York deploying on its left. The 8th New York Militia and 14th Brooklyn squeezed into line and extended the front east to the Manassas-Sudley Road. The new Federal line was immediately raked by Imboden's guns.

Col. Porter's brigade squared off against Wheat's 1st Special Louisiana Infantry Battalion. On Wheat's right, the six companies of the 4th South Carolina straddled the joint in the Federal line, facing elements of both Porter's and Burnside's brigades. The rolling tide was rapidly turning against Bee's makeshift line. Ricketts' battery arrived and unlimbered on Griffin's right, their combined twelve guns battering the Rebels. With Reynolds' battery, the number swelled to eighteen. The 71st New York also had two boat howitzers its men dragged with them. On the opposite side of the line, the 1st Minnesota extended the Federal line eastward by forming beside Sykes' Regulars. Burnside's line now outflanked the 8th Georgia by a wide margin.[1]

Although green, the Southerners battling on Matthews Hill were wise enough to realize the daunting odds. Clumps of Bee's, Bartow's, and Evans' men drifted to the rear. The fight to defend Matthews Hill had been raging for about one hour. Realizing he could no longer hold his position, Bee gave the order to fall back to Henry Hill, the ground where he wanted to make his stand all along. The orders were largely unnecessary for the 8th Georgia on the right flank, whose members were already being forced back by the fire to their front and flank. "I saw it was all up with us, and . . . everyone about me seemed to be dead or wounded," recalled a Georgian. His unit left 200 men on the field in killed and wounded—the highest regimental losses of the day. The 4th Alabama, on the left of the 8th Georgia, was the last unit to fall back. As it did, its members spotted the 69th New York of William Sherman's brigade approaching from the east. Thinking these mostly gray-clad men were reinforcements, the Alabamians moved toward them, only to be stopped in their tracks by a deadly volley that knocked down many men, including the regiment's beloved leader Col. Egbert Jones. The mortally injured Jones yelled, "Men don't run!" His soldiers briefly returned the fire, killing and wounding a few New Yorkers before withdrawing southward to Henry Hill.[2]

When the Southerners who had stood firm for so long finally turned and ran, Federal troops let out a long and hearty cheer. Rather than organize a pursuit, Burnside received permission (from Governor Sprague) to pull his brigade back to rest and reorganize. The rest of the line, particularly Col. Porter's brigade, advanced using the Manassas-Sudley Road as a guide in pursuit of the fleeing rebels. About this time, another of Gen. Heintzelman's brigades under Orlando Willcox was splashing across Sudley Ford (Howard's brigade would not finish crossing until about 3:00 p.m.). Tyler's division was approaching from the east, led by Sherman's brigade (the head of which was engaging Jones' 4th Alabama). Sherman's advance was expedited when he watched a pair of Confederate horsemen splash across the stream. Sherman shifted his troops north and east across the previously unknown ford. Col. Keyes' brigade followed Sherman across the stream.[3]

By this time, some 12,000 Federals (including brigades under Sherman and Keyes, but not those of Willcox and Howard) were on or near Matthews Hill watching while 3,000 Confederates executed their disordered escape. Visible in the southern distance on Henry Hill were mounted Rebel officers dashing back and forth trying to reform their men. Utter chaos reigned. Gen. McDowell and his staff were so excited by the tactical victory on Matthews Hill that they galloped along their lines yelling, "Victory! Victory! The day is ours!" Some Federals greeted the news with lament, for they believed the fighting was winding down and they had not yet had a chance to meet and defeat the enemy. One yelled out to McDowell, "Give us a chance at them, general, before they all run away!" McDowell shouted back, "Shut up your damned head; you'll get chances enough, maybe, before the day is over."[4]

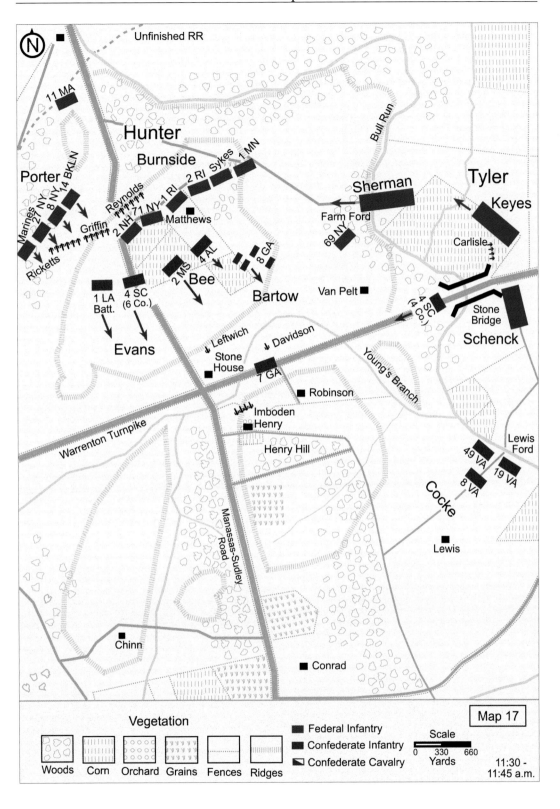

Map 17

Vegetation

Woods   Corn   Orchard   Grains   Fences   Ridges

■ Federal Infantry
■ Confederate Infantry
◪ Confederate Cavalry

Scale
0   330   660
Yards

11:30 -
11:45 a.m.

Unfinished RR

N

11 MA

Hunter

Burnside

Porter

Marines
27 NY
8 NY
14 BKLN

Griffin

Reynolds

2 NH 71 NY 1 RI

Matthews

2 RI Sykes 1 MN

Ricketts

Bull Run

Sherman

Tyler

Keyes

Farm Ford

69 NY

Carlisle

4 AL

2 MS   Bee

8 GA

Bartow

Van Pelt

4 SC
(4 Co.)

Stone
Bridge

Schenck

1 LA
Batt.

4 SC
(6 Co.)

Evans

Leftwich

Stone
House

Davidson

7 GA

Robinson

Imboden
Henry

Young's Branch

Lewis
Ford

49 VA

19 VA

8 VA

Cocke

Henry Hill

Warrenton Turnpike

Manassas-Sudley Road

Lewis

Chinn

Conrad

Map 18: Initial Actions on Henry Hill (11:30 – 11:45 a.m.)

Portions of six Confederate infantry units from five different states had stood together on Matthews Hill for about one hour of hard fighting. Now they were little more than a defeated mob. Some men ran in search of safety, some walked, and many others simply sat down. All the while, their officers attempted unsuccessfully to reorganize them for combat. Regimental structures had ceased to exist in any recognizable form because the soldiers were too intermingled to be easily extricated and reorganized. It appeared to most observers that *the* battle had been fought and the war was over.

Ironically, neither Confederate army commander was yet present on that sector of the field. Both Gens. Joe Johnston and P. G. T. Beauregard were still near Mitchell's Ford. Beauregard believed the major Federal thrust would fall against his center and right flank, and he still wanted to attack with his own right. Johnston was anxious to move to the left and the prolonged firing from that direction, together with reports from messengers, convinced him that he should. He rode off to the northwest with the words, "I am going there." Beauregard finally agreed. It was about 11:00 a.m. They ordered Jubal Early's Brigade to follow them, along with two South Carolina regiments from Gen. Bonham's Brigade and Captain Kemper's Alexandria battery.[1]

Other units were also marching for the left. Thomas Jackson's Brigade and Wade Hampton's Legion were approaching Henry Hill. Col. Hampton's 600 soldiers arrived first, having just detrained from Richmond. Hampton formed them into a battle line near the Robinson house about one-half mile from the enemy. Hampton was shocked by what he found: on the far side of the Warrenton Turnpike were heavy lines of Federal infantry with bayonets fixed. While sitting his horse in the Robinson yard, in the full presence of his men, an artillery projectile slammed into the soil under Hampton's mount, throwing him hard to the ground. The stunned colonel remounted and continued in command of his troops. About 11:30 a.m. Hampton moved forward to support Bartow's 7th Georgia

holding a hollow (the turnpike) in front of the Robinson house. Before putting his men in motion, Hampton yelled, "Men of the Legion, I am happy to inform you that the enemy is in sight!" The South Carolinian formed his soldiers in front of the Georgians. Hampton's men impressed one Georgian, who recalled that they arrived "in their best clothes and clean linen." His own comrades did not look as good, he admitted: "[We] were in our shirt sleeves, and all bedraggled and soiled with the dirt of our hard march."

New orders soon arrived for Hampton to move forward toward the Robinson house. During this leg of their journey, an increasingly intense small arms and artillery fire ripped through the South Carolina ranks. The advance continued along a lane leading toward Warrenton Turnpike. Hampton watched as what looked to be a regiment of Federal troops moved eastward along the turnpike in his direction. He ordered his men to stop and open fire, which they did to good effect.[2]

Federals north of the Warrenton Turnpike were preparing to advance on Henry Hill to complete what looked soon to be a total victory. Col. Porter's brigade under his adjutant Lt. William Averell (Porter was leading the division after Hunter fell) moved southeast toward the intersection of the Warrenton Turnpike and Manassas-Sudley Road, as did Griffin's battery. The guns unlimbered in a field within the angle formed by both roads and opened fire. Porter's men were bone-tired after their nearly eight-hour march to the field, the last mile at the double-quick. The men were so "exhausted that we could hardly stand up," recalled one New Yorker.

Instead of launching the entire brigade at Henry Hill, Averell ordered only one of the four regiments—the 27th New York—toward the Stone House on the Warrenton Turnpike. The men threw off all unnecessary accouterments except for ammunition, musket, and bayonet, formed into line, and advanced with great vigor. In their way were survivors from Col. Egbert's 4th Alabama, who had halted for a few minutes to rest. "The men, though greatly fatigued and exhausted, gallantly attacked and drove the enemy from the house, who retired in disorder behind their battery," noted a major in the 27th New York. The Alabamians continued their retreat up Henry Hill.[3]

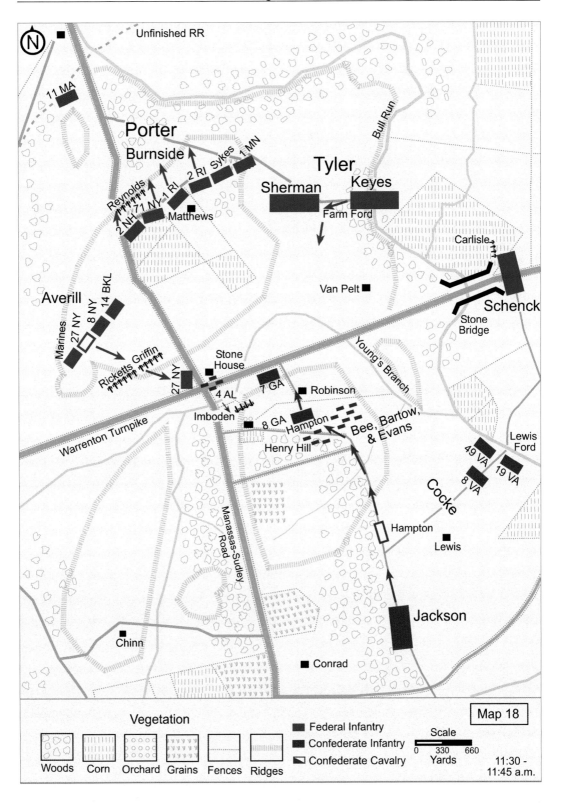

N

Unfinished RR

11 MA

Porter

Burnside

Reynolds

2 NH 71 NY 1 RI

2 RI Sykes

1 MN

Matthews

Tyler

Sherman

Keyes

Farm Ford

Bull Run

Carlisle

Schenck

Stone
Bridge

Averill

27 NY 8 NY 14 BKL

Marines

Ricketts Griffin

27 NY

Stone
House

4 AL

Imboden

Van Pelt

Young's Branch

7 GA

Robinson

8 GA

Henry Hill

Hampton

Bee, Bartow,
& Evans

Lewis
Ford

49 VA

19 VA

8 VA

Cocke

Warrenton Turnpike

Manassas-Sudley Road

Hampton

Lewis

Jackson

Chinn

Conrad

Vegetation

Woods   Corn   Orchard   Grains   Fences   Ridges

■ Federal Infantry
■ Confederate Infantry
◁ Confederate Cavalry

Scale
0   330   660
Yards

Map 18

11:30 -
11:45 a.m.

Map 19: Three Federal Regiments Defeated Near Henry Hill (11:45 a.m. – Noon)

After driving away remnants of the 4th Alabama from the Stone House, Col. Henry Slocum's 27th New York was showered by shells from Imboden's four smoothbores on Henry Hill. This was the first concentrated fire the 27th had experienced. In an effort to avoid the worst of the iron rain, the regiment veered left, moving east along the Warrenton Turnpike on a collision course with Hampton's Confederates. "We were immediately attacked on our right flank by a large force who approached by a ravine under cover of a thick growth of bushes," wrote one Federal. Volleys from the South Carolinians were followed by a charge toward the turnpike, about 200 yards distant. When Hampton's men reached the road cut they fell to their knees and fired a ragged but effective volley into the New Yorkers' right flank (No. 1 on map).

Although reports conflict, it seems men from the 7th Georgia—which was not disorganized like the battered 8th Georgia—approached the 27th New York's left and rear as the regiment battled Hampton's Legion in front. The Georgians were permitted to march within almost shouting distance because the New Yorkers believed they were Northern troops. This early in the war, many Federal regiments were dressed in gray uniforms, and some Southerners wore blue. When the Georgians began firing into their ranks, the New Yorkers thought it was friendly fire from the 8th New York. They quickly learned their mistake when the unknown unit's flag unfurled into a Southern banner and a killing volley followed. The New Yorkers exchanged fire with the South Carolinians (and likely the Georgians as well). Hampton lost another horse to hostile fire in the exchange, but jumped up and continued encouraging his men to press ahead. The 27th New York was on the verge of being trapped and destroyed. The 27th's commander, Col. Slocum, wisely pulled back his regiment northward to Buck Hill. Slocum slipped his men out of the jaws of a potentially catastrophic defeat, but suffered a thigh wound during the withdrawal.

The New Yorkers rallied near the top of the high ground, turned, and returned the fire.[1]

Continuing his piecemeal thrust at the enemy, Lt. Averell ordered the 8th New York and 14th Brooklyn toward the intersection to sweep the enemy off Henry Hill. "They went down the hill in fine style," Averell recalled. When they reached the turnpike, a junior officer ordered the New Yorkers to the left to take on Hampton (No. 2 on map). Newly arriving Southern guns on Henry Hill soon found the range, and with infantry near the Robinson house blew apart the New Yorkers. The small arms fire and shelling drove the Federals back, but not before they forced Hampton's men to also fall back south along the farm lane. The South Carolinians retreated 100 yards and reformed along a fence running parallel to the path, but at a right angle to their former position (No. 3 on map). The 7th Georgia was also forced back up Henry Hill. The short but bruising fight with Hampton's men demoralized the 8th New Yorkers. They "broke and never afterwards formed to any extent," reported Averell.[2]

Just as Evans' men had done at Matthews Hill, Hampton's South Carolinians slowed down the Federal advance for about one hour. Their stand near the turnpike discouraged a full-scale advance against Henry Hill. "[We] had an awful fight, the new and old body of the enemy crossing fire upon us," South Carolina Captain James Conner wrote to his mother. "It was terrible, and the men were falling all around . . . it was the only time in the day the men looked dashed." Hampton pulled back again, this time behind the Robinson house. There, they encountered troops from Bee's and Bartow's brigades who, according to one South Carolinian, "said that our fight at the Warrenton Turnpike had saved the army, but just how we did not know."

Hampton's fight with Porter's Federals also bought time for Bee, Bartow, and Evans to reform behind Henry Hill. "[W]e reformed & stopped in a most bewildered state, without the slightest notion of what was expected of us," remembered a confused Captain Connor. Many of the officers gave speeches: "Strike for the green graves of your sires . . . and your native land!" yelled an Alabama captain. The rattled soldiers probably did not pay much mind to their officers, and probably heard very little. Those with the presence of mind to look to the south behind them could see a long line of fresh Virginia troops approaching.[3]

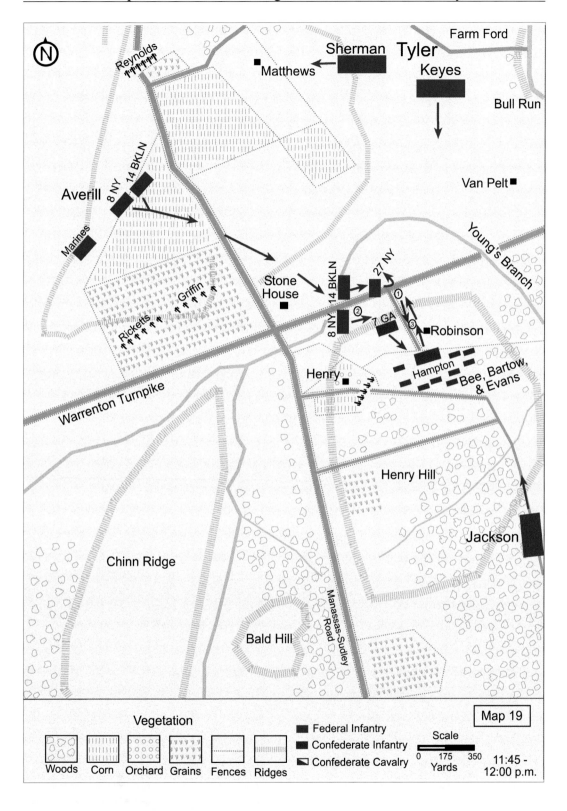

N

Farm Ford

Sherman Tyler
Matthews
Keyes

Bull Run

Reynolds

Van Pelt

Averill

8 NY

14 BKLN

Young's Branch

Marines

Griffin

Stone
House

14 BKLN

27 NY

①

Ricketts

8 NY

②

7 GA

③

Robinson

Hampton

Henry

Bee, Bartow,
& Evans

Warrenton Turnpike

Henry Hill

Jackson

Chinn Ridge

Manassas-Sudley Road

Bald Hill

Vegetation

Map 19

Federal Infantry
Confederate Infantry
Confederate Cavalry

Scale

Woods Corn Orchard Grains Fences Ridges

0   175   350
Yards

11:45 -
12:00 p.m.

Map 20: Jackson's Brigade Reinforces Henry Hill (Noon – 1:00 p.m.)

The Confederates marching north at a brisk clip were Gen. Thomas Jackson's 2,600-man brigade. Jackson was initially positioned behind Bonham at Mitchell's Ford, but was ordered that morning to provide support to Col. Cocke at Lewis' and Ball's fords on the left. The combat on Matthews Hill caught his ear. When the gunfire intensified and moved closer, Jackson double-quicked his men toward the sound of the combat without orders to do so.

The column cut its way toward Henry Hill through a wide swath of men making for the rear. Some were wounded, many were not, and all were confused about what was going on. As one Virginian put it, the soldiers told him "their commands were cut all to pieces and the day lost. Such talk was very [dis]piriting to raw troops. It was calculated to make a boy wish himself a thousand miles away . . . at his mother's house."

Nearly out of shells, Imboden had ordered his battery to the rear. As they bumped their way toward the approaching Virginians, Imboden complained to Jackson about how his men had been left without infantry support. Jackson, who appreciated men willing to fight under dire circumstances, responded, "I'll support your battery. Unlimber right here." When Imboden replied that he had only three rounds left in his limbers, Jackson told him he needed unlimbered guns to give the illusion of strength, and that he must remain there until fresh batteries arrived—even if his guns never fired another shot. Imboden immediately unlimbered on the southeastern edge of Henry Hill about 300 yards from the house. The artillery commander was down to just three guns because one was disabled during the retreat. Jackson was sizing up the deteriorating situation when Gen. Bee reached him. "General, they are driving us!" he explained. Jackson responded, "We will give them the bayonet."[1]

Jackson deployed his men in an unusual manner. Rather than place them on the crest of the hill, he aligned them on the reverse slope along the southeastern edge. Jackson didn't witness Nathan Evans' earlier deployment on Matthews Hill, but his tactical alignment on Henry Hill was similar. His position, coupled with the pine thickets bordering it, hid his men from the Federals gathered to the north and west on Dogan Ridge and Matthews Hill. If the enemy moved against Henry Hill, they would have to traverse 300 yards of open field subjected to the full firepower of Jackson's Brigade. The position also protected his men from the massed Federal artillery. Finally, the location served as a good artillery platform; after each gun fired, it recoiled below the crest of the hill, where gunners reloaded in relative safety before wheeling the piece uphill to fire again.[2]

Jackson deployed his Virginians along a 500-yard front in compact lines of two to four rows. The 4th and 27th were the first in line and deployed in the center. The 5th moved to the right (with its right near a hollow behind the Robinson house) and the 2nd to the left. The 33rd Virginia arrived last and formed on the far left. Four guns from Stanard's battery (arriving in pairs) pulled up next to Imboden's pieces, followed by four more from William Pendleton's battery, making a total of eleven guns in support of Jackson. Gens. Johnston and Beauregard rode upon the scene shortly after noon, just as Jackson was deploying his brigade. The generals brought with them additional artillery pieces that Jackson deployed in front of his infantry. With the position on Henry Hill in good hands, Imboden ordered his guns to the rear in search of additional ammunition.[3]

While Jackson was arranging his men and artillery, Beauregard and Johnston cantered behind the lines in an effort to rally the mob of men from the six battered Confederate regiments. When he encountered the remnants of the 4th Alabama, Johnston reached for its colors so he could move it into position. Its bearer yanked the flag away from the general. "Just tell me where you wish them taken and I will carry them," he snapped. Beauregard was more concerned about inspiring the men than positioning them. The Creole trotted along the lines, encouraging the tired soldiers with patriotic words and speeches. "The men brightened up, dressed their ranks and gave a rousing cheer," admitted one soldier.[4]

It was now about 1:00 p.m. The situation had dramatically changed. While McDowell had dawdled the Confederates had reformed, laying claim to a new and well-defended position on Henry Hill.

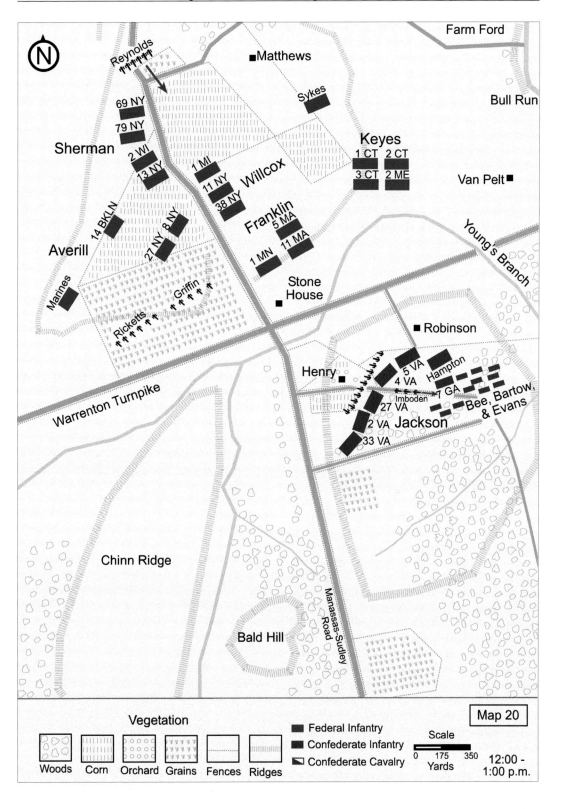

Map 20

Vegetation

| Woods | Corn | Orchard | Grains | Fences | Ridges |

■ Federal Infantry
■ Confederate Infantry
◤ Confederate Cavalry

Scale
0   175   350
Yards

12:00 -
1:00 p.m.

Map 21: Keyes' Brigade Successfully Drives Up Henry Hill (1:00 – 1:30 p.m.)

Although only Col. Burnside's and Col. Porter's (Averell's) brigades had been involved in combat, the nearly 12,000 Federal troops on and near Matthews Hill remained in place, reorganizing while the Rebels did likewise and gained strength on Henry Hill. After they watched the enemy melt away to the south, many believed the war was won. Although artillery on both sides maintained a fitful exchange that forced the infantry to occasionally drop down and hug the earth, the battlefield had to a large extent shifted into neutral and stabilized.[1]

Col. Erasmus Keyes' brigade, which had followed Sherman's brigade across Farm Ford, arrived on the Van Pelt farm about 12:30 p.m. Division commander Gen. Tyler had been "feuding" with Gen. McDowell since the botched reconnaissance at Blackburn's Ford. When Tyler arrived, he pushed the 2nd Maine and 3rd Connecticut (Keyes' brigade) southwest across Young's Branch. Little enemy resistance was encountered. Independently, Capt. Reynolds moved his guns forward to Buck Hill.[2]

Henry Hill was awash with drifting powder smoke and little could be seen of the enemy positioned there. The enemy's artillery was discernable because it was in action, and some infantry formations gathering on the right flank of Jackson's line were visible. Keyes' arrival put his brigade on a direct path into Jackson's dangling right flank and rear. Keyes decided not to wait for his other two regiments, the 1st Connecticut and 2nd Connecticut, to catch up. With the 2nd Maine on the left and the 3rd Connecticut on the right, half of Keyes' brigade stepped off on their 400-yard assault down the slope toward Warrenton Turnpike and the Southerners waiting beyond it. At some point Keyes halted his men so they could rest, take a drink from their canteens, and adjust their equipment. When they reached the top of Henry Hill near the Robinson house, the Federals discovered the 5th Virginia manning Jackson's right flank. Neither side fired. The Federals feared the gray-clad troops in front of them were Yankees because many wore the same color

uniforms as their enemy. Keyes continued advancing, hoping to identity the troops a few hundred yards in front of them.

The Virginians did not harbor any doubts about who was tramping in their direction. As one, the men of the 5th Virginia lowered their weapons and fired a deadly volley that killed and wounded a number of Keyes' men. The men from Maine and Connecticut continued moving steadily forward.

The orientation of the Federal advance also jeopardized Hampton's Legion, which was deployed behind and to the right of the 5th Virginia. Hampton later characterized his situation as very dangerous, claiming that his men were "nearly surrounded" by the twin regimental advance. The 7th Georgia of Bartow's brigade remained to reinforce this part of the line, but the weight of numbers spilling into their flanks was too much to withstand. With the situation at Matthews Hill repeating itself, the Confederates on the right side of Jackson's line began falling back. The 5th Virginia retreated about 100 yards to a hollow southeast of the Robinson house. Worried about his flanks, Jackson asked Col. Jeb Stuart if he could watch them. Stuart dutifully dispatched his 300 cavalrymen equally divided to each flank.[3]

Although pushed back, the 5th Virginia was full of fight. It reformed in the woods and opened a withering fire against Keyes' regiments. It was so intense, wrote Keyes, that "exposure to it of five minutes would have annihilated my whole line." The 3rd Connecticut reached the Robinson yard, but casualties were mounting quickly and Keyes pulled it back down the hill to the turnpike and then via a "left flank" along Young's Branch and out of the fight. The communication gap between Gens. McDowell and Tyler had sealed Keyes' fate. McDowell had a decent idea of the enemy's dispositions on Henry Hill, but Tyler failed to inform him that some of his units were going to force their way onto the high ground.

For the first time in eight hours silence fell on the field. Jackson rode along his line behind the crest of Henry Hill with a finger wrapped in a bloody handkerchief, the result of enemy fire. His horse was favoring one of its legs after sustaining a thigh wound. The Federal soldiers across the way were also waiting. Most seemed to have lost their enthusiasm for fighting, having discovered that battles were bloody and dangerous—and not as glorious as they had believed.[4]

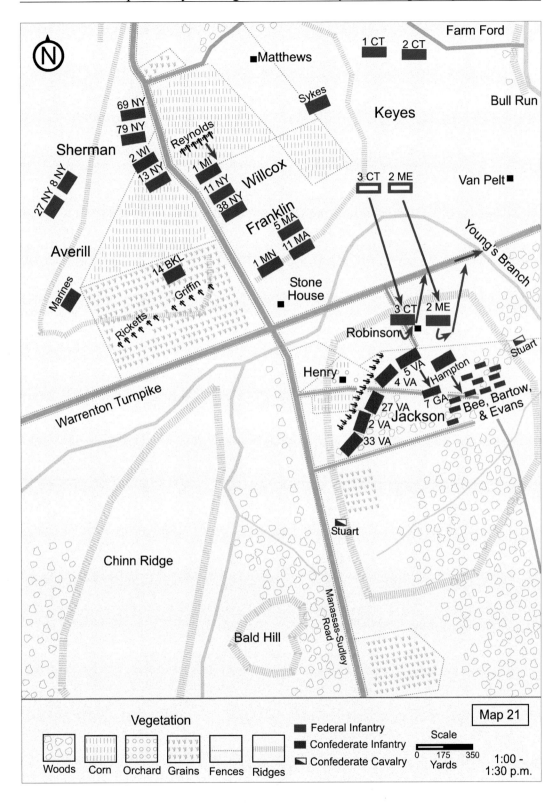

Farm Ford

1 CT   2 CT

■Matthews

Sykes

Bull Run

Keyes

69 NY

79 NY

Reynolds

Sherman

2 WI

1 MI

13 NY

11 NY

Willcox

38 NY

Franklin

5 MA

11 MA

Van Pelt ■

3 CT   2 ME

27 NY 8 NY

Averill

14 BKL

1 MN

Griffin

Marines

Ricketts

Stone
House

3 CT   2 ME

Young's Branch

Robinson

Stuart

Henry

5 VA

4 VA

Hampton

7 GA

27 VA

2 VA

Jackson

Bee, Bartow,
& Evans

33 VA

Warrenton Turnpike

Stuart

Chinn Ridge

Manassas-Sudley Road

Bald Hill

Vegetation

Woods   Corn   Orchard   Grains   Fences   Ridges

■ Federal Infantry

■ Confederate Infantry

◤ Confederate Cavalry

Scale

0   175   350
Yards

Map 21

1:00 -
1:30 p.m.

Map 22: Portions of Three Federal Brigades Unsuccessfully Attack Henry Hill (1:30 – 3:00 p.m.)

The time was roughly 1:30 p.m. After an hour of preparation, Gen. McDowell was ready for a full-scale attack against what he thought was a defeated and retreating enemy on Henry Hill, and his artillery would lead the way. He ordered his artillery chief, Maj. William Barry, to dispatch a pair of batteries to Henry Hill. Capt. Griffin vehemently protested the orders to Barry, claiming that the Zouaves could not support him and his vulnerable eleven guns. Barry pleaded with Gen. Heintzelman for support, and wrested four regiments for the enterprise: 1st Minnesota (Franklin's brigade), 14th Brooklyn and the U.S. Marine Battalion (Porter's brigade), and the 11th New York or Fire Zouaves (Willcox's brigade). When he got his orders, one of the Zouave officers yelled to his men, "Come on boys and show them what New York can do!" one soldier recalled, "and with that, the pet lambs were led to slaughter."[1]

Ricketts' battery galloped up the slope by 2:00 p.m. and unlimbered sixty yards south of the Henry house. Within seconds, enemy small arms fire from the house itself zipped around the guns. The left piece turned to face the threat and fired into the house, triggering a mass exodus as enemy sharpshooters tumbled out in search of a safer locale. The home was also occupied by four civilians. One, 85-year-old Judith Henry, was stuck in the barrage and died before nightfall.[2]

Ricketts' gunners—who were concealed on the reverse slope and could not see the enemy soldiers; nor did they have a clear view of the Confederate artillery, which was masked by vegetation—opened fire on Jackson's men just 300 yards away on the hill's southeastern edge. Griffin's guns rolled up and deployed on Ricketts' left just north of the Henry house. Their combined fire was ineffective because of the drop in the terrain and their use of long-range Parrott rifles for close-range fighting. As a result, the iron flew over the heads of the Virginians. The 11th New York formed on the down slope behind Ricketts' guns. The Marine Battalion arrived next in support, deploying on the left of the New Yorkers while the 1st Minnesota took a

position near the Manassas-Sudley Road well to the right of Ricketts' battery near the woods on the southern edge of the Henry farm. Heintzelman, who was riding with these troops, spotted a large group of men in civilian clothing in front of his infantry line drawn up in line at shoulder arms less than fifty yards away. The two sides yelled at one another in an effort to ascertain their respective identities. The 33rd Virginia, the left-most regiment of Jackson's line of battle, discovered the answer first: the newly arrived troops were Federals. The Virginians leveled their muskets and fired a hasty, ragged volley. The discharge, recalled one Virginian, was fired at a forty-five degree angle. It would not be effective, he continued, "unless they [the enemy] were nearer to heaven than they were generally located by our people."[3]

The aim of the 33rd Virginia quickly improved and Federals began to fall. Heintzelman ordered his men to dive down into the grass to avoid the deadly bullets, and their return fire was largely ineffective. Some panicked, rose to their feet, and bolted to the rear. "[T]he enemy opened a heavy but not destructive fire," wrote Col. Willcox of the 11th New York, "the zouaves returned the fire, but immediately fell back, bewildered and broken." The 33rd Virginia's volleys also killed and wounded some of Ricketts' horses and gunners. The Minnesotans also gave up ground, falling back west across the road. The Marines, deployed behind the guns, saw enough to also take to their heels. Ricketts dashed among the retreating foot soldiers, beseeching them, "For God's sake boys, save my battery!" Some of the New Yorkers within earshot and knots of men from the 1st Minnesota returned to defend the exposed pieces.[4]

As the Minnesotans retreated, the 150 troopers defending Jackson's left charged north up the Manassas-Sudley Road to hit their flank. Some infantry turned, formed into a ragged line, and fired into the charging Rebel horsemen only fifty yards away and closing fast. The muskets emptied a few saddles but the troopers continued, smashing into the panicked infantry. With sabers slashing, the riders cut their way through. Stuart was reorganizing his men for another charge when the Minnesotans reached the woods west of the road.

In less than twenty minutes the 1st Minnesota and the 11th New York each lost about forty men killed—more than any other Federal regiments engaged at First Bull Run.[5]

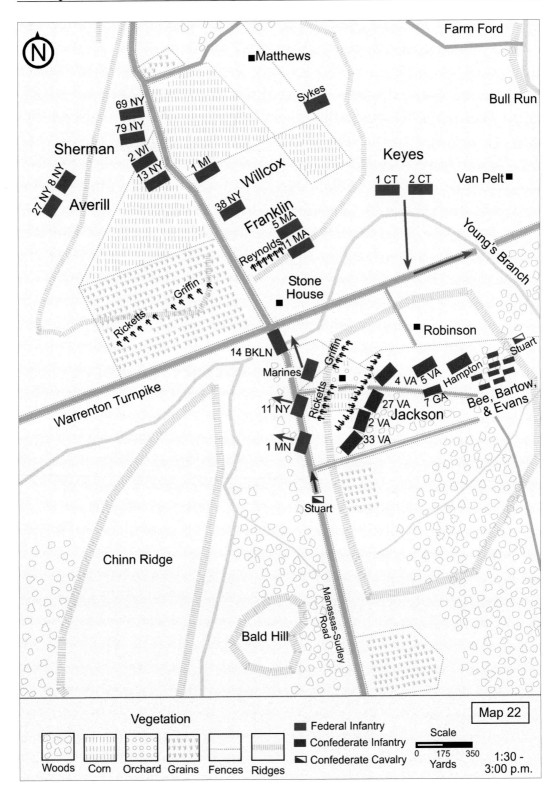

Farm Ford

Matthews

Bull Run

Sykes

69 NY

79 NY

2 WI

Sherman

1 MI

13 NY

Willcox

Keyes

27 NY 8 NY

Averill

38 NY

Franklin

5 MA

1 CT   2 CT

Van Pelt

Reynolds 1 MA

Griffin

Stone
House

Ricketts

Robinson

Young's Branch

Stuart

14 BKLN

Griffin

Marines

4 VA 5 VA

Hampton

11 NY

Ricketts

27 VA

7 GA

Bee, Bartow,
& Evans

2 VA

Jackson

1 MN

33 VA

Warrenton Turnpike

Stuart

Chinn Ridge

Manassas-Sudley Road

Bald Hill

Map 22

Vegetation

Woods Corn Orchard Grains Fences Ridges

■ Federal Infantry

■ Confederate Infantry

◨ Confederate Cavalry

Scale

0   175   350
Yards

1:30 -
3:00 p.m.

Map 23: Jackson's Troops Capture a Section of Griffin's Artillery (2:00 – 4:00 p.m.)

By 3:00 p.m., additional troops were approaching the field to reinforce both sides. Elements of southern brigades under Jubal Early, Milledge Bonham, and P. St. George Cocke were hurrying from the right side of the line toward Henry Hill. About this time history was made when Gen. Bee shouted out his famous handful of words about Gen. Thomas J. Jackson. When he spotted the 4th Alabama milling about, Bee is reputed to have pointed toward Jackson and yelled, "There stands Jackson like a stone wall. Rally behind the Virginians!" The Alabamians moved to the left of the line.[1]

On the Federal side, Oliver Howard's brigade (Heintzelman's division) was hurriedly crossing Sudley Ford in an effort to catch up with the division and so reinforce the Northern right flank. Howard and his command had marked time near the Stone Bridge during the division's move, and his men had to sprint to Sudley Ford, leaving them winded and tired when they finally arrived.

Assistance was also on the way for the vulnerable Federal batteries fighting on Henry Hill. The 14th Brooklyn, which had been detained during its march to the hill, moved toward Ricketts' battery. The 38th New York of Orlando Willcox's brigade also arrived and deployed well behind Griffin's battery, lying down to avoid the "spiteful and destructive fire from the enemy's batteries." It didn't take the cannoneers long to realize that the New Yorkers were not going to advance in an effort to take the pressure off them. The 1st Michigan, also of Willcox's brigade, together with the 5th and 11th Massachusetts of William Franklin's brigade also rushed toward the hill. The arriving Federal cannon muzzles under Griffin and Ricketts looked as "big as flour barrels," recalled one Confederate, and the newly arrived infantry beyond them looked as "thick as wheat in a field."[2]

By this time Capt. Ricketts' battery had lost so many horses it was no longer able to retreat. Griffin's battery was in only slightly better shape.

With the situation bordering on the desperate, Capt. Griffin decided on an audacious move. About 3:00 p.m., he ordered a section of the battery (two guns) shifted far to the right, well beyond Ricketts' pieces, in an effort to enfilade the Confederate guns and force them into retreat.[3]

Col. Arthur Cummings of the 33rd Virginia watched the movement and the Northern pieces dropping trail a mere 200 yards from his exposed left flank. With his men still shaken after their earlier encounter with two Federal regiments, and in no shape to withstand a sustained artillery fire from point blank range, Col. Cummings also opted for an audacious decision: he would launch an attack against the guns. "[T]he most trying position that raw men, and even the best disciplined and bravest could be placed in," explained Cummings, "was to be required to remain still, doing nothing and receiving the enemy's fire without returning it, I feared the consequences, if I strictly obeyed Gen. Jackson's orders; therefore I gave the orders to charge, contrary to his order to wait until the enemy was within thirty paces."[4]

When he spotted these Confederate reinforcements flooding to bolster Jackson's left flank, Griffin ordered his cannoneers to load their two guns with canister and fire away. Maj. William Barry, McDowell's artillery chief, rode up and ordered Griffin to hold his fire because the infantry he was firing at was his own support. A shocked Griffin refused to believe it and protested the order for several minutes, but Barry remained adamant and the two guns fell silent.[5]

The Virginians' charge was rather ragged, and to some might have looked more like an armed mob than a line of battle. As the Virginians approached, the Federal gunners realized the futility of remaining with their pieces. "That was the last of us," Griffin admitted after the battle. His guns were unsupported by infantry and severely undermanned. "Yelling like savages," the Virginians quickly closed the gap to the battery. Realizing the futility of standing by their guns, the handful of surviving gunners turned on their heels and fled to the rear, leaving the artillery in the hands of the victorious Virginians.[6]

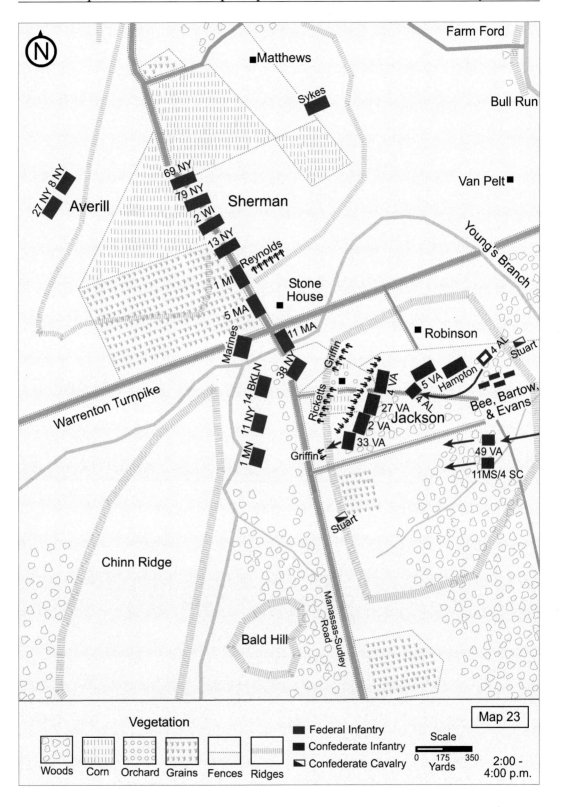

Farm Ford

Matthews

Sykes

Bull Run

69 NY

79 NY

Sherman

2 WI

Van Pelt

Averill

13 NY

27 NY 8 NY

Reynolds

1 MI

Young's Branch

Stone House

5 MA

11 MA

Robinson

Marines

Griffin

4 AL

Stuart

38 NY

5 VA

Hampton

14 BKLN

Ricketts

4 VA

4 AL

Jackson

Bee, Bartow, & Evans

11 NY

27 VA

Warrenton Turnpike

2 VA

33 VA

1 MN

Griffin

49 VA

11MS/4 SC

Stuart

Chinn Ridge

Manassas-Sudley Road

Bald Hill

Vegetation

Woods   Corn   Orchard   Grains   Fences   Ridges

Map 23

■ Federal Infantry
■ Confederate Infantry
◣ Confederate Cavalry

Scale

0   175   350
Yards

2:00 - 4:00 p.m.

Map 24: The Red-Legged Devils Clear the Field (2:00 – 4:00 p.m.)

For many Confederates on the field, the capture of Griffin's isolated guns was the turning point of the battle, but the fighting was far from over. The 14th Brooklyn, its members dressed in their French-style Chasseur uniforms, advanced quickly southwest across the Manassas-Sudley Road toward the pair of captured guns. (They had been held back to support the exposed guns.) Gen. McDowell himself ordered the regiment to "advance in line up the hill on the right of the [Sudley-Manassas] road leading through the enemy's lines." The charge to capture the pieces and subsequent celebrations had disordered the 33rd Virginia, leaving the soldiers in no shape to take on the approaching line of battle, which extended beyond its left flank (No. 1 on map). The fire opened by the troops from Brooklyn a mere forty yards distant dropped many of the Virginians to the ground. Unable to coordinate a timely defense, they fell back in disorder when the New Yorkers closed the distance and drove the Rebels from the captured guns.

The retreat exposed the left flank of the 2nd Virginia, the next regiment in Gen. Jackson's line (No. 2 on map). The 2nd's commander, Col. James Allen, tried to refuse several companies to meet the new threat. The effort, recalled a private in the 2nd Virginia, was "an unfortunate move. Few men can retire calmly under a galling fire, and the execution of this order resulted in stampeding some good soldiers." The rest of the regiment misunderstood the order and fell back with the 33rd Virginia. Allen rode after his men in an effort to get them back to the firing line, but a shell smashed a limb on a pine tree and sent giant splinters flying through the air. One of them hit Col. Allen and temporarily blinded him. After establishing a firm position on Henry Hill and driving back initial Federal advances, Jackson's left flank was disintegrating and heading for the rear (No. 3 on map).[1]

Instead of pursuing the fleeing Virginians, the New Yorkers turned their attention to the long line of Confederate artillery deployed in front of the enemy line. A single enemy regiment (14th Brooklyn) now had the left flank of Jackson's line and threatened to unravel the entire position. One of Col. Arthur Cumming's officers in the 33rd Virginia announced to Jackson, "General, the day is going against us." Jackson fixed the man with a hard stare. "If you think so, sir," he replied, "you had better not say anything about it."[2]

The hard-charging 14th Brooklyn, nicknamed the "Red-Legged Devils" because of their colorful Chasseur-pattern uniforms of red pants, trimmed jackets, blue blouses, and red kepis, created havoc all out of proportion to their numbers. As one New Yorker recalled it, "our boys were mowing them down in fine style." With the confidence of combat veterans, the 14th Brooklyn concentrated their efforts against the batteries on their left. The guns seemed especially vulnerable because no infantry support was readily visible. Jackson, however, was keenly aware of the unfolding tactical situation and was not about to be beaten so easily. Riding over to the 4th and 27th Virginia, he ordered them to prepare to charge the enemy (No. 4 on map). He also directed a few of his guns to withdraw from their vulnerable positions. "Reserve your fire until they come within 50 yards, then fire and give them the bayonet, and when you charge, yell like furies," ordered Jackson. His calm leadership inspired the green troops by encouraging them that they could successfully repel the Federal charge. Lt. Col. Francis Lackland, now in command of the 2nd Virginia, gathered about 100 men together and joined the 4th Virginia. Jackson now had more than enough men to stop and drive back the attack of the 14th Brooklyn. Once their new position was established, the Virginians opened fire.[3]

Meanwhile, Col. William "Extra Billy" Smith with three companies of the 49th Virginia, a pair of companies from the 11th Mississippi of Gen. Bee's brigade, and one company from the 4th South Carolina of Nathan Evans' brigade—about 450 men all told—slid into position on the left of Jackson's line. The 6th North Carolina of Bee's brigade, fresh off the train from Piedmont Station in their mixture of blue and gray uniforms, together with seven companies of the 2nd Mississippi, were also approaching.[4]

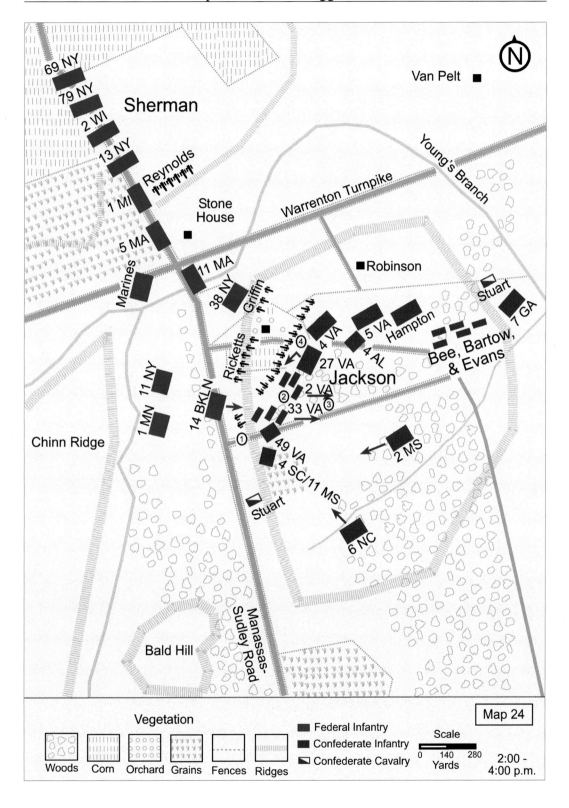

Map 24

Vegetation

| Woods | Corn | Orchard | Grains | Fences | Ridges |

Federal Infantry
Confederate Infantry
Confederate Cavalry

Scale
0   140   280
Yards

2:00 -
4:00 p.m.

Map 25: Defeat of the Red-Legged Devils (2:00 – 4:00 p.m.)

The smoke and confusion on the field hid the fact that the men of the 14th Brooklyn were in trouble as they drove toward the blazing Confederate artillery. According to the commander of the 14th Brooklyn, "We continued our advance to within forty yards of the enemy's infantry, we were then advancing up the ravine in column of division. The fire of the battalion was directed on their leading division with terrible effect, the entire division being cut down."

Maneuvering into position against the New Yorkers were portions of six Confederate regiments: 2nd, 4th, 27th, and 49th Virginia, 2nd Mississippi, and 6th North Carolina, as well as the 11th Mississippi (two companies) and the 4th South Carolina (one company). These regiments were strong in both numbers and leadership, and their members were confident of Jackson's ability, as one soldier in the 4th Virginia recalled it: "the bearing of Jackson on the field inspired the confidence of his men. . . . He rode about in that shower of death as calmly as a farmer about his farm when the seasons are good." Gen. Beauregard also rode along the line, absorbing the cheers and screams of adrenaline pumped out by his men.

The first concentrated fire to rip into the ranks of the 14th Brooklyn was a departing salvo from the Southern artillery (turned by Jackson) and small arms fire from Jackson's 2nd, 4th, and 27th Virginia regiments (No. 1 on map). The deadly fire stunned the left and center of the Brooklyn line, which staggered to a halt while officers quickly worked to redress the disorganized and thinned ranks and get them moving. After a short time the men were ordered forward once again, and once again the New Yorkers were brought to a suden halt by the withering enemy fire. The men from Brooklyn received some help when, recalled one soldier, "some of the Zouaves [11th New York] join[ed] us when the brave [James] Wadsworth came dashing up with hat in hand, and seizing the end of our colors, led the charge to the cannon's mouth."[1]

The cycle repeated itself a third time when the Red-Legged Devils made it even closer to the Confederate line. "But there were just too few New Yorkers still standing, and they were forced to finally give way and made their way to the rear," reported Lt. Col. Edward Fowler. "They then deployed and delivered their fire on us, which, together with a cross fire from the bushes and the shot and shell from their battery, were so severe that we were compelled to retire."

With the enemy retreating, Jackson ordered his men to stand up and attack. "We'll charge them now and drive them to Washington!" Jackson shouted. Moving to the left of their artillery, the 4th and 27th Virginia regiments dashed ahead toward the Federals (No. 2 on map). "[W]e were called to attention and ordered forward on the double-quick, and on an oblique move to the left over a stake and brush fence, through a skirt of pines and subject to a heavy fire of musketry. In a very few minutes we were in close contact with the enemy," a private in the 4th Virginia recalled. Hand-to-hand combat briefly ensued, for there were too many Southern soldiers to repel. Within a short time the persistent band of New Yorkers was rushing back toward the Manassas-Sudley Road (No. 3 on map).[2]

On the far left side of the Confederate line, meanwhile, the 49th Virginia, 2nd Mississippi, and 6th North Carolina were preparing to engage these same Brooklyn soldiers. "Being on my extreme left, one of the North Carolinians, recognizing me, called to me from his ranks: 'That is the enemy; shall we fire?'" recalled "Extra Billy" Smith of the 49th Virginia. "Don't be in a hurry; don't fire upon friends," replied Smith. "At that instant a puff of wind spread out the Federal flag, and I added, 'There is no mistake; give them h—l, boys!', thus giving orders most strangely to a regiment which was not under my command to begin the fight. The enemy was soon scattered and disappeared from the field."

One North Carolinian estimated that his regiment was a mere eighty yards from Ricketts' closest field piece. As a result, the subsequent small arms fire, poured into the battery from point blank range, was devastating.[3]

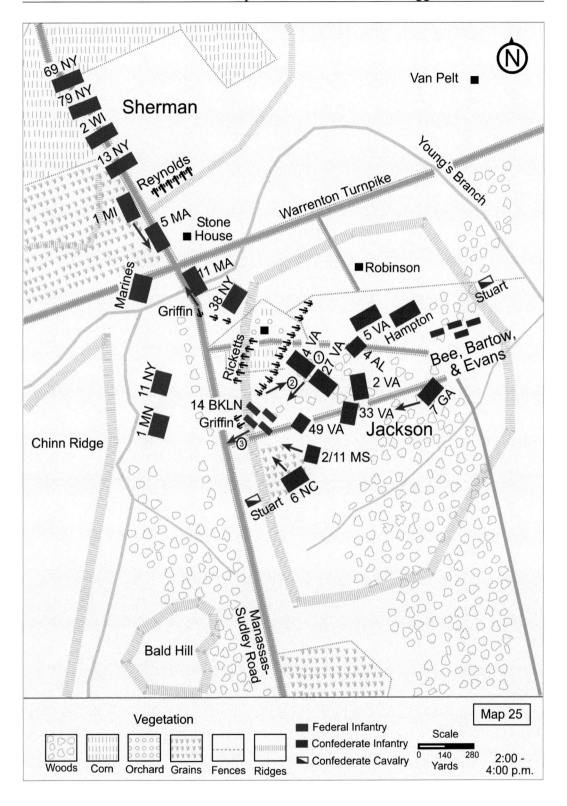

Map 26: Capture of the Federal Artillery (2:00 – 4:00 p.m.)

The Confederate infantry of the 4th and 27th Virginia moved quickly toward Ricketts' guns, their ranks bunched together into a four-deep line (No. 1 on map). According to some accounts, these Virginians hollered what would come to be recognized as the first "Rebel Yell" of the war during their rush for the battery. The Federal guns were without their commander, who was lying on the ground with a painful thigh wound. Switching to canister loads, the cannoneers cut wide swaths in the attacking lines, but the Virginians pressed forward. Without their infantry supports and with men and horses dropping to the ground all around them, the survivors took to their heels, leaving the six guns behind them. Ricketts' battery lost nearly thirty percent of its men during fighting on July 21. Griffin's three guns that had been firing to the left of Ricketts' pieces had already limbered up and rolled to safety.[1]

A quarter-mile to the south, the 6th North Carolina under Col. Charles Fisher was briefly savoring its victory over the 14th Brooklyn. Ahead and to the northwest were two recently rescued guns from Griffin's battery, defended by a small remnant of the 14th Brooklyn. The Tar Heels opened fire, killing and wounding some of the New Yorkers attempting to protect the exposed pieces. Capt. Isaac Avery, who would suffer a mortal wound in July 1863 at the head of a brigade at Gettysburg, yelled to the 6th North Carolina's Col. Fisher, "Colonel, don't you think we ought to charge?" Even without formal military experience, Fisher could see a beckoning opportunity. "Yes Captain," he replied. He turned to his regiment and yelled, "Charge!" (No. 2 on map).

The North Carolinians advanced rapidly toward the guns. A heavy small arms fire delivered by remnants of the 14th Brooklyn, 1st Minnesota, and 11th New York in the woods along their left flank tore through their ranks. The men of the 1st Minnesota were ordered to lie down in the woods to protect themselves, but the area they occupied was so small they were almost lying on top of one another. Inexperienced in war, their task was made all the more difficult by being forced to lie on their backs to load before flipping over to fire at the moving North Carolinians. The carnage on this part of the field was appalling. "[E]very horse killed and the ground covered with the bodies of the dead and wounded artillerists, and of the Brooklyn Zouaves, who were distinguished by their loose red pants," remembered one Federal soldier. To remain stationary was to encourage terrible losses, so Col. Fisher ordered his men to continue moving toward the Manassas-Sudley Road. As they did so, Fisher led a smaller group that obliqued toward the woods on the left—the location of the pesky Federals firing into their flank. A bullet slammed into Fisher's head, killing him instantly. Capt. Avery, with the main body of the attackers, continued charging toward the road. The fire directed at the regiment's front and left flank increased when bullets began zipping through the North Carolina ranks from unknown troops firing from their rear. Thinking the rounds were friendly fire, many Carolinians turned and beseeched the troops to cease firing. Some of the men later insisted that the fire was from soldiers belonging to the 4th Alabama. They also yelled to the Federals in the woods to cease firing, thinking that they too might be Confederate troops.[2]

While the North Carolinians were fighting for their lives, the 1st Michigan, part of Col. Orlando Willcox's brigade, marched south over the Warrenton Turnpike and down the Manassas-Sudley Road toward the fighting swirling on the left of the Rebel defensive line. Once they were close enough, the Wolverines fired into the exposed right flank of the 6th North Carolina. The Michiganders had already lost several men from long distance artillery fire, and so were more than ready for a fight. Their small arms fire was the last straw for the Carolinians. With their ranks ragged and depleted, and with the firing now tearing into them from three directions, Capt. Avery pulled the regiment back the way it had come (No. 3 on map) and settled the men behind Jackson's line. His withdrawal abandoned the pair of Federal cannons from Griffin's battery. The Tar Heels were spent and for all practical purposes, were out of the fight. Although their attack had initially captured Griffin's two guns, there had been no opportunity to haul them to safety. They now had nothing to show for their effort except fields sprinkled with the blue uniforms of their men.[3]

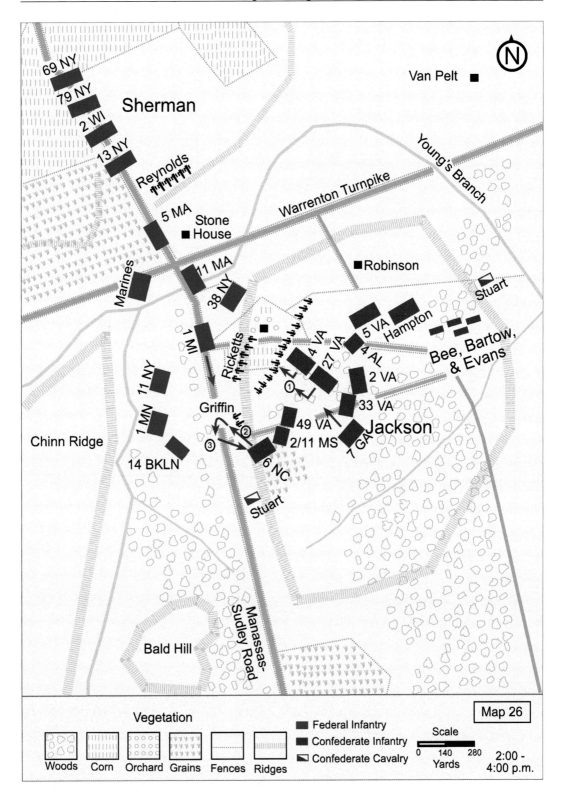

69 NY
79 NY
2 WI
13 NY

Sherman

Van Pelt ■

Reynolds

Warrenton Turnpike

Young's Branch

5 MA

Stone
House ■

Marines

11 MA

38 NY

1 MI

Ricketts

Robinson ■

Stuart

5 VA   Hampton

4 VA
27 VA   4 AL

2 VA

Bee, Bartow,
& Evans

11 NY

1 MN

Griffin

33 VA

49 VA

2/11 MS

Jackson

7 GA

Chinn Ridge

14 BKLN

① ②

③

6 NC

Stuart

Manassas-
Sudley Road

Bald Hill

Vegetation

■ Federal Infantry

Map 26

■ Confederate Infantry

◥ Confederate Cavalry

Scale

0   140   280

Yards

2:00 -
4:00 p.m.

Woods   Corn   Orchard   Grains   Fences   Ridges

N

Map 27: Federals Pour in More Troops (2:00 – 4:00 p.m.)

By the time the 6th North Carolina fell back, the hands of the clock had crossed the three o'clock hour and were moving toward 3:30 p.m. The focal point of the battle continued to swirl around the eight captured Federal cannon on Henry Hill. With the Carolinians falling back, the 1st Michigan (Willcox's brigade) turned its attention to recapturing Ricketts' guns. The Western infantrymen could see the 4th and 27th Virginia of Jackson's brigade forming a protective ring around the captured cannon. Some guessed it was only a matter of time before they would be ordered to retake them. The men went to ground to protect themselves. While in this position, Confederate shells flew over their heads. An occasional shell burst above them, showering lethal fragments among the prone soldiers. Orders arrived to stand, fire a volley, and charge the enemy. According to brigade commander Col. Orlando Willcox, the charge was a success. "The right wing fell back to reload, owing to a blundering order, but the left stood firm, expelled the enemy, and retook the battery," Willcox reported. The 1st Michigan's commander, Maj. Alonzo Bidwell, confirmed part of Willcox's claim when he wrote, "[T]he position of the enemy not being clearly understood . . . an order given at this time not clearly heard, a portion of the line fell back to reload." The determined band quickly closed on the Virginians and hand-to-hand combat erupted around the silent pieces. The fighting claimed a number of Michiganders and their flag. In danger of capture, the Michigan flag bearer used the sharpened point of the flag's staff as a lance, but was still quickly overwhelmed by the enemy. "The regiment unsupported in rear or flank, there was but one thing to be done . . . we fell back" (No. 1 on map). According to Col. Willcox, some of the men involved in the fight were from the 7th Georgia of Bartow's brigade (and some of the units on its left).[1]

When the 1st Michigan was beaten back from the guns, a band of men from the 1st Minnesota, 14th Brooklyn, and 11th New York decided to try their hand at recapturing Griffin's two pieces farther to the south just east of the Manassas-Sudley Road. Jackson's men saw them coming and opened a terrifying fire against them, throwing them back in disorder to the roadway itself. According to a Virginian, it was "a clear case, on their part, of self-imposed butchery . . . that sight was a dreadful one, and rendered ten-fold more conspicuous by the glittering of their bright red uniforms in the gleaming sun of that hot July" (No. 2 on map).[2]

The battle for the guns on Henry Hill had not yet ended. Two regiments from William Franklin's brigade, the 5th and 11th Massachusetts, approached Ricketts' captured guns on the Manassas-Sudley Road (No. 3 on map). The 11th Massachusetts led the column, with the 5th Massachusetts closely following it. Although a formidable force, the Massachusetts men were already shaken by artillery shells that rocked the column by bursting overhead and inflicting numerous injuries. One soldier believed that the 5th Massachusetts sustained most of its casualties during this period before it was able to close within small arms range. The men also saw the shocking sights of the dead and injured littering the fields, and the long line of the wounded making their way to the rear. They were rattled further when Federal horsemen rode past and yelled, "Get out of here or the Black Horse Cavalry will get you all!" Several of Ricketts' caissons galloped past the tramping Bay Staters. "For a time fearful confusion prevailed," admitted a soldier in the 11th Massachusetts. At a time like this, officers can make or break a unit, and the officers on this day showed their effectiveness by calming their men and keeping them in line.

Although the 5th and 11th Massachusetts constituted two-thirds of Col. Franklin's brigade command (the third regiment was the 1st Minnesota, hundreds of yards to the south), some of the men did not see Franklin and after the war wrote bitterly about his "absence." These soldiers resented being sent into battle without their brigade commander riding with them. Franklin made matters worse when he wrote in his after-action report that the two regiments, while occupying their position north of the Warrenton Turnpike, "were slightly exposed to the fire of the enemy's battery on the left [Imboden's], and were consequently thrown into some confusion . . . they fired without command . . . closed in mass."[3]

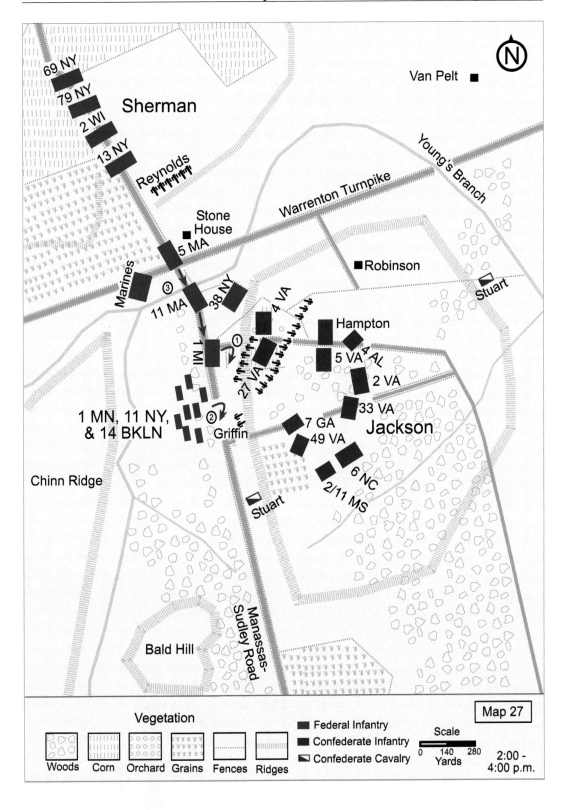

N

Van Pelt ■

69 NY
79 NY
2 WI
13 NY

Sherman

Reynolds

Young's Branch

Warrenton Turnpike

Stone
House
■
5 MA

Robinson ■

Stuart

Marines
11 MA

③

38 NY

4 VA

Hampton

②
①

27 VA

5 VA

4 AL

1 MI

2 VA

33 VA

1 MN, 11 NY,
& 14 BKLN

②
Griffin

7 GA
49 VA

Jackson

6 NC

Chinn Ridge

2/11 MS

Stuart

Bald Hill

Manassas-
Sudley
Road

Map 27

Vegetation

Woods Corn Orchard Grains Fences Ridges

■ Federal Infantry
■ Confederate Infantry
◥ Confederate Cavalry

Scale

0   140   280
Yards

2:00 -
4:00 p.m.

Map 28: Ricketts' Guns are Recaptured (2:00 – 4:00 p.m.)

The 5th and 11th Massachusetts regiments crossed Manassas-Sudley Road under a heavy artillery fire. An officer yelled inspirational words, swung his sword toward the enemy, and led his men up the embankment. When he looked back, he was shocked to see many men moving toward the road rather than up the slope. He halted the advance and aligned his men again, the 5th Massachusetts on the left and the 11th Massachusetts on the right. This time, both regiments moved slowly but steadily eastward toward the enemy.

Ahead of the 5th Massachusetts was the right front of the 4th Virginia and 27th Virginia. Both fired into the advancing regiment. The 11th Massachusetts on the 5th's right found a softer spot in the Southern line, striking the left flank of the 4th Virginia and likely part of the 27th Virginia near Ricketts' guns. A withering artillery and small arms fire raked the Confederate line (No. 1 on map). Capt. Thompson McAllister, who had gallantly led his company of the 27th Virginia against Ricketts' battery a few minutes earlier, ordered his men to "fall back and rally . . . Every other man except the wounded and their attendants, rallied immediately some one hundred and fifty yards in the rear" (No. 2 on map). The original owners of the prized cannon reclaimed their guns. Some of the Federals tried to pull the guns to safety, but they were abruptly stopped by their leaders and ordered back into line to prepare for a Confederate counterattack.[1]

Farther south, the right of the 2nd Virginia advanced to recapture Griffin's two guns, but was forced back (No. 3 on map), likely because of fire from the 11th Massachusetts. For some reason, Col. Franklin minimized the valiant efforts of the two Massachusetts regiments. "[W]ith the help of some other regiments on their right, the enemy was driven from the guns three times. It was impossible, however, to get the men to draw off the guns, and when . . . attempts were made, we were driven off by the appearance of the enemy in large force with heavy and well-aimed volleys of musketry."[2]

Gen. Jackson's entire line on Henry Hill was now jumbled, tired, bloodied, and disordered. Southern army leader Gen. P. G. T. Beauregard knew the position was critical, and cast about for reinforcements. The 5th Virginia and Hampton's Legion, which had held the right side of the Henry Hill line until being driven back earlier in the fighting, answered the call. Pointing to the guns, Beauregard personally led the reinforcements westward toward the fighting. His final words before launching them into action were "Give them the bayonet!" The 5th Virginia advanced on the left side of Hampton's men (No. 4 on map). As they approached the Henry house, the Virginians and South Carolinians made out the 11th Massachusetts aligned near Ricketts' guns. The Southerners drove the Massachusetts soldiers from the guns on two occasions, but both times the Bay Staters returned to defend the guns.

"[We] again engaged the enemy, driving them out of a farm yard and ourselves taking possession of it," wrote Capt. James Conner of Hampton's Legion. "They returned to take it, and the firing was hot and heavy." The approach of the enemy units overlapped the 11th Massachusetts' right flank (No. 5 on map). As one Southerner recalled, "the shouts of the combatants, the groans of the wounded and dying, and the explosion of shells made a complete pandemonium . . . the atmosphere was black with smoke." The Virginians surged forward to claim the guns; it was the second time that Ricketts' pieces had fallen into enemy hands that afternoon. The gray-clad 11th Massachusetts' troubles were not at an end. As they fell back, their own comrades confused them with Jackson's advancing Virginians and South Carolinians and fired into their already torn ranks.[3]

Just one hour earlier, it looked as though Gen. McDowell was presiding over a major victory on Henry Hill. Within that short time, the tactical tables turned and it was his men streaming from the high ground. In rapid piecemeal succession, nine of his regiments had been driven back in defeat. A majority of his original 13,000 men who crossed at Sudley Ford that morning had been killed, wounded, captured, or were no longer in the ranks. Ambrose Burnside's men, roughly handled on Matthews Hill, were resting in the rear, Erasmus Keyes' brigade had been engaged and withdrawn, and Robert Schenck's brigade did not have orders to cross Bull Run. That left McDowell with two available combat brigades under William T. Sherman and Oliver O. Howard.

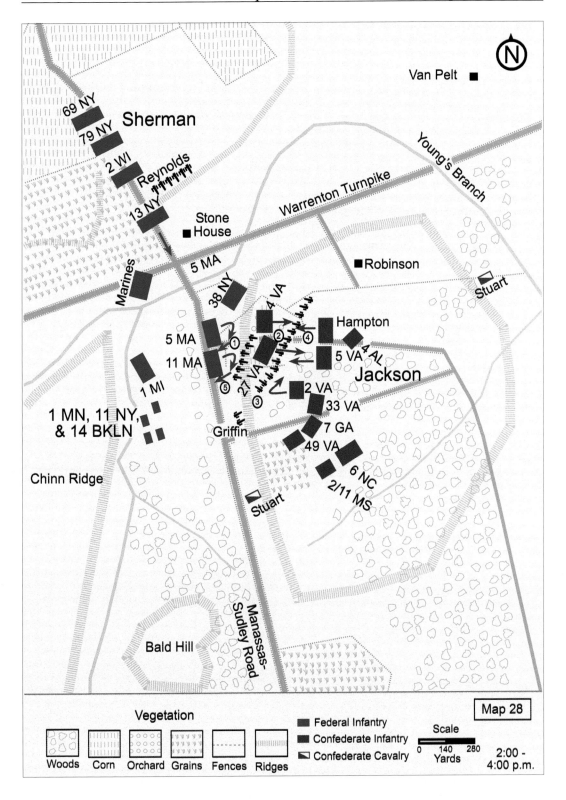

Van Pelt ■

69 NY
79 NY
Sherman
2 WI
Reynolds
13 NY

Young's Branch

Warrenton Turnpike

Stone
■ House

■ Robinson

Stuart

5 MA

Marines

38 NY

4 VA

Hampton

5 MA
11 MA

1 MI

5 VA
4 AL

Jackson

27 VA

2 VA

33 VA

1 MN, 11 NY,
& 14 BKLN

Griffin

7 GA

49 VA

Chinn Ridge

6 NC
2/11 MS

Stuart

Bald Hill

Manassas-Sudley Road

Vegetation

| Woods | Corn | Orchard | Grains | Fences | Ridges |

■ Federal Infantry
■ Confederate Infantry
▷ Confederate Cavalry

Scale
0   140   280
Yards

Map 28

2:00 -
4:00 p.m.

Map 29: Sherman's Brigade Fights for Henry Hill (2:00 – 4:00 p.m.)

On the right of the Federal line, remnants of the 1st Michigan and 11th New York (Willcox's brigade), 1st Minnesota (Franklin's brigade), and the 14th Brooklyn (Porter's brigade) reformed and moved east toward Griffin's two captured guns. Opposing them was an equally makeshift force composed of remnants from the 4th South Carolina and 1st Louisiana battalion (Evans' brigade), 7th Georgia (Bartow's brigade), and 4th Alabama (Bee's brigade) (Nos. 1 and 2 on map).

As the Alabamians moved to engage the enemy, a Southern battery retreating from the front appeared out of the smoke and confusion to cut the regiment in two. Gen. Bee led the 100 or so men closest to him toward the approaching enemy, the unit's battle flag firmly in his hands. He was returning the banner to the flag bearer when a bullet sliced into his abdomen. A group of soldiers gathered around the mortally wounded general. He died early the next day, with Capt. Imboden holding his hand. Bee was the highest ranking officer on either side killed in the battle. Col. Bartow was also cut down about the same time leading the 7th Georgia. On foot, with his cap in hand and yelling to his men to follow him (his horse had been shot earlier), the colonel was struck in the chest by a bullet that lodged in or near his heart. "They have killed me, but never give up the field," he supposedly uttered before dying. He was the first brigade commander killed in action during the Civil War.

Despite these high profile Southern losses, the motley assemblage of troops poured a heavy fire into the attacking Federals and drove them back. "We reformed near the road and advanced again to the top of the hill and were again compelled to retire," wrote the commander of the 14th Brooklyn, "firing as we retreated." The Federals fell back west beyond the Manassas-Sudley Road. Henry Hill was once again in Confederate hands.[1]

With his several efforts rebuffed, McDowell decided on a new strategy. William Sherman's brigade would move directly against Henry Hill while Howard's brigade occupied Chinn Ridge, about 500 yards to the west, where it could flank the Southern forces holding the Henry Hill line.

Howard's rookie troops, however, were bone-tired after their long ten-mile march under a blazing hot sun (occasionally at the double-quick) and needed time to rest. Time, however, was a commodity in short supply.[2]

Col. William Sherman's large 3,000-strong brigade (13th New York, 69th New York, 79th New York, 2nd Wisconsin—Battery E, 3rd U.S. Artillery remained east of Bull Run) was rested and ready for combat. It crossed Bull Run hours earlier about 11:30 a.m. and had done little since that time except make its way fitfully south along the Manassas-Sudley Road. Like many officers who fought that day, Sherman carved out a stellar Civil War career. At First Bull Run, however, he would make the same mistake many of his fellow officers made: sending units into the fight piecemeal.

The 13th New York was thrown toward Henry Hill first—the tenth Federal regiment to try its hand at capturing the hill—while the balance of Sherman's brigade continued marching south to attack Henry Hill from the west. Crossing Warrenton Turnpike east of the crossroads, the New Yorkers spun off to the left of the road and waited there for direction. "We marched down a long hill, and partly up another when we stopped to wait for further orders," wrote Charles Brown of the 13th New York a few days after the fighting. "The enemy's shot and shell fell around us and our battery's shot & shell flew over our heads." After lying in place for several minutes, but which surely must have felt much longer for each man in the ranks, "two of our companies were ordered up to support a battery." The rest of the regiment soon followed. "We rushed up a hill [Henry], and took up a position about thirty rods [roughly 166 yards] from a house and orchard in which was posted a strong force of the rebels," continued Brown.

Huffing their way to within seventy-yards of the house, the men were ordered a second time to lie down (No. 3 on map). When they spotted troops ahead of them, they leveled their muskets and opened fire. "You're firing on friends!" yelled a voice through the smoke, causing the New Yorkers to hold their fire. The troops on the receiving end were not friends but members of Hampton's Legion, who unleashed several volleys into the prone unsuspecting New Yorkers. When the expected orders to charge failed to materialize, the two sides held their ground and emptied their firearms into one another for the next half hour.[3]

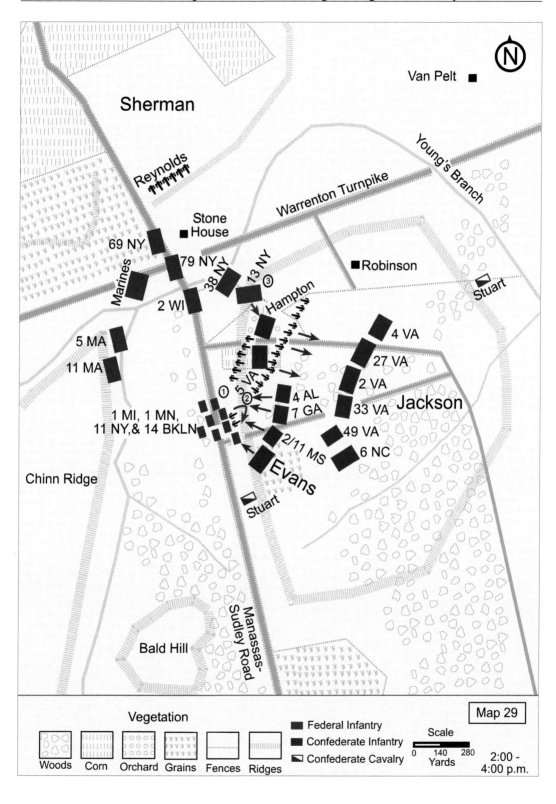

Van Pelt ■

Sherman

Reynolds

Young's Branch

Warrenton Turnpike

Stone
■ House

69 NY

79 NY

38 NY

13 NY ③

Marines

2 WI

Hampton

Robinson

Stuart

5 MA

11 MA

4 VA

27 VA

2 VA

5 VA

① ②

4 AL

7 GA

33 VA

Jackson

1 MI, 1 MN,
11 NY,& 14 BKLN

49 VA

6 NC

2/11 MS

Evans

Chinn Ridge

Stuart

Manassas-
Sudley Road

Bald Hill

Vegetation

Woods Corn Orchard Grains Fences Ridges

■ Federal Infantry
■ Confederate Infantry
◥ Confederate Cavalry

Scale
0   140   280
Yards

Map 29

2:00 -
4:00 p.m.

Map 30: Attack and Defeat of Two of Sherman's Regiments (2:00 – 4:00 p.m.)

While the 13th New York angled southeast, Col. Sherman's remaining three regiments marched south on the Manassas-Sudley Road with the 2nd Wisconsin in the lead, followed by the 79th and 69th New York. Sherman may have hoped the 13th New York's lone thrust up the north face of Henry Hill would distract the enemy while his other regiments slipped farther south to attack the high ground from the west. The plan failed (as most similar plans would during the war) because of poor coordination.

The gray-clad men of the 2nd Wisconsin deployed along the Manassas-Sudley Road facing east, climbed over the embankment bordering it, and headed straight for Ricketts' guns (No. 1 on map). Enemy fire, likely from the 5th Virginia, greeted their arrival. Confused by the disordered nature of close-in combat, the Wisconsin men began falling back. More fire ripped through the ranks of the Badgers, who were mistaken for the enemy. The men threw themselves to the ground to avoid the flying lead while their officers did their best to stop the friendly fire. "This regiment [2nd Wisconsin] ascended to the brow of the hill steadily, received the severe fire of the enemy, returned it with spirit, and advanced delivering its fire," reported Sherman in his report. "This regiment is uniformed in gray cloth . . . and when the regiment fell into confusion and retreated toward the road there was an [sic] universal cry that they were being fired on by our own men."

When they again reached the road, the Wisconsin officers ordered their men to move eastward back up the hill. A small ravine divided the regiment into two distinct groups. When the Wisconsin troops opened fire on the enemy to their front, screams that they were shooting their friends reached them. It was not so. As their fire slackened, the 5th Virginia and Hampton's Legion opened fire. Falling into disorder and with no troops behind them or on their right, the Badgers drifted down the slope to the road. Sherman admitted in his report that the regiment was "repulsed in disorder." To the men of the 79th New York (and perhaps some from the 69th New York as well), the large groups of gray-clad soldiers moving in their direction from the high ground looked suspiciously like an enemy attack. The New Yorkers opened fire, though their effectiveness in downing Badgers is not known.[1]

Sherman's launch of his third regiment, the 79th New York or Highlanders, continued the piecemeal attack against the 5th Virginia and Hampton's Legion. The brigade commander recalled how Confederate artillery shells tore through the Highlanders' ranks when they were ordered to "cross the brow of the hill and drive the enemy." While marking time west of the road, the New Yorkers were unable to respond to an unseen deadly fire landing in their ranks, so the order to advance was greeted by many with relief (No. 2 on map). "All feelings of fear or even nervousness at once vanished; every man felt himself a hero, and our only thought was to get at the enemy and drive him from the field," remembered the regiment's historian. Like the 2nd Wisconsin before them, which had already ascended the hill and been driven back down, the Highlanders were met by a devastating Confederate fire about mid-way up the slope. When the line began to waver, the officers screamed, "Rally, boys, Rally!" It might have been at this point when Wade Hampton exclaimed, "Isn't it terrible to see that brave officer trying to lead his men forward, and they won't follow him."

The New Yorkers, however, reformed and both sides exchanged fire. Sherman noted that "the Seventy-ninth . . . charged across the hill, and for a short time the contest was severe. They rallied several times under fire, but finally broke and gained the cover of the hill." As had happened several times that day, the Confederates yelled out, "Cease Firing! You're shooting your own men!" The claim caused considerable confusion; some men knew it to be a ruse, others were not so sure. The issue was settled when the Rebels fired a devastating volley followed by a second round into the New Yorkers. "[A] shower of bullets crashed through our already torn and bleeding ranks!" wrote one New Yorker. "This caused us to waver again, and after receiving another volley . . . we turned and sought cover under the hill." The 79th New York sustained the highest casualties of any Northern regiment at Bull Run. One of the dead was Col. James Cameron, brother of Secretary of War Simon Cameron. "As we passed down we saw our Colonel lying still, in the hands of Death," remembered one New Yorker.[2]

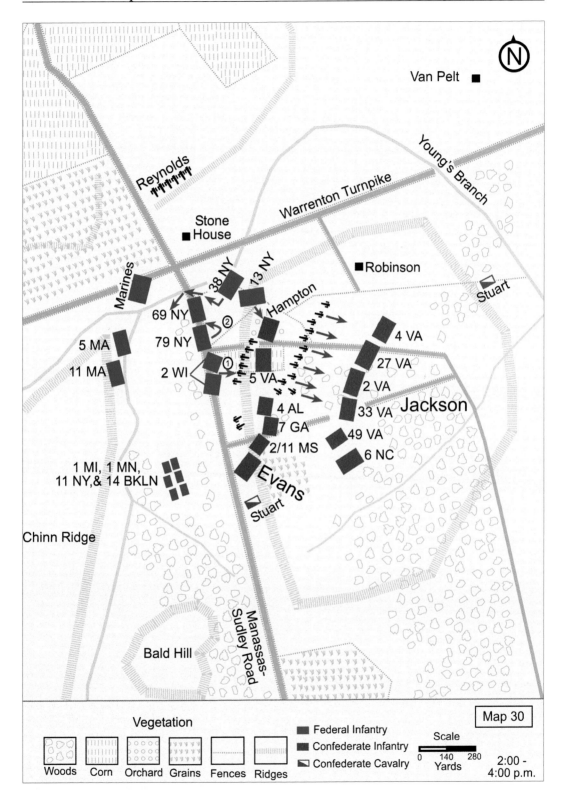

Van Pelt ■

Young's Branch

Reynolds

Warrenton Turnpike

Stone
■ House

Robinson ■

Marines

38 NY

13 NY

Hampton

Stuart

69 NY

②

4 VA

5 MA

79 NY

①

27 VA

11 MA

2 WI

5 VA

2 VA

Jackson

4 AL

33 VA

7 GA

49 VA

2/11 MS

6 NC

1 MI, 1 MN,
11 NY,& 14 BKLN

Evans

Stuart

Chinn Ridge

Manassas-
Sudley Road

Bald Hill

Vegetation

Woods   Corn   Orchard   Grains   Fences   Ridges

■ Federal Infantry
■ Confederate Infantry
◣ Confederate Cavalry

Scale

0   140   280
Yards

Map 30

2:00 -
4:00 p.m.

Map 31: Recapture of the Federal Guns (2:00 – 4:00 p.m.)

The bitter fighting to hold Henry Hill against the assaults from four different Federal regiments exhausted the 5th Virginia and Hampton's Legion and thinned their ranks considerably. There was no time to rejoice, however, for another line of Yankees were now visible emerging from the lingering powder smoke. The 38th New York of Orlando Willcox's brigade had been hovering north of Henry Hill for some time. While Sherman's regiments were being defeated in detail, the 38th New York moved west across the Manassas-Sudley Road and then south, maneuvering into position on the right side of Sherman's fragmented brigade line (No. 1 on map), forming south of Sherman's last intact regiment, the 69th New York (No. 2 on map). Looking behind them, the New Yorkers cheered when a section of Reynolds' battery under Lieutenant J. Albert Monroe, rumbled up, and dropped trail.

Demonstrating some semblance of a coordinated advance, the 38th and 69th New York regiments stepped within range and opened fire on the Confederate defenders. After a prolonged engagement of about forty minutes, their fire forced the exhausted Southern troops to withdraw (No. 3 on map). The 38th New York's Lt. Col. Addison Farnsworth recalled it this way in his report: "A well-directed and destructive fire was immediately opened upon the enemy by my regiment . . . and after a sharp conflict he was forced to retreat in disorder with great loss, seeing shelter in the woods whence he had previously emerged."[1]

To the Federal troops, it looked as though their advance and slugfest had collapsed the entire Confederate defensive line atop Henry Hill. Capt. Thomas Meagher of the 69th New York yelled to his Irishmen, "Come on boys! You have got your chance at last!" His men were more exhausted than some because they had been denied baggage wagons, and so had carried items that few others in the army had to shoulder. Throwing off their loads, they prepared for additional action. The organized attack continued, with the 38th New York and 69th New York surging forward with a cheer.

Gen. McDowell rode behind the 38th New York, watching them as they advanced eastward. His presence "inspired" the New Yorkers. The early progress of the 69th was impeded by some of the survivors of the 79th New York, who were still milling about the area. The two regiments (38th and 69th New York) were joined in their advance by remnants of the 1st Michigan, 1st Minnesota, 14th Brooklyn, and 11th New York (No. 4 on map).

The coordinated drive soon placed Ricketts' guns back in Federal hands. The Northern troops continued advancing, some toward the Henry House and others for Griffin's two guns to their right (south). Details of men from the 38th New York pulled Ricketts' pieces as far as 200 yards to the Manassas-Sudley Road. After a host of failed charges, the hill was finally in Northern hands. McDowell had thrown thirteen regiments against Henry Hill, and all but two were essentially spent. Only Col. Oliver Howard's brigade was fresh, and it was deploying for action near the John Dogan house north of the Warrenton Turnpike.[2]

Many men unschooled in the ways of combat congratulated themselves for winning the battle. Their hopes were quickly dashed when the New Yorkers on Henry Hill spotted additional Southern troops moving into view. Gen. Joe Johnson had overseen the rush of reinforcements toward the hill. These men included elements of three regiments from Col. P. St. George Cocke's Brigade (8th, 18th, and 28th Virginia), which had been defending Ball's and Lewis' fords and were now approaching from the east (No. 5 on map), and the 2nd and 8th South Carolina of Milledge Bonham's Brigade from Mitchell's Ford, which arrived a short time later advancing north up the Manassas-Sudley Road (No. 6 on map). Col. Arnold Elzey's Brigade (temporarily under Gen. E. Kirby Smith) was fresh off the trains from Piedmont Station and arrived a short time later, followed by Jubal Early's Brigade, which had spent the day in reserve on the far right of the Confederate line. Many of Jackson's and Hampton's men who had been streaming to the rear saw the heavy reinforcements, halted, and joined the new arrivals.

It was now about 3:30 p.m., and some 7,000 fresh Southern infantry were marching hard to join the battle.[3]

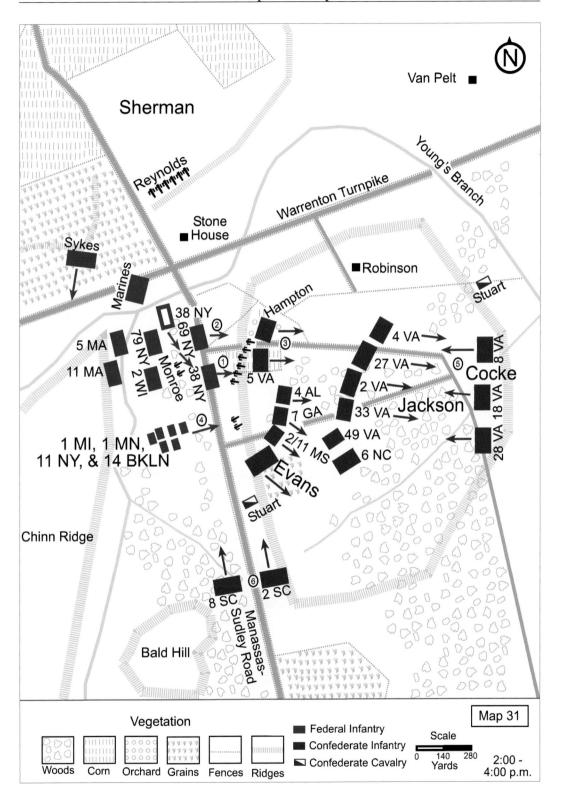

Van Pelt ■

N

Sherman

Reynolds

Young's Branch

Warrenton Turnpike

Stone
House ■

■ Robinson

Sykes

Stuart

Marines

Hampton

38 NY

69 NY

② ③

4 VA

8 VA

5 MA

79 NY

38 NY

① ⑤

Cocke

11 MA

2 WI

Monroe

5 VA

27 VA

2 VA

4 AL

33 VA

Jackson

18 VA

7 GA

④

49 VA

1 MI, 1 MN,
11 NY, & 14 BKLN

2/11 MS

6 NC

28 VA

Evans

Stuart

Chinn Ridge

8 SC   ⑥   2 SC

Manassas-Sudley Road

Bald Hill

Vegetation

Woods   Corn   Orchard   Grains   Fences   Ridges

■ Federal Infantry

■ Confederate Infantry

◥ Confederate Cavalry

Map 31

Scale

0   140   280
Yards

2:00 -
4:00 p.m.

Map 32: The Confederates Counterattack (2:00 – 4:00 p.m.)

McDowell's situation was deteriorating rapidly. The initial approach of the 38th New York below the Warrenton Pike heartened many survivors gathered on the right of the Federal line. Those men—remnants from the 1st Michigan (Willcox) and other regiments—believed the New Yorkers were moving to bolster their exposed position. Instead, the 38th assaulted Henry Hill to the north with the 69th New York. The bloodied and disorganized Federals holding the right flank were already exposed to long range fire from east of the Manassas-Sudley Road[1] (No. 1 on map).

Three other regiments from Cocke's Brigade (8th, 18th, and 28th Virginia) arrived and deployed on Henry Hill as survivors from the 5th Virginia and Hampton's Legion streamed to the rear. Officers tried to rally them, and many from Hampton's unit formed on the right of the 18th Virginia. These Virginians had been guarding Ball's Ford, while the 8th Virginia watched Lewis' Ford. Both regiments had received orders about 2:00 p.m. to leave the crossing points on Bull Run and "go into action as speedily as possible." The men didn't need much prodding, for they were "so anxious to get at the Yankees that it [was] impossible to keep them in line."[2]

The 8th Virginia, moving in on the right of the 18th Virginia, drove toward the 69th New York near the Henry House (No. 2 on map). The 18th Virginia hit the 38th New York farther south near Griffin's pair of abandoned guns (No. 3 on map). To the Federals, the sweeping enemy counterattack likely looked unstoppable. The New Yorkers tried to stand, were too tired and disorganized to do so, and began streaming to the rear. The 13th New York (Sherman's brigade) had been in position north of Henry Hill. Cocke's onslaught made the 13th's situation untenable, or so its officers believed, and that regiment also retreated (No. 4 on map).

The 8th Virginia halted near the Henry house, but the 18th Virginia continued all the way to the Manassas-Sudley Road. According to one Federal, "an attempt was made to rally the men and form line regardless of regiments, but every one was giving orders, and pandemonium

reigned supreme. The enemy . . . approached . . . and poured a volley into this howling mob; it was then 'Skiddoo,' every man for himself." The attack cleared Henry Hill of Federals and swept the road of enemy troops.[3]

Farther south along the Manassas-Sudley Road, Southern reinforcements were reaching the field. The 28th Virginia of Cocke's Brigade, which had been guarding Ball's Ford, advanced west and struck and repulsed the 1st Michigan, wounding and capturing Col. Orlando Willcox. When the recently arrived 8th and 2nd South Carolina regiments of Milledge Bonham's Brigade (the balance remained at Mitchell's Ford) and Capt. Kemper's battery from the south dispersed the last Federals there (No. 5 on map). "On crossing the road a battery open[ed] on us from the right, compelling us (with the example of others retreating) to retire from the field in disorder, the greater portion of the Army then being in rout," Lt. Col. Fowler of the 14th Brooklyn wrote. The South Carolinians continued north and met the 18th Virginia on their right front, exhausted after its fight with the last enemy defenders on Henry Hill. South and west of the Palmetto men, three of Arnold Elzey's four regiments were deploying on Bald Hill (No. 6 on map). After two hours of almost constant combat, the fight for Henry Hill was at an end. McDowell had few fresh troops readily at hand to throw into the fight. The nine Federal guns still on the high ground were once again in Confederate hands.[4]

By 4:00 p.m., McDowell was resigned to defeat. His handling of his army—the piecemeal feeding of troops into the fight, the two-hour delay, the loss of Ricketts' and Griffin's guns, and the failure to launch diversionary attacks to siphon off enemy reinforcements—threw away his initial advantage in numbers and position. Most of his engaged units had been tactically beaten, and many regiments had disintegrated during the hard fighting and withdrawal toward the Warrenton Turnpike. To prevent a complete collapse, McDowell directed Col. Miles at Centreville to advance to the Stone Bridge to cover the army's retreat. From Secretary of War Simon Cameron, McDowell requested all available troops from Washington to move in his direction as quickly as possible.[5]

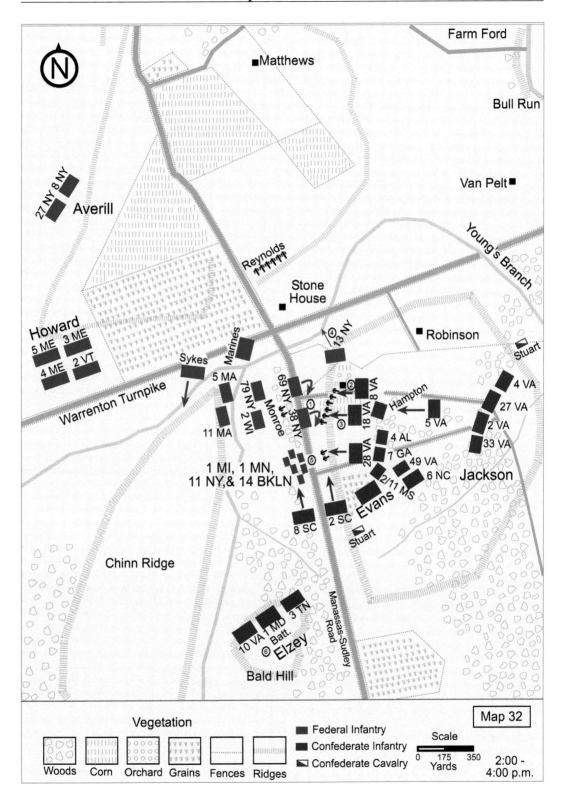

Farm Ford

■Matthews

Bull Run

N

Van Pelt■

27 NY 8 NY

Averill

Young's Branch

Reynolds

Stone
House

Howard
5 ME 3 ME
4 ME 2 VT

Robinson

13 NY

Stuart

4 VA

Sykes

Marines

5 MA

69 NY 38 NY

79 NY 2 WI

Monroe

Hampton

27 VA

8 VA

2 VA

18 VA

5 VA

33 VA

Warrenton Turnpike

11 MA

4 AL

7 GA

28 VA

49 VA

6 NC Jackson

1 MI, 1 MN,
11 NY,& 14 BKLN

2/11 MS

8 SC 2 SC Evans

Stuart

Chinn Ridge

10 VA 1 MD 3 TN
Batt.
Elzey

Manassas-Sudley Road

Bald Hill

Vegetation

Woods Corn Orchard Grains Fences Ridges

■ Federal Infantry
■ Confederate Infantry
◣ Confederate Cavalry

Map 32

Scale
0   175   350
Yards

2:00 -
4:00 p.m.

Map 33: Howard's and Elzey's Brigades on a Collision Course (4:00 – 4:15 p.m.)

McDowell still believed he had an outside chance to turn defeat into at least a stalemate. His last card was Oliver Howard's brigade of four regiments, which was in position north of the Warrenton Turnpike on Dogan Ridge. McDowell's plan was to push Howard south along Chinn Ridge, turn east, and strike what he believed was the Confederate flank and rear east of the Manassas-Sudley Road.

About 4:00 p.m., Howard organized his men near the Dogan house, the 2nd Vermont and 4th Maine in the first line and the 3rd and 5th Maine behind them. He marched his first line south onto Chinn Ridge while his second line waited near the turnpike. Howard, too, fed his men piecemeal into battle. They were tired, having marched since the middle of the night along hot and dusty roads. "Most were pale and thoughtful. Many looked up into my face and smiled," he recalled. McDowell had sent the U.S. Regular battalion under Maj. George Sykes to help shore up the Manassas-Sudley Road sector. When Howard's advance began, Sykes' men were on his left on Buck Hill.[1]

Col. Joseph Kershaw, commander of the 2nd South Carolina (Bonham's Brigade), watched from along the Manassas-Sudley Road as Howard's men tramped south. Kershaw swivelled his regiment and the 8th South Carolina next to him in the direction of the enemy to avoid being flanked. Kemper's Alexandria battery, which had seen action at Blackburn's Ford, was deployed in the ill-fated position of Griffin's two captured guns. The Confederates opened a brisk fire on the approaching enemy infantry, with Sykes' Regulars on the left side of the Federal line bearing the brunt of this frontal and flanking fire.[2]

Additional Southern reinforcements were arriving to support the Carolinians. Col. Arnold Elzey's Brigade was the last from Johnston's army to reach the field. Gen. E. Kirby Smith was in charge of getting Johnston's men on the trains at Piedmont, but when his own brigade didn't make it to the trains on time he joined Elzey and assumed command by virtue of rank, a decision that angered Elzey. The men double-quicked through a thick coating of road dust that covered their shoes, coated their uniforms and exposed skin, and was inhaled into their lungs. When Smith fell wounded while discussing troop placement with Kershaw, Elzey resumed command. Once on Bald Hill, he deployed his men west of Kershaw's position, from left to right as follows: 10th Virginia-1st Maryland battalion-3rd Tennessee. The men were tired from their long rail journey, and the fast march from the Lewis house worsened their ordeal. Elzey sent the four guns of Beckham's battery west to the Chinn house, where they unlimbered. Jubal Early's Brigade was also at hand, marching northwest toward Bald Hill, and part of Jeb Stuart's cavalry was riding to take up station on the left of the strengthening Confederate wing.[3]

Once he was sure the troops approaching Chinn Ridge were in fact Federals—one of Howard's flags' bobbed into view at the top of the high ground—Elzey ordered his men, who by this time had advanced a short distance into a patch of woods, to open fire. "Stars and Stripes! Stars and Stripes! Give it to them, boys!" Elzey shouted. If he initially believed he overlapped the enemy position, Howard was soon disabused of that notion. Beckham's battery and small arms fire began raking the right side of Howard's front line and knocked it into a state of disorder. Howard rode back to the turnpike to bring up his remaining two regiments. What he found there horrified him: the two green regiments were disintegrating. Both had been shaken by long range artillery and scattered small arms fire. Many mistook retreating Federal cavalry for "Black Horse Cavalry" (generic for Rebel horsemen). Only the diligent work of Howard and other officers stopped the panic, but about one-half of the 5th Maine had simply melted away. Howard eventually got the 3rd Maine and what was left of the 5th moving south to relieve his embattled first line on Chinn Ridge.[4]

The reinforcements could not arrive too quickly. The 3rd Maine relieved the 2nd Vermont on the firing line, while the remnants of the 5th Maine slid into position on the right side of the 4th Maine. This arrangement put the newcomers even closer to Beckham's battery, which was firing as rapidly as its gunners could sponge and load. It was "a hot place," admitted Howard. "Every hostile battery shot produced confusion."[5]

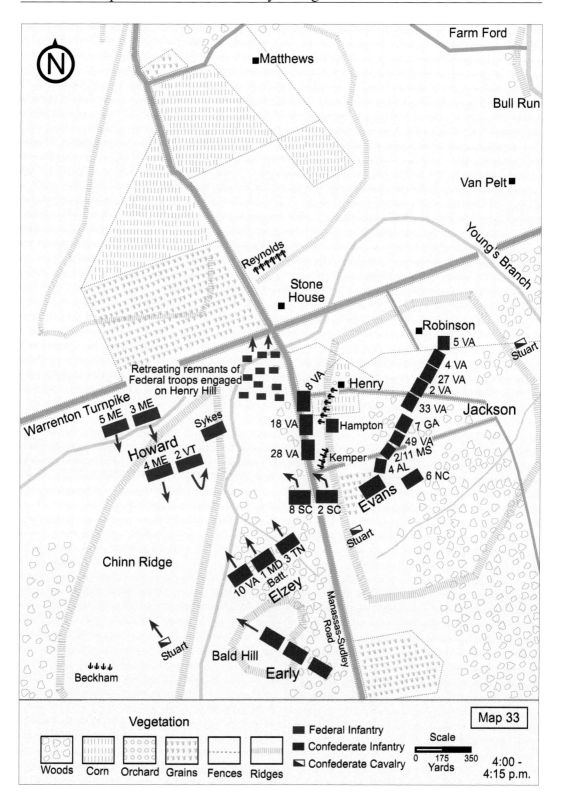

Farm Ford

■Matthews

Bull Run

Van Pelt■

Young's Branch

Reynolds

Stone
House

Robinson
5 VA
4 VA
27 VA
2 VA
8 VA
Henry
33 VA   Jackson
Hampton   7 GA
18 VA
49 VA
2/11 MS
28 VA   Kemper   4 AL
6 NC

Retreating remnants of
Federal troops engaged
on Henry Hill

Warrenton Turnpike
5 ME 3 ME   Sykes

Howard
4 ME 2 VT

8 SC 2 SC   Evans

Stuart

Stuart

Chinn Ridge

10 VA 1 MD 3 TN
Batt.
Elzey

Manassas-Sudley Road

Stuart

Beckham

Bald Hill
Early

Vegetation

Woods Corn Orchard Grains Fences Ridges

■ Federal Infantry
■ Confederate Infantry
◨ Confederate Cavalry

Scale

0   175   350
Yards

Map 33

4:00 -
4:15 p.m.

Map 34: Howard Retreats (4:15 – 4:30 p.m.)

Jubal Early marched his newly arrived (to this sector) brigade off Bald Hill onto Chinn Ridge to the left of Arnold Elzey's three regiments, straightened his line of battle, and advanced north toward Howard's position. Early's thrust extended the Confederate ring of fire, which was now slicing through Howard's regiments from their left and front (No. 1 on map). The 3rd and 4th Maine regiments, on the left side of Howard's line, fired blindly into the woods sheltering Elzey's troops, "though wholly ignorant of whether our efforts were any use or not," admitted a regimental historian. "Our men fought well and stood the fire like heroes," remembered one of the soldiers. In reality, the Maine men found themselves in a very difficult position, and they did not hold it for long. One shell exploded directly above the 3rd Maine, sending its men scurrying north on Chinn Ridge until they found cover behind the brow of the hill. To its credit, the regiment quickly reformed and returned to its former position.[1]

A mistake on the field ended Col. Howard's Civil War combat debut. With the Confederates advancing toward his position, Howard ordered a portion of one regiment to refuse one flank. His directive was construed to mean a general withdrawal by the entire regiment—something the rest of the men gladly complied with. When the officers learned of the mistake, they desperately attempted to stem the rearward tide, to no avail. By this time, Howard was well aware his position on Chinn Ridge was precarious. With the Confederates advancing in overwhelming numbers on his left and along his front, Howard decided a withdrawal was the best decision and joined the retreat (No. 2 on map).[2]

When Elzey realized the New Englanders were retreating north on Chinn Ridge, he ordered his men to follow (No. 3 on map). According to a soldier in the 1st Maryland, the advance was "not in a very regular line, but each one striving to be the foremost." Everything progressed as expected until the men stumbled upon a sprawling field of blackberries. Since many of the men had not eaten for nearly thirty-six hours, they stopped to fill their mouths

with the ripe fruit. The frustrated officers worked hard to get the men moving again, for it was a matter of honor that they pursue the enemy. It took some doing, but they finally got the men moving again, but not before the troops grabbed handfuls of the berries every time they brushed past a bush. Many soldiers spent the next few days pulling painful thorns from their hands.[3]

Col. Howard halted his men on the northwest corner of Chinn Ridge behind a thicket, where he hoped to reform his broken ranks (No. 4 on map). Climbing the ridge, Elzey's men spotted the reforming enemy, leveled their muskets, and fired into them while Beckham's battery found the range and pounded them anew. Early's Brigade continued its march northeastward, sweeping along the top of the ridge. "It was no use," wrote a soldier in the 3rd Maine. "All the other troops had left, and the rebels were coming upon us in overpowering numbers." Howard ordered another retreat about 4:30 p.m., but this one was different. His men completely broke under the strain, flooding north as fast as they could run. Standing on the heights, Elzey's men watched with glee as the Federals fled en masse in full retreat.[4]

There was one exception to the rout now underway: Maj. Sykes' Regulars. Sykes' command was the only organized body of Federal troops remaining south of the Warrenton Turnpike. The Regulars gamely held their position under a galling enfilading fire against their center and left from Virginia and South Carolina troops stationed along the Manassas-Sudley Road. Elzey's pursuit against Howard's retreating masses threatened Sykes' right flank and rear, and made his position untenable. Realizing the dangerous nature of his position, and without any hope of support, Sykes ordered an "about face" and marched his men north toward the turnpike (See No. 5 on map).[5]

With Howard's troops streaming north and Sykes' Regulars falling back, Gen. McDowell's final options for continuing the battle were exhausted. There were no more troops to throw against the advancing Confederates. McDowell and his staff desperately tried to stop the flood of panicked men near the Matthews house, without success. The Federals had been beaten, and there was nothing left to do but leave the field of battle as fast as possible. "It was no use to do anything more," one of McDowell's staff officers observed, "and they might as well start home."[6]

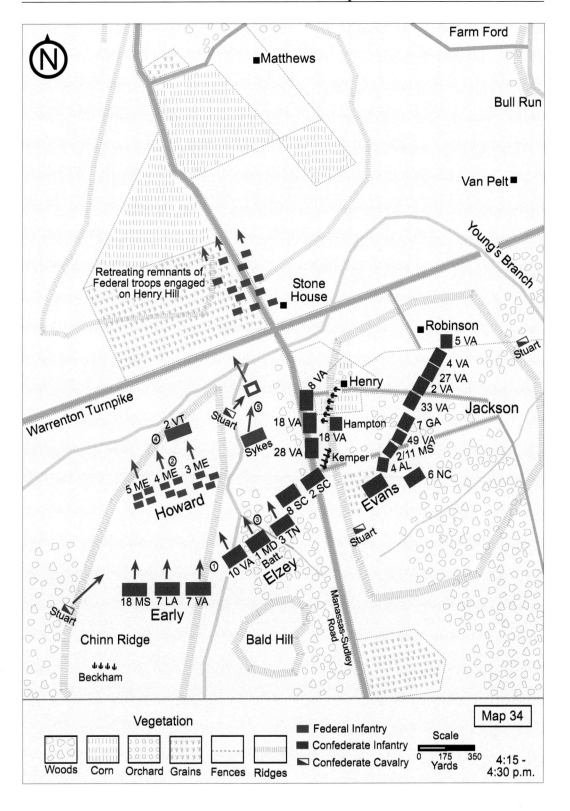

N

Farm Ford

■Matthews

Bull Run

Van Pelt■

Retreating remnants of
Federal troops engaged
on Henry Hill

Stone
House

Young's Branch

Warrenton Turnpike

■Robinson

5 VA

Stuart

4 VA
27 VA
2 VA

8 VA   ■Henry

33 VA   Jackson

18 VA   Hampton   7 GA

2 VT   Stuart   ⑤

18 VA   49 VA

④   Sykes   28 VA   Kemper   2/11 MS

②   4 AL   6 NC

5 ME 4 ME 3 ME

Howard   8 SC 2 SC   Evans

③   Stuart

①   10 VA 1 MD 3 TN
Batt.   Elzey

18 MS 7 LA 7 VA

Stuart   Early

Manassas-Sudley Road

Chinn Ridge   Bald Hill

Beckham

Vegetation

■ Federal Infantry
■ Confederate Infantry
◨ Confederate Cavalry

Map 34

Scale

0   175   350
Yards

4:15 -
4:30 p.m.

Woods Corn Orchard Grains Fences Ridges

Map 35: Fighting North of Blackburn's Ford (7:30 a.m. – 4:00 p.m.)

McDowell needed to freeze in place the four Confederate brigades guarding the Bull Run fords so they could not reinforce their embattled comrades on Henry Hill. The task of feinting to hold the enemy was given to a pair of brigades led by Col. Israel Richardson (Tyler's division) and Col. Thomas Davies (Miles' division).[1]

Richardson had pushed his four regiments near the Butler house when Tyler's guns opened fire early on July 21. Richardson likely savored the opportunity to take another shot at the enemy, for he had unsuccessfully fought them here on July 18. He ordered the 3rd Michigan into line of the road leading to the ford, with seven companies of the 1st Massachusetts aligned on the right side (the three remaining Massachusetts companies were on skirmish and guard duty). His remaining two regiments, the 2nd Michigan and 12th New York, were posted north of the Butler house. Two four-gun batteries, Co. M, 2nd U.S. Artillery under Capt. Henry J. Hunt and Co. G, 2nd U.S. Artillery under Lt. Oliver Greene, galloped into position, unlimbered, and opened fire on the enemy batteries on the far side of Bull Run. Col. Davies' brigade—the 16th, 18th, 31st, and 32nd New York regiments—deployed east of the road on Richardson's left flank (No. 1 on map).[2]

The Confederates on the far side of Bull Run watched with growing concern as the enemy gathered in strength. The four Southern brigades protecting the crossings were arrayed as follows: Milledge Bonham at Mitchell's Ford; James Longstreet at Blackburn's Ford; David R. Jones at McLean's Ford; and Richard S. Ewell at Union Mills. Bonham sent at least two scouting teams north toward the Butler house to ascertain enemy strength. During the mid-morning hours Longstreet, concerned about the growing losses enemy guns were inflicting on his men, sent most of his brigade across the stream to capture them (No. 2 on map). When he realized the Federals were in strength, Longstreet returned his soldiers to their positions on the south shore.[3]

Division leader Miles arrived on the scene about 11:00 a.m. Unhappy with Davies' deployment, he ordered the 16th and 31st New York forward to a farm lane facing Little Rocky Run, pulled back the 18th New York into a supporting position, and left the 32nd New York along the Manassas-Centreville Road. He also rearranged the artillery. Richardson ordered his men to dig in to strengthen their position.[4]

Except for some fitful artillery fire, several hours passed without serious action. This convinced Gens. Johnston and Beauregard (as did the fact that the Federals were throwing up defensive works) that the threat here was a feint. By this time, the Confederates were fighting to hold the high ground on Henry Hill. Sometime between 1:00 and 2:00 p.m., two of Bonham's regiments, the 2nd and 8th South Carolina, together with Kemper's battery, were pulled away from Mitchell's Ford to reinforce Henry Hill.[5]

Col. David R. Jones's Brigade guarding McLean's Ford was ordered at 11:30 a.m. to cross the creek and test Federal strength (No. 3 on map). A similar order at 7:15 a.m. had been recalled. Jones marched as fast as possible, but his men were still tired from the morning reconnaissance, and many were recovering from a measles outbreak. When he reached Little Rocky Run about 3:00 p.m., Jones placed the 18th Mississippi on his left and the 5th South Carolina on the right, leaving the 17th Mississippi in reserve (No. 4 on map).

When the South Carolinians and the Mississippians advanced, the 16th and 31st New York turned to the left to face them. Six Federal guns were also redeployed to meet the unexpected Southern troops. The 18th Mississippi had trouble keeping up with the Carolinians, and the 17th Mississippi fired into the 18th's rear. Davies called up the 18th New York and 32nd New York to bolster his line. Despite a heavy fire against their front and scattered fire against their rear, the South Carolinians refused to budge. Three times Jones ordered them to retreat, but the men stood tall for another forty-five minutes before doing so. Davies pulled his men back a short time later.

Jones' Brigade lost fourteen killed and sixty-two wounded in this action, which was to have been coordinated with a similar move by Ewell and Longstreet. (Beauregard had been trying to direct an offensive against the Union left for hours, but his orders were ill-conceived and poorly written.) Ewell claimed he never received any orders to launch his attack.[6]

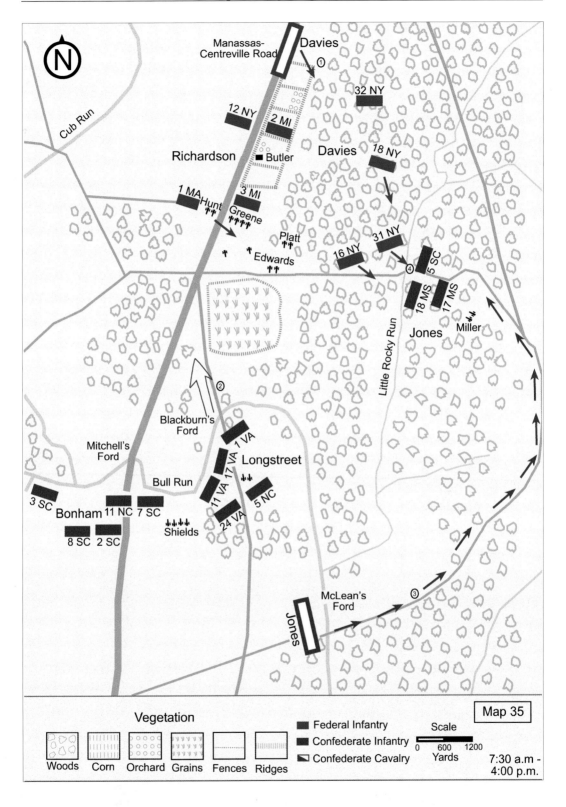

Map 36: The Federal Retreat (4:30 – midnight)

The Federals retreated across Bull Run using the same fords they had crossed earlier that morning. Sherman's and Keyes' brigades (Tyler's division) waded Farm Ford. The remnants of Heintzelman's and Hunter's (now Porter's) divisions crowded across Sudley Ford—which meant they would once again tramp the longer eight-mile route to the Cub Run. The delay that would ensue offered the enemy time to reform and possibly get into a position to cut off the retreat. Many units were so disorganized and confused that their officers simply instructed them to reassemble in their old camps near Centreville. The retreat was anything but orderly, but it was not yet panic-stricken. The enemy withdrawal, wrote one Confederate, "reminded me of nothing so much as a swarm of bees."[1]

Even the lowliest Southern foot soldier realized a golden opportunity when he saw one. The Federals were in complete disarray, trudging back the way they had come. This was the time to end the war. Some infantry turned the captured guns around and fired a few parting shots at the Federals. Gen. Beauregard ordered the 28th Virginia of Col. Cocke's Brigade to move first. The Virginians marched up Matthews Hill without finding any Federal troops and halted near the Matthews house. Jubal Early's Brigade advanced north across the Warrenton Turnpike all the way to Poplar Ford without finding opposition. Jeb Stuart's cavalry galloped after the retreating Federals and caught up with the rearguard crossing Sudley Ford, capturing scores of prisoners. The presence of Sykes' Regulars near the ford, formed into a square to ward off cavalry, coupled with the prisoners they had to escort to the rear, ended Stuart's pursuit.[2]

Beauregard knew enough about military tactics to try and intercept the head of the column rather than push after the rearguard. He sent the 18th Virginia of Cocke's now widely scattered brigade across Lewis Ford and then north toward the Stone Bridge. The 2nd and 8th South Carolina of Bonham's Brigade, together with Capt. Kemper's battery, also moved north to cut off the Federals. Although the enemy was in sight the South Carolinians waited for orders before attacking (though they did capture New York Congressman Alfred Ely). By the time they received orders to engage, the Federals were well on their way back toward Centreville. About 6:00 p.m., Capt. Kemper's gunners found a good platform and opened fire on the suspension bridge across Cub Run. Their accurate fire created panic on and around the bridge, as one Rhode Island soldier recalled: "It was the first time that day that I had seen anything to startle me. Before the third shell struck near us, every man as far as the eye could reach seemed to be running for [his] very life." Kemper's shells overturned a wagon that closed the bridge to traffic. The gunners turned their attention to the defenseless mass of Federal wagons and guns huddled near the bridge. Many later called the decision "barbarous cruelty."[3]

A makeshift Southern cavalry battalion under R. C. Radford hit a band of Federals milling about the Spindle house, where the remnants of Porter's and Heintzelman's divisions reached the Warrenton Turnpike just west of the bridge over Cub Run. Cutting and slashing, the cavalry rode into the yard, scattering troops and capturing several guns from Cpt. James H. Carlisle's Co. E, 2nd U.S. Artillery. Panic began to slowly infiltrate several areas along the retreat. It could have been much worse for the Federals. When Beauregard received reports that a sizeable Federal force was moving across McLean's Ford on his far right to attack his flank and rear, he diverted large numbers of troops who would otherwise have marched hard to intercept the retreating Federals. The "threat" was David R. Jones' repulsed Confederate brigade re-crossing the creek.[4]

By about 7:00 p.m., all of the Federals had moved beyond Cub Run. Left behind was the large Parrott rifle that had opened the fight so many hours earlier. As the Northern troops trudged toward Centreville, they could see Col. Richardson's brigade (Tyler's division) and Col. Miles' division guarding the roads.

When Longstreet was ordered to join in the pursuit, he rapidly crossed the run and moved north toward Centreville. Bonham inserted his brigade on the road leading to Centreville, however, clogging the route. Night quickly fell and Longstreet halted his men for about an hour and returned them to the run.

The battle of Bull Run (Manassas) was finally at an end.[5]

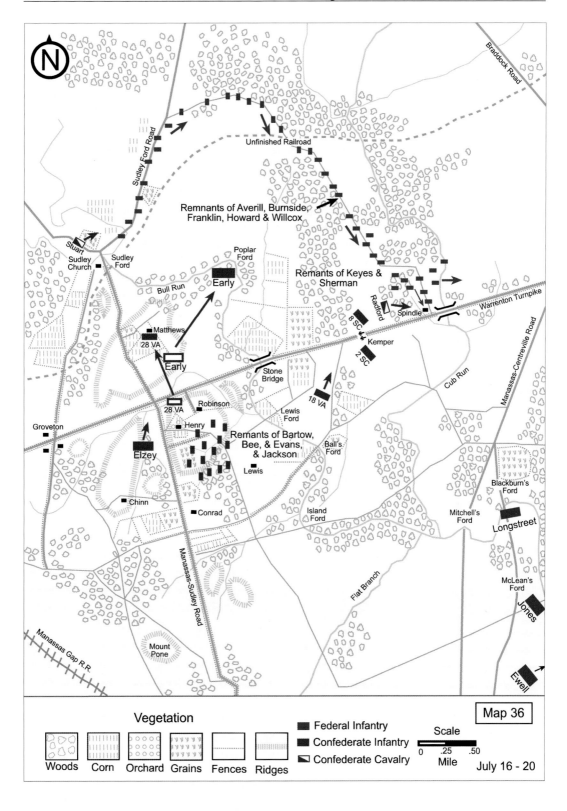

Braddock Road

Sudley Ford Road

Unfinished Railroad

Stuart

Sudley
Church

Sudley
Ford

Poplar
Ford

Bull Run

Early

Remnants of Averill, Burnside,
Franklin, Howard & Willcox

Remants of Keyes &
Sherman

Radford

Spindle

Warrenton Turnpike

Matthews

28 VA

Early

28 VA

Robinson

Henry

Remants of Bartow,
Bee, & Evans,
& Jackson

Lewis

Stone
Bridge

Lewis
Ford

18 VA

8 SC

Kemper

2 SC

Cub Run

Manassas-Centreville Road

Groveton

Elzey

Chinn

Conrad

Ball's
Ford

Island
Ford

Blackburn's
Ford

Mitchell's
Ford

Longstreet

Manassas-Sudley Road

Flat Branch

McLean's
Ford

Jones

Manassas Gap R.R.

Mount
Pone

Ewell

Vegetation

Woods   Corn   Orchard   Grains   Fences   Ridges

■ Federal Infantry

■ Confederate Infantry

◥ Confederate Cavalry

Scale

0   .25   .50

Mile

Map 36

July 16 - 20

First Bull Run (Manassas) Summation

By the time the shooting ended, thousands of dead and wounded dotted the fields from Sudley Ford to the north to Chinn Ridge to the south. The largest concentrations of killed and maimed were on Henry Hill and Matthews Hill.

Gen. McDowell's Federal army lost 481 men killed, 1,011 wounded, and 1,216 missing (and presumably captured) for a total loss of 2,708. Gen. Heinzelman's division sustained the greatest losses with 1,582 from all causes, and Hunter's [Porter's] division the least with 809.

On the Confederate side, Gen. Beauregard's and Gen. Johnston's armies lost a combined 378 killed, 1,489 wounded, and 30 missing for a total of 1,897. Of this total, Johnston's army—which did most of the fighting on July 21—lost 270 killed, 979 wounded, and 18 missing. Beauregard's army accounts for the remainder of these numbers with 108 killed, 510 wounded, and 12 missing.[1]

Although the Federal army had been beaten, some of its commanders were still full of fight. Riding into Centreville during the evening of July 1, Gen. Tyler was "astonished at the demoralization which presented itself on every side." He was also unhappy with Col. Dixon Miles' division, which formed the reserve. "[E]ven the reserve seemed demoralized," Tyler observed, "its commanding general was maudlin drunk." When he found Gen. McDowell, Tyler insisted that he gather as many of the division and brigade commanders as he could find and hold a counsel of war to determine whether the army should remain in Centreville. The army commander was so exhausted during this discussion that he fell into a deep sleep. He was finally roused by an aide who informed him that the group had determined that it was folly to try and hold the small town. Riders were dispatched to order the troops to continue their retreat, only to find that many were already on the move. It is unlikely that any amount of pleading could have convinced them to turn and fight.

McDowell rode to Fairfax Court House and composed a hasty telegram to Washington to informing the War Department of his decision to continue retreating to the capital. "The men

having thrown away their haversacks in the battle and left them behind, they are without food," he explained. "The larger part of the men are a confused mob, entirely demoralized." He also informed the department that he would attempt to hold the town, although "it was the opinion of all the commanders that no stand could be made this side of the Potomac." Although McDowell later reconsidered his decision, it is doubtful whether he could have rallied many men to his cause. All this was a deep disappointment to Gen. Winfield Scott, who had hoped that McDowell would hold Centreville, or at the very least Fairfax Court House. As the magnitude of the army's disintegration became clear, Scott understood the need to return the troops to the Washington defenses. President Lincoln took the news badly, spending the night stretched out on a couch reading and listening to reports of the unfolding disaster.

The Confederacy had not only won the first major battle of the war, but had also captured invaluable equipment. According to McDowell's after-action report, his army lost 25 artillery pieces (Johnston put the number at 28). While some of the guns were small and older iron smoothbores, most were modern rifled pieces the South desperately needed. Johnston also reported that his men captured 5,000 muskets, nearly 500,000 cartridges, ten stands of colors, 64 artillery horses, 26 wagons, and "much camp equipage, clothing, and other property abandoned in their flight."[2]

One of the battle's enduring myths is the claim that numbers of Northern civilians watched the battle and were swept up in the chaotic Federal retreat. According to historian John Hennessy, there were spectators, to be sure, but the vast majority of them got no closer to the battlefield than Centreville. Those who made it closer to the action (mainly politicians) stopped near Schenck's position by Bull Run. And of those, only Congressman Alfred Ely fell into Southern hands. Ely spent the next six months in a Richmond prison and wrote about his experiences in 1862, soon after his release.[3]

Why did the Federal army lose First Bull Run; or put another way, why did the Southern army emerge victorious? According to historians, there are a number of reasons why McDowell lost.

First, Gen. Robert Patterson was unable to hold Johnston's army in the Shenandoah Valley.

When the latter reached Manassas, the size of the two opposing forces became roughly equal and the Confederates had a mobile reserve (although McDowell had planned on facing an enemy about the size of the one he actually fought).

Second, if McDowell had quickly marched on Bull Run rather than wait for supplies for two days around Centreville on July 19 and 20, he almost certainly could have crushed the outnumbered Beauregard before Johnston's army arrived.

Third, although McDowell had an army of almost 35,000 men, he only managed to get 15,000 – 18,000 into the battle. Unfortunately from the Northern perspective, these numbers were further minimized because the men were fed bit by bit into the action rather than advanced in larger, stronger attacks. The rest of McDowell's army waited in reserve for orders.

Fourth, while McDowell's battle plan was sound, he fatally erred by not putting the flanking divisions (Hunter's and Heintzelman's) at the head of the column, rather than behind Tyler's division (whose leader expressed reticence to cross in force after receiving orders to do so), which had only a short distance to march.

Finally, McDowell's lack of large scale combat experience (which was true of every other officer of note on the field that day) was on full view on July 21. He underestimated the difficulties of complex offensive action and moving large bodies of inexperienced men over long distances, and he waited too long (about one and one-half hours) to press the retreating enemy after crushing them on Matthews Hill. His decision to send Ricketts' and Griffins' guns across the pike, thereby negating their longer range advantage, was also a mistake.[4]

The Federal army was reorganized and given to Gen. George McClellan, who had won minor victories in Western Virginia. McDowell was given a division and later a corps and participated in the Second Bull Run Campaign. He was court-martialed for his actions during this campaign and exonerated. Shipped to the West coast in 1864, he commanded the Department of the Pacific through war's end.

Division leader Col. Miles, who had behaved rather oddly during the battle (and who Tyler believed was clearly drunk immediately thereafter), was the subject of a Court of Inquiry.

The findings, handed down on November 6, 1861, found that while Miles was indeed intoxicated, he had been given brandy by a surgeon because he was ill that day. According to the court, "evidence cannot be found sufficient to convict Colonel Miles of drunkenness before a court-martial." Miles was allowed to remain in the army.

On the Southern side, Gens. Beauregard and Johnston were lucky to have had aggressive leaders like Nathan Evans, Bernard Bee, and Thomas Jackson handling matters on the Confederate left while they were involved on the right flank. Evans' decision to rush his men to defend Matthews Hill absorbed the initial Federal thrust behind the Confederate left flank, disorganized the attackers, threw them off their game plan, and bought precious time for Bee, Bartow, Jackson, and others to join in the combat or take up a defensive stand on Henry Hill.

Despite the important victory, both army leaders soon quarreled with President Jefferson Davis. The bickering resulted in Beauregard's banishment to the Western Theater; Johnston also bitterly feuded with Davis but remained with the army until he was critically wounded the following spring at Seven Pines. He was permanently replaced by Gen. Robert E. Lee.[5]

The men had plenty of time to think about what had transpired during those fateful days in July. Some, like members of Francis Bartow's Brigade, chose to recognize their fallen leader by erecting the first battlefield monument. The marble shaft, which sat on the exact location of Bartow's mortal wounding, was dedicated on September 5, 1861, during a somber ceremony witnessed by thousands. The monument was subsequently vandalized by Federal soldiers when they occupied this area in 1862. Only the base now exists.

While many men regretted their decision to volunteer, a large number remained committed to their cause. This can be summed up by a portion of a letter from Sergeant A. C. McPherson of the 7th Georgia (Bartow's Brigade) to his brother: "The particulars of the battle you will find in the Richmond papers, fuller than I can give them; but I will say that it was a terribly, bloody battle, and I was in it. I have seen the horrors of war, in all its blood and terror. My curiosity is satisfied; but I am as anxious to again brave its perils to defend our country and repel her invaders."[6]

August–September 1861

Map 37: Retreat to Washington (July 22)

The wagons carrying the shattered bodies of the Federal wounded began rumbling into the forts near the Potomac River about 3:00 a.m. on July 22. Bands of stragglers, many of whom were lightly wounded, followed. Onlookers watched with incredulity as one particular soldier trudged past, rifle in hand, with one of his arms shot off below the elbow. That so many of these men were able to weather the twenty-five mile trek from the battlefield defied belief. Behind the wagons and wounded marched units that retained some semblance of order. Many were in fairly good fighting trim, considering what they had just experienced.[1]

The men thought they would return to their old camps along the Potomac River between the high ground of Alexandria and Arlington. The position, however, was fairly low in the center and too close to the river, which made it difficult for troops to maneuver easily from one sector to another. To make matters worse, many of the forts and defensive works south and west of the capital were incomplete. When he arrived at his headquarters on the morning of July 22, McDowell—who had been in the saddle for thirty-two hours—mounted the steps to the porch, plopped his large frame into a rocking chair, and fell asleep. When he awoke, his entire demeanor exuded defeat and bewilderment. He soon snapped out of his depression and began preparing for the defense of Washington.

In the city, Gen. Winfield Scott assumed control over the military situation. He dismissed suggestions that the enemy was advancing and ordered engineers to strengthen Forts Albany, Corcoran, Ellsworth, and Runyon. Scott also ordered McDowell to send the returning troops across the Potomac to Washington except for fifteen three-year regiments, which Scott wanted left on the Virginia side of the river.[2]

Every Confederate, from commanders Joe Johnston and P. G. T. Beauregard down to the lowest private in the army, was elated by the stunning victory on the plains of Manassas. Confederate President Jefferson Davis, himself a

decorated Mexican War veteran and former Secretary of War, arrived on the field in time to bask in the glow of victory. There was still daylight left and more damage to inflict if the army could organize itself to launch an effective pursuit. After a discussion with his chief lieutenants, Davis agreed to order Bonham's Brigade forward toward Centreville. (Bonham's was the closest brigade to the enemy and was the freshest in hand.) The onset of evening shadows brought with it caution. Perhaps it was best, thought the Confederate high command, to wait until morning to launch Bonham toward the defeated enemy. Rain arrived with the darkness and continued into July 22, soaking the men and making the roads impassible to columns of men and their wheeled vehicles. The advance would have to be delayed for at least another day.[3]

For the Federals, the finger pointing began almost as soon as the sun set behind the Blue Ridge Mountains. Among the first to be singled out was the elderly Gen. Patterson, who had failed to keep Joe Johnston's army in the Shenandoah Valley. Without his help, Beauregard's small command at Manassas would almost surely have been crushed in the fighting at Bull Run. McDowell was next in line. Although he had not selected his immediate subordinates, and he believed he was forced to venture forth to give battle with troops not yet ready for the task, on his broad shoulders would fall the brunt of the criticism and blame. Many of President Lincoln's advisors restated their faith in McDowell at a cabinet meeting on July 22, but everyone in the room knew he had to be removed from command of the army. McDowell would retain his rank, would not be ostracized, and would be allowed to continue serving with the army.

Also on July 22, Gen. George B. McClellan received a telegram from Washington: "Circumstances make your presence here necessary. Charge Rosecrans or some other Gen. with your present department and come hither without delay." Only 34 years old, McClellan impressed Gen. Scott. He had graduated second in his 1846 West Point class and served with distinction during the war with Mexico. Scott regularly corresponded with McClellan during the early days of the Civil War, and his small victory over Confederate Gen. Robert E. Lee in Western Virginia branded him as a man destined for high command.[4]

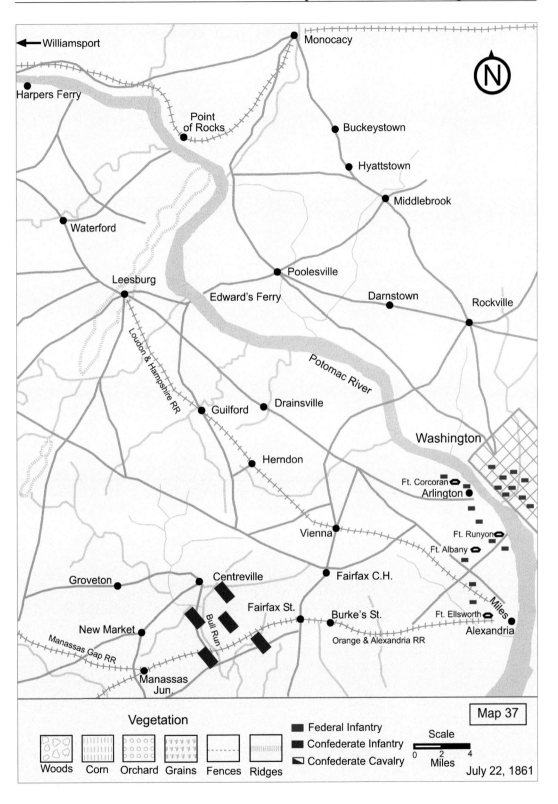

←Williamsport

N

Harpers Ferry

Point
of Rocks

Monocacy

Buckeystown

Hyattstown

Middlebrook

Waterford

Poolesville

Leesburg

Edward's Ferry

Darnstown

Rockville

Loudon & Hampshire RR

Potomac River

Guilford

Drainsville

Herndon

Washington

Ft. Corcoran

Arlington

Vienna

Ft. Runyon

Ft. Albany

Groveton

Centreville

Fairfax C.H.

Fairfax St.

Bull Run

Burke's St.

Ft. Ellsworth

New Market

Manassas Gap RR

Orange & Alexandria RR

Miles

Alexandria

Manassas
Jun.

Vegetation

Woods   Corn   Orchard   Grains   Fences   Ridges

■ Federal Infantry
■ Confederate Infantry
◨ Confederate Cavalry

Scale

0   2   4
Miles

Map 37

July 22, 1861

Map 38: Positions Around Washington (Mid-August)

Gen. McClellan arrived in Washington on July 26 and he wasted little time getting about the monumental task of whipping a defeated army into shape. The young commander was dismayed by the unorganized conditions in and around Washington. To him, at least, all was chaos. The army units were understrength, poorly trained, and woefully organized and distributed. Morale was low, and public drunkenness was rampant. A number of regiments were preparing to leave for home when their enlistments expired. Fortunately, the enemy had not pursued and Washington was in no immediate danger. McClellan issued a stream of orders, with the matter of discipline first on his agenda. The soldiers were driven out of the Washington saloons and anyone found drunk was punished. Drilling consumed most of the men's time. New units were integrated into the army, with a new regiment arriving every few days. McClellan's command swelled from about 50,000 men to nearly 80,000 by early November. On August 17, the War Department merged the Departments of Northeastern Virginia, Shenandoah, and Washington into the Department of the Potomac, and three days later, McClellan renamed his growing assemblage of units The Army of the Potomac.[1]

The passage of calm weeks allowed the army to grow stronger not just in number but in training, organization, and morale. By the end of September, it occupied a broad semi-circle in northern Virginia stretching from Alexandria in the south to Langley in the north, with both flanks anchored on the Potomac River. The defensive line included a number of powerful forts. Samuel Heintzelman's division occupied the left at Fort Lyon, near Alexandria, while William F. "Baldy" Smith's division anchored the right side at the Chain Bridge.[2]

The Southerners discovered that victory disorganized armies nearly as effectively as did defeat. Unable to mount an effective pursuit after the July 21 battle, Joe Johnston and P. G. T. Beauregard shifted their men along a line stretching from Flint Hill in the north running south through Fairfax Court House, Fairfax Station, and Sangster's Cross Roads. Johnston established his headquarters at Centreville, with advance outposts at Munson's and Upton's hills closer to the Federal defenses. A series of small actions allowed the Federals to claim these heights and Lewinsville (see Map 39). Nathan Evans' Brigade moved northwest as far as Leesburg. By early fall 1861, it was obvious to Johnston that McClellan's defensive perimeter around Washington was too strong to attack. He pulled his units back toward Centreville.[3]

McClellan slowly and methodically transformed his growing army into a well-disciplined unit. Officers who had performed poorly like Daniel Tyler, David Hunter, and Dixon Miles, were shipped elsewhere. McDowell was kicked down the ladder and given command of a division. Of the original men who led a division into battle on July 21, only Gen. Samuel Heintzelman remained in place. William Franklin, who had commanded a brigade at Bull Run, was elevated to division command. Other divisions went to Fitz John Porter, Charles Stone, Don Buell, George McCall, William F. Smith, Joseph Hooker, Edward Sumner, Silas Casey, Nathaniel Banks, John Dix, and Louis Blenker. Eight of these divisions manned the defenses west and southwest of Washington. The growing number of divisions convinced McClellan of the need to organize his army into corps, but he would wait until later that winter to do so. The delay allowed him time to evaluate the progress of his divisional officers.[4]

Changes were also in the works for the Confederates. Realizing that the army's organization did not provide for an adequate defense of Virginia, the War Department issued an order on October 22, 1862 creating the Department of Northern Virginia under the command of Gen. Joseph Johnston. The department was divided into three regions: the Potomac District (under the command of Gen. P. G. T. Beauregard); the Aquia District (under Gen. T. H. Holmes); and the Valley District (under Gen. Thomas "Stonewall" Jackson). The order also created infantry divisions. The First Division was assigned to Gen. Earl Van Dorn, the Second to Gen. Gustavus Smith, the Third to Gen. James Longstreet, and the Fourth division to Gen. E. Kirby Smith.[5]

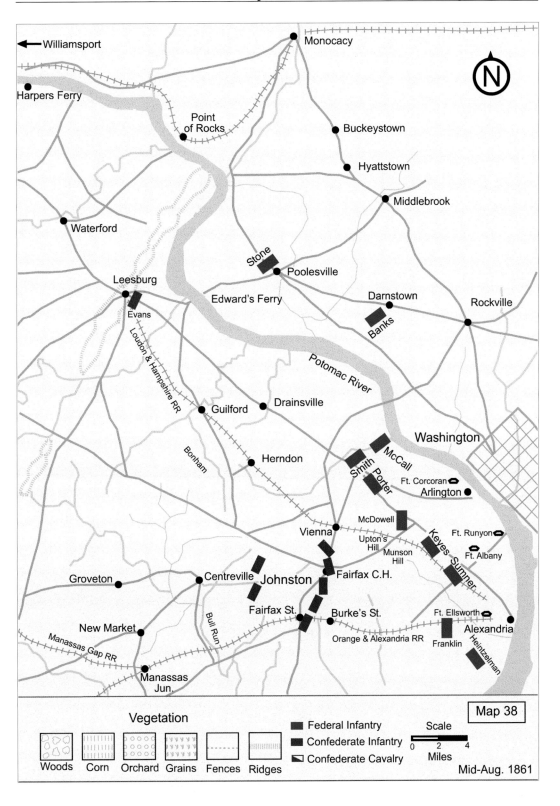

Williamsport

Monocacy

N

Harpers Ferry

Point
of Rocks

Buckeystown

Hyattstown

Middlebrook

Waterford

Stone

Poolesville

Leesburg

Edward's Ferry

Darnstown

Rockville

Evans

Banks

Loudon & Hampshire RR

Potomac River

Guilford

Drainsville

Washington

Bonham

Herndon

McCall

Smith

Porter

Ft. Corcoran

Arlington

McDowell

Vienna

Upton's
Hill

Munson
Hill

Ft. Runyon

Keyes

Sumner

Ft. Albany

Groveton

Centreville

Johnston

Fairfax C.H.

Fairfax St.

Burke's St.

Ft. Ellsworth

Bull Run

New Market

Orange & Alexandria RR

Franklin

Alexandria

Manassas Gap RR

Heintzelman

Manassas
Jun.

Map 38

Vegetation

Federal Infantry

Scale

Confederate Infantry

0   2   4

Confederate Cavalry

Miles

Woods   Corn   Orchard   Grains   Fences   Ridges

Mid-Aug. 1861

Map 39: Skirmish at Lewinsville (September 11)

The forts ringing Washington were a strong deterrent to a Confederate attack, but they did not deter Southern troops from roaming uncomfortably close to the capital.

On September 10, a pair of Federal regiments conducted a reconnaissance from the Chain Bridge on the Potomac River west to Lewinsville, Virginia, a strategic crossroads town about six miles west of Washington. The move resulted in the death of four of Jeb Stuart's Confederate cavalry and the wounding of four more. The following day, Col. Isaac Stevens was ordered to march with 1,800 men back to Lewinsville to reconnoiter. His force, composed of the 79th New York and 3rd Vermont, four companies of the 65th New York, two companies of the 3d Vermont Infantry, five companies of the 19th Indiana Infantry, four guns from Capt. Charles Griffin's Battery D, 5th U.S. Artillery, and about fifty cavalry Regulars and forty volunteers, left camp at 7:30 a.m. and reached Lewinsville about 10:00 a.m.[1]

When no enemy presence was immediately discovered, Stevens posted guns along three of the roads with detachments from the 19th Indiana and the 3d Vermont to support them. The rest of the infantry waited about one-third of a mile south of the town facing Falls Church. Confident with these arrangements, Stevens scouted for a suitable site to construct a light fort. When "single individuals and small bodies of men were seen to be observing us at safe distances," Stevens ordered his mounted troops to push them back. By 2:15 p.m., Stevens was ready to return to the safety of the Washington forts. To his dismay, it would take forty minutes for his picket forces to rejoin the main body, and by that time, the enemy would be upon them.[2]

The Confederate pickets observing Stevens' Federals transmitted information back to Jeb Stuart, who decided "to surprise them." The cavalier gathered together as many troops as he could lay his hands on. These amounted to one company of his own 1st Virginia Cavalry, 300 infantry from the 13th Virginia, and two guns from the Washington Artillery of New Orleans. Stuart's men were on the way to Lewinsville by

noon. Although he did not know it, he was outnumbered about five to one. Still, Stuart would not have been deterred for the country was "favorable to retreat and ambuscade." With the idea of striking the Federals from two sides, Stuart split the 300 infantry from the 13th Virginia into two columns. One marched northwest on the road from Falls Church to Lewinsville, while the other moved in the opposite direction, or southeast, along the road leading to Lewinsville.[3]

Stuart slipped his Virginians as close as possible and ordered his men to pick off the enemy cannoneers so they could not operate their gun. When all was ready, the Southerners opened fire. Although the Federal gunners did their best to man their piece, the zipping bullets made the task all but impossible. When one of the gunners toppled over with a shot through the head, the Federals quickly withdrew the cannon. As the Virginians advanced, some men of the 19th Indiana halted their withdrawal and rushed back to fire on the enemy. This impulsive action resulted in the capture of three Hoosiers, including an officer.[4]

Unsure of the nature of the developing threat, Stevens repositioned two of Griffin's guns to fire on the pursuing enemy soldiers. Griffin's two remaining pieces unlimbered about 600 yards behind them. After firing about forty rounds, the guns closest to the enemy withdrew behind Griffin's second set of guns, which then opened fire. The first two cannon unlimbered joined in. All four fired together for the next several minutes.[5]

Realizing that he should be at the front, Gen. William F. "Baldy" Smith galloped in that direction, picking up two guns of the 3rd New York Battery under Capt. Thaddeus P. Mott along the way. Smith ordered Mott to drop trail on a small hill one mile east of Lewinsville while knots of Stevens' men rushed past toward Fort Ethan Allen. Conditions were ripe for a repeat of the disorganized Union retreat at Bull Run (on a much smaller scale), but Federal officers calmed their men and marched them away from Lewinsville. They reached their camps about 5:30 p.m.[6]

The affair was another inauspicious Federal display. The skirmish cost five men killed, an equal number wounded, and six captured. Gen. McClellan put a positive spin on the expedition when he wrote, "Our men came back in perfect order and excellent spirits. . . . We shall have no more Bull Run affairs."[7]

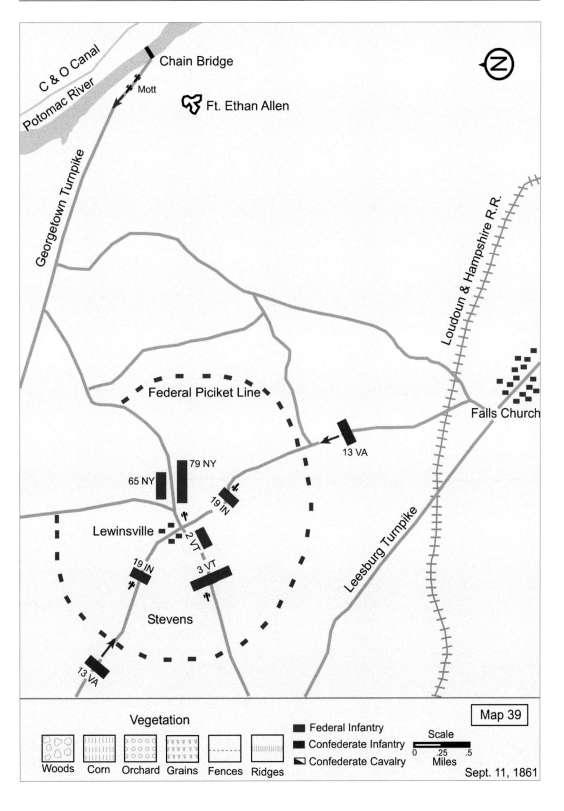

Map 39

Sept. 11, 1861

Ball's Bluff

Map 40: McCall's Reconnaissance to Dranesville (Mid-October 1861)

Skirmishing in Northern Virginia ebbed and flowed through the fall months. Gen. George B. McClellan claimed a small victory when his men occupied Munson's and Upton's hills. The positions were too close to the Federal lines to allow Southern forces to continue to hold them.

Finally conceding that he did not have the men or the supplies to attack Washington, Gen. Joe Johnston moved his army west to Centerville, where the brigades fanned out in a wide arc north and south of the town. The men immediately went to work building new defenses. On October 18, Gen. James Wadsworth of Gen. McDowell's Federal division moved west without orders to Fairfax Court House, which had been abandoned (along with valuable supplies) by the Southerners. During this time, McClellan ordered Gen. Samuel Heintzelman, whose division occupied Alexandria at the southern portion of the Federal defensive line, to venture forth to Occoquan Creek to reconnoiter. Heintzelman ordered part of Col. Israel Richardson's brigade forward, but his effort was a "perfunctory, unsatisfactory effort," writes one modern historian.[1]

One of McClellan's concerns was an enemy movement around his right flank at Langley, a Potomac crossing near Poolesville, Maryland, followed by a quick strike against Baltimore. After severing communications between Washington and the Northern states, the enemy might then march on the capital. Gen. Charles Stone, whose division occupied the Poolesville area, paid close attention to the Virginia side of the river, particularly around Leesburg, for evidence of an enemy buildup. The Rebels were present there, but were building what appeared to be defensive works. Neither a pontoon bridge nor boats to cross the wide Potomac were evident. Gen. Winfield Scott did not think much of this threat, and his disagreement led to a growing conflict with McClellan that resulted in each tendering his resignation. Lincoln accepted neither. Nathaniel Banks' division, meanwhile, marched from Sandy Hook and Buckeystown to Hyattstown and Darnestown to link Stone's division with McCall's division.[2]

The strategic stalemate continued through August and September. Around midnight on October 16-17, Col. Shank Evans ordered his brigade to abandon its strong defensive position near Leesburg. Evans established a new defensive line about seven miles south of town where the Carolina Road (modern Rt. 15) crosses Goose Creek near Oatlands Plantation. Federal observers across the Potomac were somewhat puzzled the next day when they discovered that the Confederates appeared to have abandoned the strategically significant position. Curiously, Evans' own superior, Gen. P. G. T. Beauregard, had not been informed of the withdrawal and was not pleased. He sent a note to Evans asking why he had left, then informed him that he could remain in his new position, but one of his regiments had to man the strong Leesburg defenses.[3]

Evans' disappearance caught McClellan's attention. On October 19, he threw McCall's division of Pennsylvania Reserves northeast toward Dranesville to reconnoiter, urging him to pay attention to his vulnerable left flank. McCall got underway as ordered, dropping off one brigade under Col. John S. McCalmont about six miles from Langley at Difficult Creek, and George Meade's brigade left the column as it approached Dranesville. McCall reached the town and with John Reynolds' brigade marched another four miles. McClellan arrived later in the day, pulled Reynolds back to Dranesville, and ordered McCall to map the area and return to Langley the next day. When McCall protested that he needed more time, McClellan agreed to allow him to remain there until the morning of October 21.[4]

A mulatto who had fled from the 13th Mississippi (Evans' Brigade) was taken to McClellan with a report that Evans would retreat if attacked. Thinking McCall's move north toward Leesburg might have threatened Evans, McClellan thought another move from the east might force Evans to desert Leesburg. McClellan sent a telegram to Gen. Stone on October 20 informing him of McCall's reconnaissance and directing him to "keep a good lookout upon Leesburg, to see if this movement has the effect to drive them away. Perhaps a slight demonstration on your part would have the effect to move them."[5]

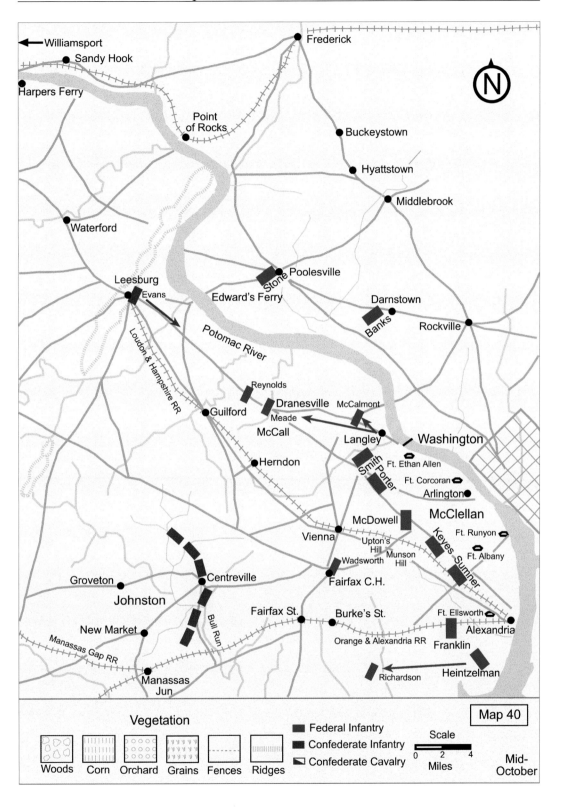

Williamsport
Sandy Hook
Harpers Ferry
Frederick
Point of Rocks
Buckeystown
Hyattstown
Middlebrook
Waterford
Poolesville
Leesburg
Evans
Stone
Edward's Ferry
Darnstown
Banks
Rockville
Loudon & Hampshire RR
Potomac River
Reynolds
Dranesville
McCalmont
Guilford
Meade
McCall
Langley
Washington
Herndon
Smith
Porter
Ft. Ethan Allen
Ft. Corcoran
Arlington
McDowell
McClellan
Ft. Runyon
Vienna
Upton's Hill
Keyes
Sumner
Ft. Albany
Wadsworth
Munson Hill
Groveton
Centreville
Fairfax C.H.
Johnston
Bull Run
Fairfax St.
Burke's St.
Ft. Ellsworth
New Market
Manassas Gap RR
Orange & Alexandria RR
Franklin
Alexandria
Manassas Jun
Richardson
Heintzelman

Vegetation

Woods   Corn   Orchard   Grains   Fences   Ridges

Federal Infantry
Confederate Infantry
Confederate Cavalry

Scale
0   2   4
Miles

Map 40

Mid-October

Map 41: Philbrick's Reconnaissance (October 20)

When Nathan Evans discovered that Gen. Beauregard was unhappy about the move that left Leesburg vulnerable, he marched his brigade back to its original defensive line.[1]

Gen. Charles Stone received McClellan's telegram about 11:00 a.m. on October 20 and had two of his brigades in motion by that afternoon. Gen. Willis Gorman's brigade, along with the 7th Michigan and some cavalry, moved to Edwards Ferry, which was already occupied by Battery I, 1st U.S. Artillery (now under Lt. George Woodruff). A battalion of the 20th Massachusetts, the 42nd New York, and a section of Battery B, 1st Rhode Island Artillery (under Capt. Thomas Vaughn) made their way upriver to Conrad's Ferry. Four companies of the 15th Massachusetts moved to a point on the Maryland side of the river opposite Harrison's Island and Ball's Bluff; another company was already on the island.

Stone knew Evans' scouts were watching these movements, but that they might not be enough to encourage him to abandon Leesburg. In a bolder move, Stone pushed two companies of the 1st Minnesota across the river at Edwards Ferry shortly before dusk. The Minnesota troops remained on enemy soil for only about fifteen minutes before returning to the Maryland shore. It is doubtful whether most of the men even left the boats, but those who did flushed out several Confederate pickets—enough to get the word to Evans that Federal troops had crossed the river. Satisfied he had performed the ordered feint, Stone ordered most of his troops back to their original camps.[2]

While the two companies of the 1st Minnesota shipped back to the Maryland shore at Edwards Ferry, Capt. Chase Philbrick was rowing in the opposite direction near Harrison's Island with about twenty volunteers of the 15th Massachusetts to see if the demonstration had triggered a Confederate withdrawal. When he reached the Virginia side, Philbrick led his men downriver, made his way up the path to the top of the bluff, then moved cautiously in the direction of Leesburg. It was dark when he reached a slight ridge about three-fourths of a mile from the river and two miles from Leesburg, where the full moon revealed what appeared to be an enemy camp in the distance. The Federals edged within 130 yards of the camp, which appeared to be unprotected. Deciding he had gleaned enough information, Philbrick ordered his men back to the boats. He reached Harrison's Island about 10:00 p.m. "A very nice little military chance seemed to have been brought out by that reconnaissance," wrote Stone. "News was brought that there was a small camp without pickets. And it seemed to me one of those pieces of carelessness on the part of the enemy that ought to be taken advantage of." Although he was not in a position to launch a full-scale operation across the river, Stone could send a strong raiding party.[3]

Stone ordered Col. Charles Devens to recross the river with four companies of his 15th Massachusetts (he took across five companies, about 300 green troops), and attack the enemy camp at first light. While Devens was moving, Col. William Lee was to march to the Maryland side opposite Ball's Bluff with two companies of his 20th Massachusetts (about 100 men) and two mountain howitzers and provide assistance, if needed. Col. Edward D. Baker, commander of the California Brigade (later called the Philadelphia Brigade) received orders at 12:45 a.m. to march at once for Conrad's Ferry, and arrive there no later than sunrise.

To divert the enemy's attention from the landing at Ball's Bluff, Stone ordered a feint at Edwards Ferry. Thirty-four men of the 3rd New York Cavalry and two companies of the 1st Minnesota recrossed the Potomac River there about 7:00 a.m. on October 21. Recent showers had swollen the river, making its currents treacherous and fording dangerous, at best. Boats were pressed into service for the endeavor. Stone was able to rustle up a small, four-oared "whale-boat" that could carry about 16 men. This, with the two skiffs used by Philbrick, swelled the number of men that could be transported during each trip to 30-35.

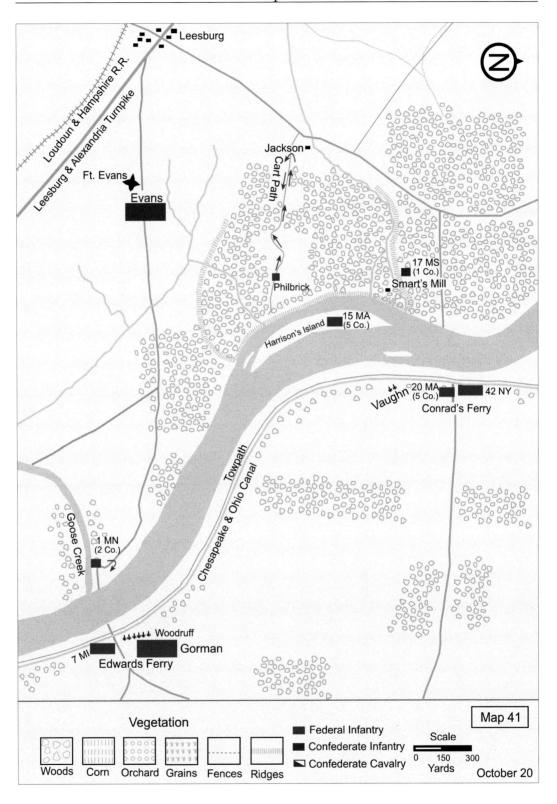

Vegetation

Woods   Corn   Orchard   Grains   Fences   Ridges

■ Federal Infantry
■ Confederate Infantry
◣ Confederate Cavalry

Map 41

Scale

0   150   300
Yards

October 20

Map 42: Initial Actions (7:00 – 8:00 a.m., October 21)

The crossing near Harrison's Island teemed with activity as the sun rose on October 21. Col. Devens' five companies of the 15th Massachusetts began crossing about midnight. With access to only three boats capable of collectively transporting only thirty men per trip, Devens' entire force did not make it to the Virginia bank until 4:00 a.m. Once on Southern soil, Devens advanced to an open field, where he halted his men until Col. William Lee with his two companies of the 20th Massachusetts could arrive to provide support. As soon as it was light enough to see, Devens ordered his men to advance along the winding cart path. It did not take him long to discover that what Capt. Philbrick had thought were tents, in fact were only trees. According to Devens' later testimony, "…at the head of the rise here was a single row of trees—I think of fruit trees…the light coming through between part of the branches of the trees gave very much the appearance of a row of tents."

Leaving his men in the woods, Devens and Philbrick, together with a couple of scouts, quietly advanced to observe Leesburg. When they did not see any enemy, Devens sent an aide back to Gen. Stone informing him of the mistake and indicating he would remain in position until reinforced. Stone immediately ordered the remaining companies of the 15th Massachusetts across the river to Smart's Mill, just north of the bluff to strengthen Devens for what now had become an expanded reconnaissance. Devens knew that a large boat, capable of carrying sixty to seventy men per trip, had been procured, so he was confident that at least 500 soldiers could be transported each hour.[1]

While Devens was discovering Phillbrick's mistake, the feint at Edwards Ferry was underway as planned. Throwing out two companies of the 1st Minnesota as a skirmish line, Maj. John Mix approached the Leesburg Road with his troopers. Mix had two jobs. His first was to advance up the Edwards Ferry Road in order to draw Confederate attention to himself and away from the Ball's Bluff raiding party, and his second was to reconnoiter toward

Goose Creek. His was a very small force for such a dangerous mission. After proceeding about two miles along the Edwards Ferry Road, the Federal horsemen briefly engaged a group of Southern infantry, probably from the 13th Mississippi, and both sides opened fire with only about thirty yards separating them. Unsure of the size of the enemy force, and in accordance with his orders, Maj. Mix pulled his men back toward the ferry.[2]

About 8:00 a.m., meanwhile, Col. Devens learned that at least one company of Confederate infantry was on his right flank. The enemy was Company K of the 17th Mississippi, operating on picket duty near Smart's Mill. When he learned of the crossing of 15th Massachusetts, the Southern company's commander, Capt. William Duff, collected his men and moved between the Union force and Leesburg. What he did not know was that his forty men would soon be facing 300 Federals. When the two forces met each other, Devens advanced Company H under Philbrick to attack them, while Company A circled to the right to get into the rear of the Mississippians. Seeing Company H's approach, and worried that he was outnumbered, Capt. Duff pulled his men back toward the road to draw the Federal attackers away from their supporting line. Duff's men had been present at the Battle of Manassas and experienced some limited action there. Their yells to the Federals to halt were ignored. When the Bay Staters stepped within sixty yards, Duff ordered his men to open fire. The volley cut down a number of Federal troops.

Devens ordered Company G forward to reinforce Philbrick's men on the front line. Before that company had moved far, however, Rebel cavalry was reported on its left. Fearing the troopers could cut off Philbrick's men, Devens recalled them. Duff was also pulling his infantry back about this time. The little skirmish claimed one Federal soldier killed, nine wounded, and two missing; three Confederates fell wounded. Although it did not amount to much, the sharp little affair served notice to Col. Evans that Federals were moving inland from the river in some strength. The skirmish was also valuable for Devens, for it proved the enemy was aware of his presence and that he was now in a more vulnerable position.[3]

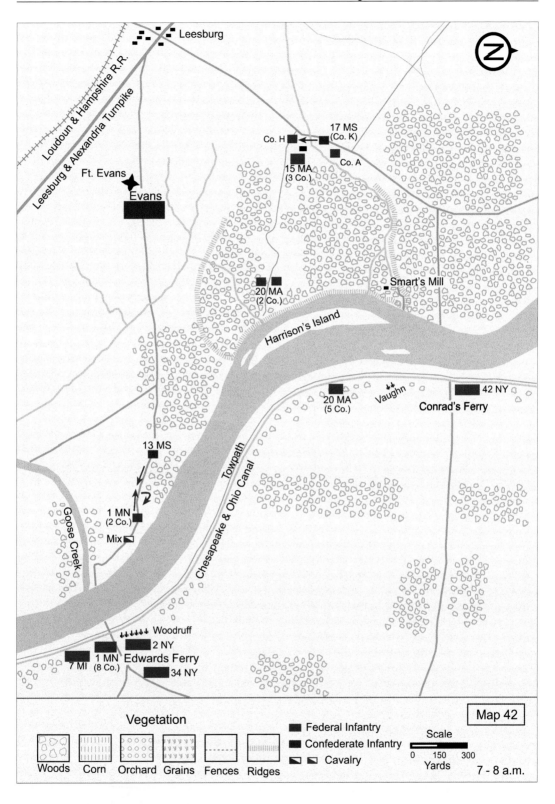

Leesburg

Loudoun & Hampshire R.R.

Leesburg & Alexandria Turnpike

17 MS
(Co. K)

Co. H

15 MA
(3 Co.)

Co. A

Ft. Evans

Evans

20 MA
(2 Co.)

Smart's Mill

Harrison's Island

20 MA
(5 Co.)

Vaughn

Conrad's Ferry

42 NY

13 MS

Towpath

Chesapeake & Ohio Canal

1 MN
(2 Co.)

Mix

Goose Creek

Woodruff

2 NY

7 MI

1 MN
(8 Co.)

Edwards Ferry

34 NY

Vegetation

Federal Infantry

Confederate Infantry

Cavalry

Scale

Map 42

Woods   Corn   Orchard   Grains   Fences   Ridges

0   150   300

Yards

7 - 8 a.m.

Map 43: Initial Attacks on the 15th Massachusetts (11:00 a.m.)

The bloodied 15th Massachusetts battalion fell back a short distance, and then continued all the way to the bluff, where the two supporting companies of the 20th Massachusetts were deployed. Devens remained there only briefly, however, then moved his companies back to their previous position. An aide informed him that he was to remain there, for the remainder of the regiment was on its way to reinforce him. Devens threw out a skirmish line on each flank and across his front.[1]

Rather than take direct command of the Ball's Bluff sector, Gen. Charles Stone ordered Col. Edward Baker, a U.S. Senator and personal friend of President Abraham Lincoln, to move his 1st California (made up largely of men from Pennsylvania) to Harrison's Island and oversee the entire operation. "In case of heavy firing in front of Harrison's Island," instructed Stone, "you will advance the California regiment of your brigade or retire the regiments under Cols. Lee and Devens upon the Virginia side of the river, at your discretion, assuming command on arrival."[2]

On the Virginia side of the river along Edwards Ferry Road, meanwhile, Col. Nathan Evans received a flurry or reports about Federal troops crossing the Potomac at multiple locations. The activity at Edwards Ferry was clearly within view, and Evans could hear the rattling small arms fire between Capt. Duff's Mississippians and Col. Devens' Massachusetts soldiers. He knew that George McCall's division near Dranesville to the east was no longer a threat, so he could freely deal with the Federal crossings at Edwards Ferry and Ball's Bluff. Because he did not know where the major thrust would be launched, Evans wisely decided to act with caution.

He reinforced Capt. Duff with four companies (two from the 18th Mississippi, and one each from the 13th Mississippi and 17th Mississippi) and three undersized companies of Virginia cavalry. The entire force was put under the command of Col. W. H. Jenifer, Evans' cavalry leader. Evans retained the balance of the three Mississippi regiments at Fort Evans. A fourth regiment, the 8th Virginia, was stationed to the east guarding Burnt Bridge on the Leesburg-Alexandria Turnpike.[3]

Col. Jenifer received his orders about 9:00 a.m. and immediately moved toward Ball's Bluff with approximately 320 men. Apparently stretching the intent of his orders, Jenifer decided to go over to the offensive around 11:00. What he did not know was that, by then, the number of Federals had swelled to about 625 with the arrival of the remainder of Devens' 15th Massachusetts. The Confederates were also sending reinforcements. Evans ordered all but one company of the 8th Virginia to march to the support of Jenifer's force though the Virginians did not arrive until after Jenifer had fought the morning's second skirmish.

By 11:00 a.m., Jenifer's line was facing east and prepared to attack. He deployed one company of the 18th Mississippi on the skirmish line. Another held the right side of the line, with Capt. Duff's company of the 17th Mississippi extending the line left (or north), followed by a company of the 13th Mississippi and the cavalry. It was a long and thin line with gaps between each man. When Jenifer realized that a stout fence precluded a saber charge by his cavalry against Devens' men, he dismounted one company and sent it forward with the infantry. His men skirmished on foot from behind a fence until Jenifer ordered it torn down so that his horsemen could get through and charge the Union force. When they did this, the Federals fell back a short distance and regrouped. Jenifer then pulled his men back as well. Following a lull in the fighting, the 8th Virginia arrived at about 12:30 and the stage was set for the morning's third skirmish.[4]

Off to the southeast, meanwhile, most of Gen. Willis Gorman's Federal brigade was crossing the river as quickly as the boats could carry them. Having heard from Baker that he was crossing more troops at Ball's Bluff, Gen. Stone had decided to cross additional troops at Edwards Ferry in case they might be needed.

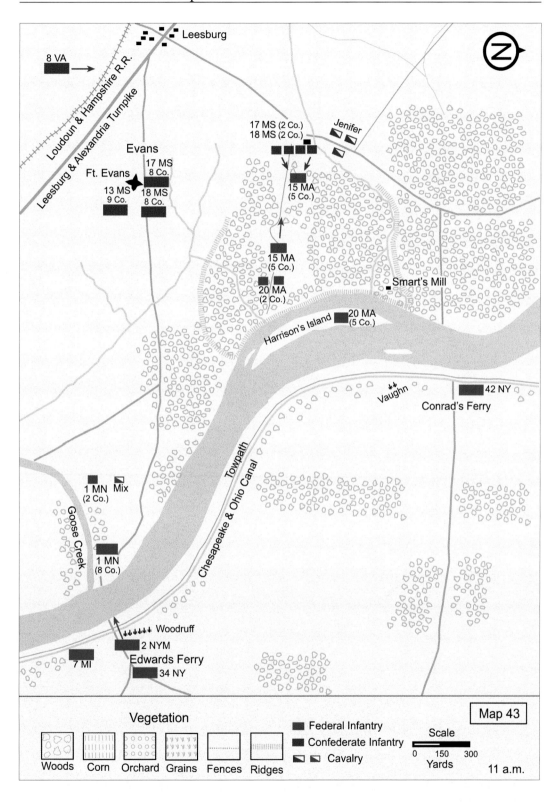

8 VA

Leesburg

Loudoun & Hampshire R.R.

Leesburg & Alexandria Turnpike

Evans

Ft. Evans

17 MS
8 Co.

13 MS
9 Co.

18 MS
8 Co.

17 MS (2 Co.)
18 MS (2 Co.)

Jenifer

15 MA
(5 Co.)

15 MA
(5 Co.)

20 MA
(2 Co.)

Smart's Mill

20 MA
(5 Co.)

Harrison's Island

Vaughn

42 NY

Conrad's Ferry

Towpath

Chesapeake & Ohio Canal

Goose Creek

1 MN
(2 Co.)

Mix

1 MN
(8 Co.)

Woodruff

2 NYM

7 MI

Edwards Ferry

34 NY

Vegetation

Woods   Corn   Orchard   Grains   Fences   Ridges

■ Federal Infantry
■ Confederate Infantry
◨ ◨ Cavalry

Map 43

Scale

0   150   300
Yards

11 a.m.

Map 44: Continued Attacks on the 15th Massachusetts (1:00-2:15 p.m.)

When orders arrived to support Col. Jenifer's command, the undersized 8th Virginia moved quickly past Fort Evans and, according to Jenifer, formed behind his men in a supporting role. The Virginians later moved to the front, with the four Mississippi companies shifting to the right to make room for them on the firing line. Capt. Duff's company moved to form on the left of the 8th Virginia. By now it was near 1:00 p.m. For the first time, the Confederates (numbering about 700 men) outnumbered Devens' complete 15th Massachusetts regiment (No. 1 on map).[1]

A soldier in the 15th Massachusetts recalled the beginning of the fighting: "[W]e saw an officer ride in front of their infantry and wave his hand. Immediately the [Confederate] infantry advanced . . . at the same time a rushing sound was heard in the woods on our left . . . the next minute a large body of them dashed upon us. . . . It was impossible for so few of us, situated as we were, to withstand such a force." But withstand the attack they did, holding their ground in most places while the fighting raged back and forth for about an hour. With the Southerners attacking his front and pressing against both flanks, Col. Devens increasingly worried about being surrounded. About 2:00 p.m., he ordered his men to withdraw to the cleared field near the edge of Ball's Bluff (No. 2 on map).[2]

While the 15th Massachusetts was slugging it out with the Virginians and Mississippians, five more companies of the 20th Massachusetts reached the bluff on the Virginia side of the river and remained on the eastern edge of the clearing. Two of them (D and H) were placed on the flanks.

The 20th Massachusetts was reinforced by a pair of 12-pounder mountain howitzers which had been detached from the 2nd New York State Militia and were manned by a mixed crew from that unit and Battery I, 1st U.S. Artillery. These small 12-pounder guns, weighing only 500 pounds apiece, were perfect for the close-in fighting that would occur that afternoon. Their light weight made the ascent up the far bank fairly easy. Seeing the guns on the bluff, deployed and ready for action, tremendously boosted the men's morale.[3]

Col. Edward Baker spent three to four hours seeking the best and fastest way to get his troops across the river. Baker ordered his men to find as much rope as they could to be spliced together, so a line could be stretched across the river to expedite the crossing. Orders also went out to scrounge up as many boats as possible. One was a large canal boat from the Chesapeake and Ohio Canal. One eyewitness noted that Baker, "took charge of the matter and got some 500 men, and with very great labor got the boat out of the canal and pulled it over the tow-path into the river. Colonel Baker stood by all the time very quiet." Baker personally crossed to Ball's Bluff about 2:15 p.m. Before setting foot on Virginia soil, he seemed to already have decided to commit his small force to battle. "[H]urry all [men] you can!" Baker yelled to one of his commanders. "Get everything that can float. Cross every man you can into Virginia." The men of the 1st California crossed next. This unit was part of Col. Baker's own brigade. One company crossed prior to Baker's arrival on the bluff.[4]

Some of the officers believed the Federal left flank was most vulnerable because of certain terrain features, including a ravine that could permit the enemy to encircle that portion of the line. When Baker reached this part of the line, he conferred with Capt. Casper Crowninshield of the 20th Massachusetts, who led a skirmish company in this sector. When Crowninshield told Baker his men could defend this area with another company, the Senator ordered one up from the 1st California.[5]

Confederates were keenly watching the build up on Ball's Bluff. The increased Federal activity worried the commander of the 8th Virginia, Col. Eppa Hunton, who was running low on ammunition. Hunton sent several messages to Col. Evans notifying him of the activity and seeking reinforcements. Evans was concerned about Edwards Ferry—where Willis Gorman's Federal brigade had crossed and now potentially threatened the Confederate right flank—and had dispatched the 13th Mississippi about 1:30 p.m. to keep an eye on Gorman. Evans now had but two regiments left in reserve at Fort Evans.[6]

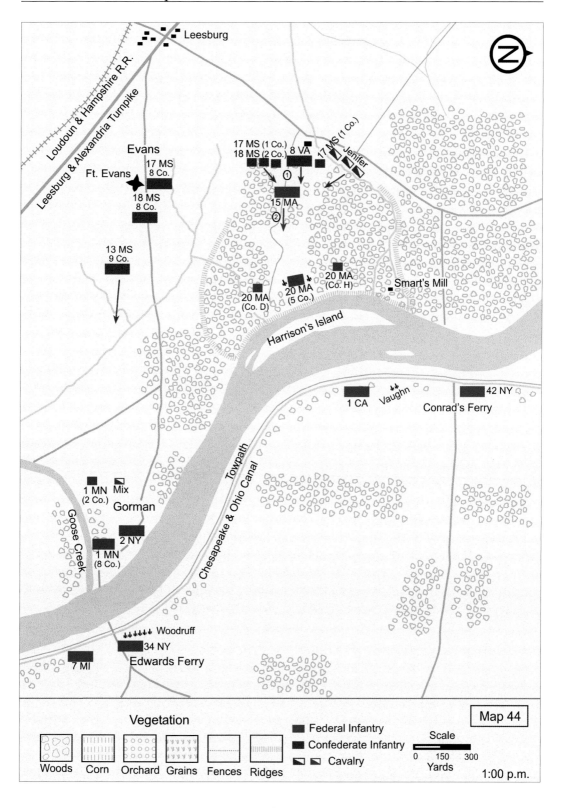

Leesburg

Loudoun & Hampshire R.R.

Leesburg & Alexandria Turnpike

Evans

Ft. Evans

17 MS
8 Co.

18 MS
8 Co.

13 MS
9 Co.

17 MS (1 Co.)
18 MS (2 Co.)

8 VA

17 MS (1 Co.)

Jenifer

①

15 MA

②

20 MA
(Co. H)

Smart's Mill

20 MA
(Co. D)

20 MA
(5 Co.)

Harrison's Island

1 CA

Vaughn

Conrad's Ferry

42 NY

Towpath

Chesapeake & Ohio Canal

1 MN
(2 Co.)

Mix

Gorman

Goose Creek

2 NY

1 MN
(8 Co.)

Woodruff

34 NY

Edwards Ferry

7 MI

Vegetation

Woods   Corn   Orchard   Grains   Fences   Ridges

Federal Infantry

Confederate Infantry

Cavalry

Scale

0   150   300
Yards

Map 44

1:00 p.m.

Map 45: *Federal Defensive Line Takes Shape (3:00 p.m.)*

Excited about the prospects of a full-scale fight, Col. Edward Baker showed considerable exuberance. "I congratulate you on the prospects of a battle," he gushed to Col. William Lee of the 20th Massachusetts when he arrived atop the bluff. Federal reinforcements continued streaming onto the high ground above the Potomac River, including additional companies of the 1st California and a James rifled cannon belonging to Battery B, 1st Rhode Island Light Artillery but commanded by Lt. Walter Bramhall of Company K, 9th New York State Militia (later known as the 6th New York Independent Battery). Lt. Frank French of the regular battery commanded the two mountain howitzers.[1]

Col. Baker threw his energies into organizing the Federal defense, but the line ultimately formed was a jumbled command affair that seemed to ask for trouble. The bloodied 15th Massachusetts withdrew across the open field from the west and took up a new position just inside the woods on its northern fringe and at a right angle to the Federal line along the bluff. In the northern edge of the woods, a pair of companies from the 15th Massachusetts formed at a 45 degree angle to the rest of the 15th's line, roughly facing the Mississippi companies they had battled earlier. Half of the 1st California deployed on the left of the five 20th Massachusetts companies, except for three companies from the 1st California held in reserve behind the northern portion of the line and another thrown farther to the left to scout the high ground beyond the ravine. A company of the 20th Massachusetts also took up a position on the far left of the line, while yet another company was thrown out in the woods north of the field to watch for rebels in that sector.[2]

The Southerners opened the new round of fighting with a "spitting" fire from across the field, which the Federals promptly returned. The fight was getting underway when the last regiment to actually cross the river, the 42nd New York, reached the crossing point to Ball's Bluff. Its commander, Col. Milton Cogswell, was shocked by the chaos he found there. "I found the greatest confusion existing," he wrote. "No

one seemed to be in charge, nor any one superintending the passage of troops, and no order was maintained at the crossing." Cogswell received orders to cross about 2:00 p.m. The West Point graduate was in a foul mood that began with his arrival at the disjointed crossing site. Matters were not helped by the fact that he would be under the command of a military novice in Edward Baker. When Cogswell arrived, Baker strode up to greet him. "Col. Baker welcomed me on the field, seemed in good spirits, and very confident of a successful day," Cogswell later wrote.[3]

Cogswell had reason enough to grouse about the confusion that reigned at the crossing site, but things seems to be looking up for the Federals. As the soldiers of the 42nd New York made their way across, another Massachusetts regiment arrived at the crossing site behind them. When the commander of 19th Massachusetts, Col. Edward Hincks, saw the same confusion Cogswell had just waded through, he took charge and created some semblance of order.[4]

While the Federals were reinforcing the Virginia side of the river, Col. Erasmus Burt of the 18th Mississippi received orders between 2:00 and 2:30 p.m. to move toward Ball's Bluff to attack the Federal left flank. Already shy two companies that were fighting with Col. Jenifer's force on the western side of the clearing, Burt ordered his men to double-time for the two-mile trip to the bluff. He arrived about the same time as the remainder of the 1st California.[5]

Throughout the day, a steady stream of telegraph messages carried information from Gen. Charles Stone to Gen. George B. McClellan. Often the messages served little than to add to the confusion, for the information was often ambiguous and sometimes outright erroneous.[6]

Company C was the first company of Cogswell's 42nd New York to arrive on the bluff. It was quickly dispatched to the right, where some Confederates (possibly Capt. Duff's company of the 17th Mississippi) had gained the riverbank and were firing into the arriving New Yorkers. The two sides battled for about thirty minutes before the Confederates were recalled westward to rejoin the main body.

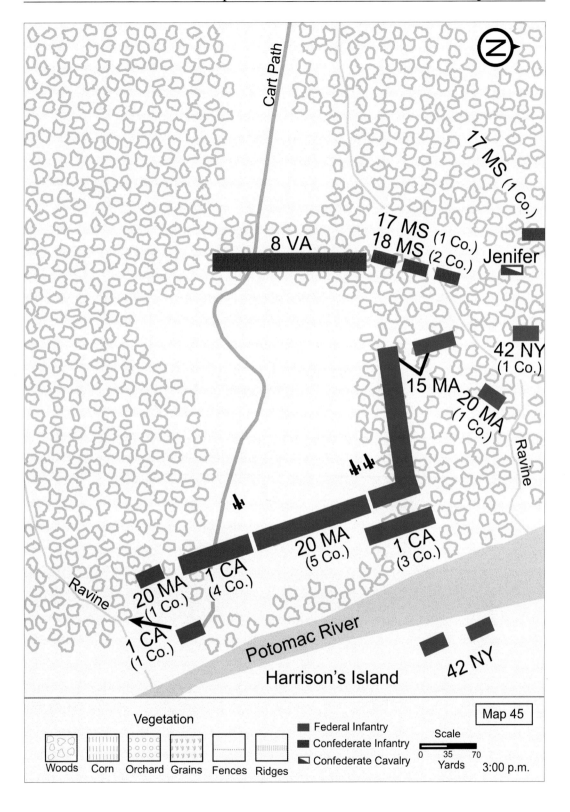

8 VA

17 MS (1 Co.)

17 MS (1 Co.)
18 MS (2 Co.)

Jenifer

Cart Path

42 NY
(1 Co.)

15 MA

20 MA
(1 Co.)

Ravine

20 MA
(5 Co.)

1 CA
(3 Co.)

Ravine

20 MA
(1 Co.)

1 CA
(4 Co.)

1 CA
(1 Co.)

Potomac River

Harrison's Island

42 NY

Vegetation

Woods   Corn   Orchard   Grains   Fences   Ridges

Federal Infantry
Confederate Infantry
Confederate Cavalry

Scale

0   35   70
Yards

3:00 p.m.

Map 45

Map 46: The Fight between the 1st California and 8th Virginia (4:00 p.m.)

Col. Milton Cogswell of the 42nd New York was angry when he surveyed the battlefield that afternoon. Col. Edward Baker had rebuffed Cogswell when he offered his opinion of the Federal defensive line. "I frankly told him that I deemed [it] very defective, as the wooded hills beyond the ravine commanded the whole so perfectly, that should they be occupied by the enemy he [Baker] would be destroyed," recalled Cogswell. "I advised an immediate advance of the whole force to occupy the hills, which were then not occupied by the enemy. I told him that the whole action must be on our left, and that we must occupy those hills." Cogswell was right. The Federal position was a poor one, and commands were fragmented all along the line.

Baker's men were fighting along an open field with heavy woods on both sides and with elevated ground on the left. Worse, their backs faced a steep bluff and swift unfordable river. Baker, however, ignored the advice and ordered the West Pointer to "take charge of the artillery, but without any definite instructions as to its service." A frustrated Cogswell placed two of his arriving companies behind the main line of the 20th Massachusetts and 1st California.[1]

While the Federal officers were arguing, a wholesale realignment of the Confederate line was taking place. Four Mississippi companies reunited on the left (north) end. Most of the 8th Virginia moved left (south) of the cart path. Two or three companies were on the line's extreme right flank. In the woods in front of the Virginians were two companies of the 1st California (A and D), probing through the heavy terrain to determine Southern strength. They found the right of the 8th Virginia when the Virginians fired on them from the top of the slope that roughly marks the site of today's parking lot. The rest of the Virginians heard the scattered shooting and opened fire through the trees. The 1st California companies suffered severely and within less than thirty minutes lost two-thirds of their men. Retreat seemed the only option. But the Federals were not the only ones anxious to retreat. The firing was so heavy

against the right side of the 8th Virginia that Col. Eppa Hunton, its commander, ordered Lt. Col., Charles Tebbs to shift about one-quarter of the regiment back a couple hundred yards to regroup. Tebbs either completely misunderstood the order or lost some control, for his men pulled back toward Leesburg, many of them in a panic-stricken flight.

It was about 3:30 p.m., and Hunton was attempting, with good success, to keep the panic from spreading. As he withdrew the 8th Virginia, the 18th Mississippi arrived behind them. Hunton likely felt both relief and exasperation when they arrived, for he had sent several messengers for help and ammunition. Col. Nathan Evans had developed a negative attitude toward both the 8th Virginia and its leader. Although Evans finally dispatched the 18th Mississippi to reinforce Hunton (and later sent the 17th Mississippi), Evans seems to have done so grudgingly. He purportedly told one messenger, "Tell Hunton to hold his ground till every d__n man falls." Bad blood had existed between the two since Evans superceded Hunton in command earlier that year.[2]

It was at this point that Federal Lt. Walter Bramhall appeared at the top of Ball's Bluff and assumed command of the James rifle. Col. Evans' men opened fire on the horses, cannoneers, and howitzers. "The horses became frantic," wrote Col. Lee of the 20th Massachusetts, "the leading horses broke the traces, and they all rushed down the hill, dragging the limber after them." Bramhall dropped trail near the two howitzers.[3]

Col. Baker hoped that both McCall's division and Willis Gorman's brigade were absorbing some of the enemy's attention. They were not. Though Gen. Stone did not know it—and believed that McCall might be on his way—McCall was following his orders from McClellan and marching back toward his camp at Langley, and Gorman was cooling his heels on the Virginia side of the river across from Edwards Ferry. Neither were doing anything to worry Evans. Gorman, in fact, was digging in rather than moving toward the enemy.[4]

Stone sent yet another message to Baker at 3:45 p.m. In it, he referred to Baker's situation on Ball's Bluff: "If satisfied with it hold on, & don't let the troops get fatigued or starved while waiting." Stone's point of view had changed from his earlier "move forward" to "hold on." Baker, however, would not live to see the message.[5]

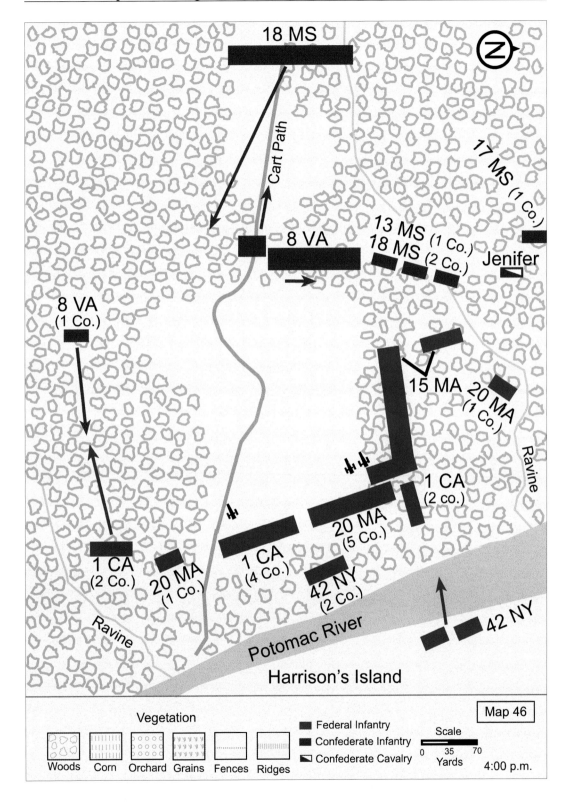

Map 47: Advance and Defeat of the 18th Mississippi (4:15 p.m.)

As the 18th Mississippi maneuvered into position, many of its men may have thought back to the same day three months ago when, as part of Gen. David R. Jones' brigade, they had defended McLean's Ford during the Manassas Campaign. Although they had crossed Bull Run and engaged the enemy, their participation had been relegated to little more than a brief mention in newspapers. During their wait near Fort Evans, some of the men wondered if they would miss yet another battle. The men cheered heartily when they learned that they were being sent forward about 2:30 p.m. to attack the enemy's left flank. Evans expected the 18th Mississippi would fall upon the Federal flank while Hunton's 8th Virginia and Jenifer's motley command attacked the enemy front. Struck from two directions, Evans hoped the Federals would retreat across the river and end the threat to Leesburg.[1]

The Mississippians, "with the steady tread of veterans," noted an early historian of the battle, "marched over the field to the woods." Moving into battle on the right of the 8th Virginia, the Mississippians wheeled to the right to strike the Federal position on the flank. When the Southerners mounted the elevation overlooking the left flank of the Federal position, a storm of minie balls ripped through their ranks, dropping many to the ground. One of them was the regiment's commander Col. Erasmus Burt, fell with a gunshot wound to the belly. As Burt was helped down from his horse, he turned to White and said in a calm voice, "Go tell Colonel Jenifer I am wounded and shall have to leave the field." He lingered in agony for several days before dying on October 26.

The heavy fire was delivered by the 15th Massachusetts, situated on the northern (opposite) side of the clearing. Because of the terrain, the Bay Staters could see the left side of the advancing line of Mississippians, but the Mississippians could not see them. The two howitzers at the far end of the field added their weight to the combat. Elijah White, who would earn fame in subsequent battles under the Confederate flag, called this volley "the best

directed & most destructive single volley I saw during the war." The regiment's second in command, Lt. Col. Thomas Griffin, pulled the shaken regiment back into the woods to reform its shattered ranks and reinstate calm within the ranks. Griffin divided the regiment into two battalions.[2]

By 4:30 p.m., Col. Edward Baker was in a position to end the small fight and claim a Federal victory. With the repulse of the 8th Virginia, about one-third of which was falling back west, and the sharp defeat of the 18th Mississippi, the battlefield had stabilized in Baker's favor. Neither of the Southern units was ready to reenter the fight. The shift of the Mississippians to the right left a gaping hole between them and the Virginians. If the 20th Massachusetts and 1st California had driven forward at this time, the odds are they would have driven the disoriented Southern forces from the field. Baker, however, seems not to have realized the opportunity in his immediate front. The window to drive the enemy from the field closed when the 17th Mississippi from Fort Evans approached to plug the gap in the Confederate line.[3]

Gen. George B. McClellan received a string of messages about the shifting situation at Ball's Bluff. Demonstrating a streak of aggressiveness late in the day, McClellan ordered Charles Stone to advance and capture Leesburg. An accidental skirmish had evolved into a full-scale strategic advance. By the time Stone received this communication (about 4:30 p.m.), his men were already heavily engaged. If they could defeat the Confederates at Ball's Bluff, an easy march into Leesburg would naturally follow. Stone, however, did not know the contents of McClellan's message because it was encoded, and he did not have the key. Even if he had, there was only about ninety minutes of daylight left. The 2,500 men of Willis Gorman's brigade already on the Virginia side, directly across from Edwards Ferry, would have to wait until the morrow to march on Leesburg.[4]

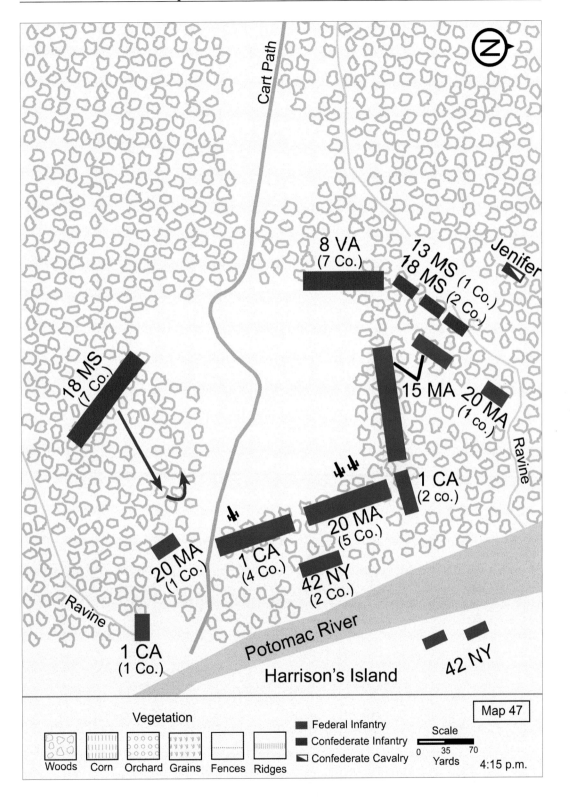

Cart Path

8 VA
(7 Co.)

13 MS (1 Co.)

18 MS (2 Co.)

Jenifer

18 MS
(7 Co.)

15 MA

20 MA
(1 co.)

Ravine

1 CA
(2 co.)

20 MA
(5 Co.)

20 MA
(1 Co.)

1 CA
(4 Co.)

42 NY
(2 Co.)

Ravine

1 CA
(1 Co.)

Potomac River

Harrison's Island

42 NY

Vegetation

Woods   Corn   Orchard   Grains   Fences   Ridges

■ Federal Infantry
■ Confederate Infantry
◥ Confederate Cavalry

Scale

0   35   70
Yards

Map 47

4:15 p.m.

Map 48: Additional Reinforcements Reach the Field (4:30 p.m.)

Lt. Col. Thomas Griffin of the 18th Mississippi sent Company H to scout toward the river and get on the Federal far left. The men crept around the Federal line to the edge of the bluff, turned north, and headed straight toward the Federal left flank. About this time, Col. Edward Baker seems to have finally realized the vulnerability of his left flank. Two companies of the 15th Massachusetts were shuttled left to bolster the threatened sector. Four companies of Federals now directly faced seven companies from the 18th Mississippi. Throughout this period, fighting on Baker's right flank was light and fitful.[1]

After its initial bloody repulse and reorganization, those seven companies of the 18th Mississippi shifted to their right to occupy the high ground above the ravine. They used the depression to securely shuttle troops into position in the thick woods. The men did not need to worry, for the woods were so thick that no one could see far in any direction. A Mississippi private recalled that he could not see the enemy, but when it came time to fire, he and his comrades left fly "volley after volley into this obstruction that hid our view." Col. Isaac Wistar of the 1st California claimed that the Mississippians charged a total of five times down the ravine toward the Federal position, and were thrown back each time.[2]

Two more companies from Col. Milton Cogswell's 42nd New York arrived and were moved promptly to the left. They "arrived on the field, cheering most heartily," remembered Cogswell, but by this time the Confederates "had obtained too strong possession of the hills to be dislodged."[3]

Before its problematic withdrawal, the 8th Virginia on the western edge of the open field maintained an effective fire against the Federals across the field in front of it, knocking down both men and horses with its accurate fire. Some of the Federal officers, including Cols. Baker, Cogswell, and William Lee were happy to see Bramhall's piece arrive, and helped wheel it into position. It too became the focal point of enemy small arms fire though it and the mountain howitzers did good service during the course of the fight.[4]

About this time in the battle, a series of firefights erupted, with companies often fighting independently of one another. According to a Federal officer in the 20th Massachusetts, "the fight was made up of charges" where company commanders would "rush out in front & cry 'forward' & their companies would follow them at full speed under a tremendous fire till they were obliged to fall back." As the woods and field filled with powder smoke, Southern reinforcements in the form of the 17th Mississippi arrived and deployed for action.[5]

On the right side of the Confederate line, members of the 18th Mississippi continued applying pressure against the Federal left flank. The escalating fighting there triggered a disaster for the Federals when Southern small arms severely wounded Col. Isaac Wistar of the 1st California and killed Col. Baker, who was standing in the open field near the 1st California's position. Capt. Crowninshield of the 20th Massachusetts left a good account of what transpired: "[W]e heard a tremendous cheering on our left . . . the men there were giving way, at the expected charge of the enemy. . . . We drove them back by a good shower of bullets. The bullets flew about very thick, and I saw many of my men fall all about me. . . . Col. Baker came down near me and cheered on the men . . . he was shot. He got up again and then fell, struck by eight balls, as I afterwards learned." The Federal commander at Ball's Bluff was dead. Unfortunately for the Federals, Baker fell without designating a second in command.[6]

When word of Baker's death spread through the ranks, men on the left began drifting toward the river. Capt. Louis Bieral refused to allow his dead commander's body to fall into the hands of the enemy. "Do you wish to leave the body of our beloved Col. in the hands of the enemy?" he is said to have yelled. Bieral shot a rebel stooping over Baker's body and ran forward to the corpse, while others engaged in hand-to-hand combat around the prone colonel.[7]

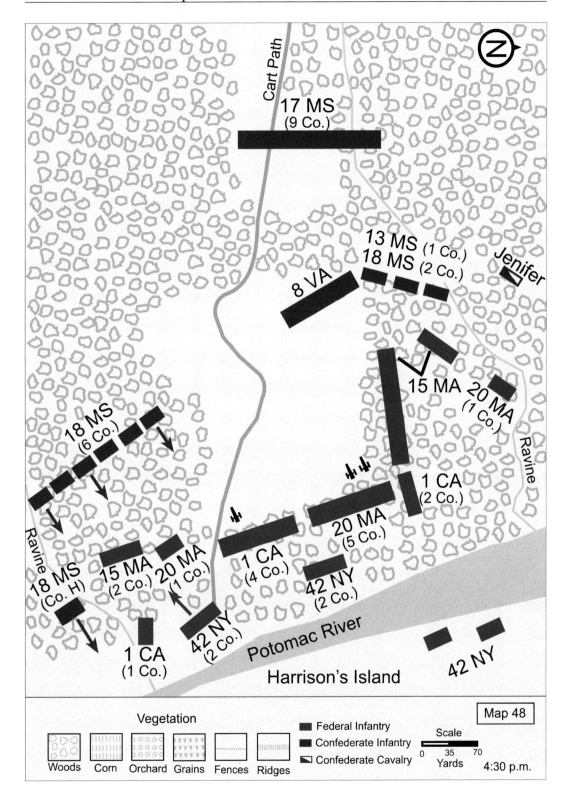

Cart Path

17 MS
(9 Co.)

13 MS (1 Co.)
18 MS (2 Co.)

Jenifer

8 VA

15 MA

20 MA
(1 Co.)

Ravine

18 MS
(6 Co.)

1 CA
(2 Co.)

20 MA
(5 Co.)

Ravine

18 MS
(Co. H)

15 MA
(2 Co.)

20 MA
(1 Co.)

1 CA
(4 Co.)

42 NY
(2 Co.)

42 NY
(2 Co.)

1 CA
(1 Co.)

Potomac River

Harrison's Island

42 NY

Vegetation

Woods   Corn   Orchard   Grains   Fences   Ridges

■ Federal Infantry
■ Confederate Infantry
◥ Confederate Cavalry

Scale

0   35   70
Yards

Map 48

4:30 p.m.

Map 49: Federals Attempt to Break Out (5:00 p.m.)

Col. Charles Devens of the 15th Massachusetts learned of Col. Edward Baker's death when he was summoned to the middle of the defensive line to meet with Col. William Lee of the 20th Massachusetts. Col. Milton Cogswell of the 42nd New York joined the officers. Because he had seniority, Cogswell assumed command of the Federal forces on the field at Ball's Bluff. All three were in agreement that the situation was deteriorating quickly and the Federals needed to slip out of the situation. Lee was in favor of retreating across the Potomac River to safety, but the scarcity of boats precluded that route. Cogswell put his faith in Willis Gorman's brigade on the Virginia side of the river and believed that the men on the bluff could cut through the Confederates and unite with Gorman's men at Edwards Ferry. The move would have been feasible earlier in the fight but by this time the 18th Mississippi was standing in the way and the fresh 17th Mississippi was moving up into position on the far side of the cleared field. Nearly two full enemy regiments barred the way.[1]

As Cogswell prepared his attempted breakout, he ordered Devens to move the 15th Massachusetts from the far right side of his line leftward, forming in front of the 20th Massachusetts. Devens' men faced southward in a column of fours and arrived without significant incident in their new position. Devens was pleased by their comportment during this complicated movement. Two companies of the 42nd New York took up a position on the left of the 15th Massachusetts with its front facing northwest across the field. This odd arrangement makes sense to a modern historian: the New Yorkers would lead the breakout, and when the last man had moved, Devens' men would turn to their right and follow them up the slope toward today's parking lot.

Confederates from the 8th Virginia and Jenifer's command discovered the withdrawal from their front and moved quickly to fill the woods where the 15th Massachusetts had been. About this time, men from the 42nd New York watched as an officer rode through the woods toward them. Just like at Bull Run, a case of mistaken identity occurred, for the men of the 42nd New York were in their pre-war militia gray uniforms. Thinking they were his own men, a hat-waving and possibly intoxicated Lt. Charles Wildman of Nathan Evans' staff ordered the New Yorkers forward to attack some Confederates he had mistaken for Union troops. In turn mistaking Wildman for one of their own officers, the New Yorkers cheered and rushed into the woods, only to be met by deadly Confederate fire.[2] In the midst of this confusion, Col. Cogswell attempted to oversee the operation. He found "our lines pressed severely, [and] ordered an advance of the whole force on the right of the enemy's line." The two Massachusetts regiments (the 15th and 20th) did not participate in the advance. According to Col. Devens, his men of the 15th began moving in that direction, but absent direct orders, he called them back. The failure of the Massachusetts troops to add their weight to the move doomed the success of the breakout.[3]

Col. Eppa Hunton had been dealing with a lack of ammunition for some time. Having gotten the 8th Virginia back into the fight, he temporarily solved the ammunition problem by redistributing the meager number of cartridges among his men so that each had at least one or two rounds before going back into action. When all was ready, Hunton prepared the Virginians to charge across the open field. "Relying almost solely upon the bayonet," Hunton later reported, his men "rushed upon and drove back a heavy column of the enemy just landed and captured the two howitzers." A company of the 20th Massachusetts advanced to recapture the guns. "If bullets had rained before, they came in sheets now," recalled a Federal officer, though bullets could hardly have come "in sheets" from a unit as low on ammunition as the 8th Virginia was. Other Confederates, probably Company D of the 13th Mississippi which had arrived late, had to have been involved. Another Union soldier wrote, "We charged across the field about half way, when we saw the enemy in full sight . . . in their dirty gray clothes, their banner waving, cavalry on the flank. For a moment there was a pause. And then, simultaneously, we fired & there came a murderous discharge from the full rebel force." While this fighting on the northern edge of the field was unfolding, the 17th Mississippi moved to add its weight to the action.[4]

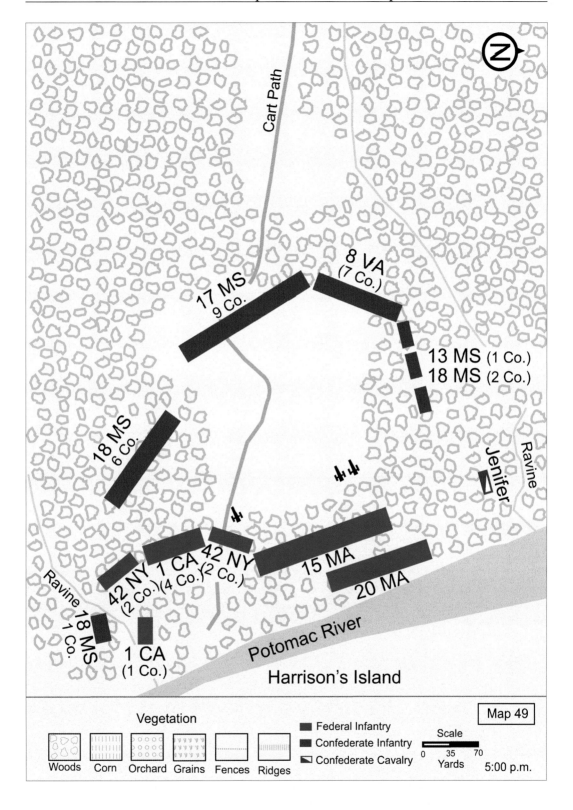

Harrison's Island

Potomac River

8 VA (7 Co.)

17 MS 9 Co.

13 MS (1 Co.)
18 MS (2 Co.)

18 MS 6 Co.

Jenifer

Ravine

Ravine

42 NY (2 Co.)   1 CA (4 Co.)   42 NY (2 Co.)

15 MA

20 MA

18 MS 1 Co.

1 CA (1 Co.)

Cart Path

Vegetation

Woods   Corn   Orchard   Grains   Fences   Ridges

Federal Infantry
Confederate Infantry
Confederate Cavalry

Scale
0   35   70
Yards

Map 49

5:00 p.m.

Map 50: Federal Defeat (5:30 p.m.)

Out of ammunition and energy, the 8th Virginia was ordered to lie down to rest and avoid Federal bullets. The 17th Mississippi's commander, Col. Winfield Featherston, may have realized that the battle hung in the balance when he yelled to his troops, "Forward Mississippians, & drive them into the Potomac or into eternity!" When his men reached the edge of the field, Featherston ordered them to halt and fix bayonets. The men swept across the clearing yelling like "wild Indians." Ahead were scores of discharging Federal muskets on the opposite side of the field that killed and wounded Mississippians with each step. On the right, some of the men of the 17th Mississippi could make out a line of Confederate infantry sweeping ahead in the same direction. It was the 18th Mississippi. For the first time that afternoon, the Confederates were moving and attacking in unison.[1]

The surge of some 1,000 Confederate infantrymen quickly overwhelmed the exhausted and confused Federals. According to Col. Featherston, the Mississippians drove "to within 40 or 50 yards of their line, when we poured in a close and deadly fire, which drove them back, and continued to advance . . ." The Federal line began breaking apart. Their only hope was to try and escape the way they had come—down the bluff and to the boats. A resigned Col. Cogswell finally gave the order for a full retreat to the river. Col. Devens asked that he repeat the order in the presence of a witness, for he did not want to be blamed for the unfolding fiasco.

There was still some fighting going on, particularly on both Federal flanks, as some Massachusetts and New York companies fought to stave off the pending annihilation of the small force on the bluff. Capt. William Bartlett of the 20th Massachusetts noted, "[E]very man that was left sprang forward . . . both sides were surprised to see each other . . . we stood looking at each other . . . for some twenty seconds, and then they let fly their volley at the same time we did . . . they [the bullets] came in sheets . . . it is surprising that anyone could escape being hit . . . we were driven back again." Lt. Bramhall

ordered his men to throw the James Rifle over the side of the bluff, lest the Southerners capture it. He was seriously wounded, however, and order never seems actually to have been carried out though many men apparently thought it was.[2]

The battle now entered a new and gruesome stage. Beaten and demoralized Federal troops tried desperately to escape in any way they could. His infantry, reported Col. Featherston of the 17th Mississippi, continued "loading and firing until the enemy were driven to seek shelter beneath a high bluff immediately upon the brink of the river, and some of them in the river itself." One Southern soldier recalled how the side of the bluff was rubbed smooth by so many men sliding down it. About 300 Federals realized that the enemy was already upon them and set their arms down in surrender.

Col. Lee of the 20th Massachusetts was so demoralized by the sudden turn of events that he simply sat down and awaited capture. His men helped him navigate the steep slope, but he eventually fell into Confederate hands. Col. Cogswell was also among the captured. Turning away from the fast-flowing river, many soldiers ran north or south along the riverbank hoping to elude the pursuing enemy. Some, including Col. Lee, were captured upriver by Southern cavalry. Many of the Federals sought to find a way back across the river in a boat, but most either took to the water or concealed themselves at the base of the steeper parts of the bluff trying to escape from the sheets of Confederate bullets raining down upon them. Hundreds of men jumped in the water in an attempt to swim across the Potomac. Many perished as a result, their heavy clothes and accouterments dragging them under the swift water. The chaos and spread of death worsened when the Mississippians lining the bluff opened fire on the helpless men packed below, slaughtering scores. "[W]e arrived at the brink of the bluff & fired down on them," was how one private casually recalled the mass killing.[3]

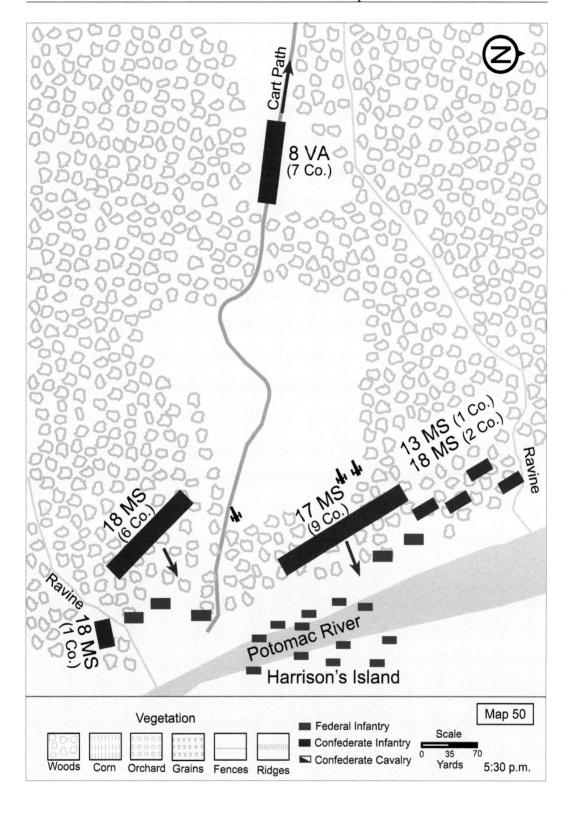

Cart Path

8 VA
(7 Co.)

13 MS (1 Co.)
18 MS (2 Co.)

Ravine

18 MS
(6 Co.)

17 MS
(9 Co.)

Ravine

18 MS
(1 Co.)

Potomac River

Harrison's Island

Vegetation

Woods   Corn   Orchard   Grains   Fences   Ridges

Federal Infantry
Confederate Infantry
Confederate Cavalry

Map 50

Scale

0   35   70
Yards

5:30 p.m.

Map 51: Aftermath / Edwards Ferry (October 22)

The Ball's Bluff fighting was small by comparison to later battles, but its significance was not. For the only time in American history a sitting U.S. Senator had been killed in combat. Four Federal regimental commanders crossed over the Potomac River to Ball's Bluff; one was killed, and two were captured. Federal losses were staggering: just over 1,000 of the 1,700 on the field were killed, wounded, or captured—about one-third of the entire casualties suffered at Bull Run. The number of captured constituted the largest segment in both raw numbers and percentage (553, or nearly half). Confederate losses were significantly lower at 149 from all causes.[1]

In addition to the hundreds of captured enemy, Col. Nathan Evans' men collected "1,500 stand of arms, three pieces of cannon, one stand of colors, a large number of cartridge boxes, bayonet scabbards, and a quantity of camp furniture." The Confederates spent days combing the battlefield for anything useful. Some Confederates dragged hooks along the bottom of the river to snag dead bodies in order to rifle through pockets and relieve the drowned or killed Federals of valuable military equipment.[2]

Gen. Charles Stone, who had delegated so much authority to Edward Baker, a politician with limited prior military experience, was quickly made the scapegoat of the fiasco. The small force had been soundly whipped. Col. Evans spent the battle near the Edwards Ferry Road and through both good luck and the hard fighting of his soldiers, won a decisive victory that maintained his grip along the Potomac.[3]

Stone received word of Baker's death about 6:45 p.m. We know that because he immediately penciled a note to Gen. George McClellan: "Col. Baker has been killed at the head of his Brigade. I go to the right at once." Stone encountered the party carrying Baker's body as he made his way upstream. He stopped briefly to converse with the men, and then continued his journey. Along the way he passed streams of beaten and demoralized Federal soldiers. Many had thrown away their muskets during their mad dash to escape. Knapsacks and other accouterments were also in short supply. Stone "began to fear that we had had a disaster."[4]

Stone also worried about the safety of Willis Gorman's brigade at Edwards Ferry. Was it just a matter of time before the victorious Confederates fell upon Gorman and repeated their victory at Ball's Bluff? Stone turned the Harrison's Island sector over to Col. Edward Hinks of the 19th Massachusetts. There was some confusion about whether the 42nd New York should remain on Harrison's Island or return to Maryland, which consumed Stone for a while before he rode as fast as possible to the ferry.[5]

McClellan's reply, written at 10:00 p.m., ordered Stone to hold Edwards Ferry "at all hazards." Both men knew that Gen. Nathaniel Banks was sending reinforcements, and McClellan directed Stone to use his discretion on the disposition of those men. A couple of regiments from Banks' division arrived between 3:00 and 4:00 a.m. on October 22 and immediately crossed the river.[6]

October 22 was a rainy, dreary day. Although Stone had about 4,500 men at Edwards Ferry by midday, Col. William Barksdale maneuvered his 600 men of the 13th Mississippi into position to attack the Federal forces. The audacious Southerners emerged from the woods in front of the Federal positions "yelling like Demons and driving our pickets ahead of them in double quick time." Barksdale wisely aborted the attack when Federal artillery opened fire on his men and he fully realized the extent of the enemy strength. At least he could say his men had played a role in the short victorious campaign.[7]

Without a good reason to continue risking the lives of his men, Gen. McClellan ordered Stone to abandon the position at Edwards Ferry around nightfall on October 23. The last boat pushed off from the Virginia shore about 4:00 a.m. on October 24, bringing the Ball's Bluff campaign to an end.[8]

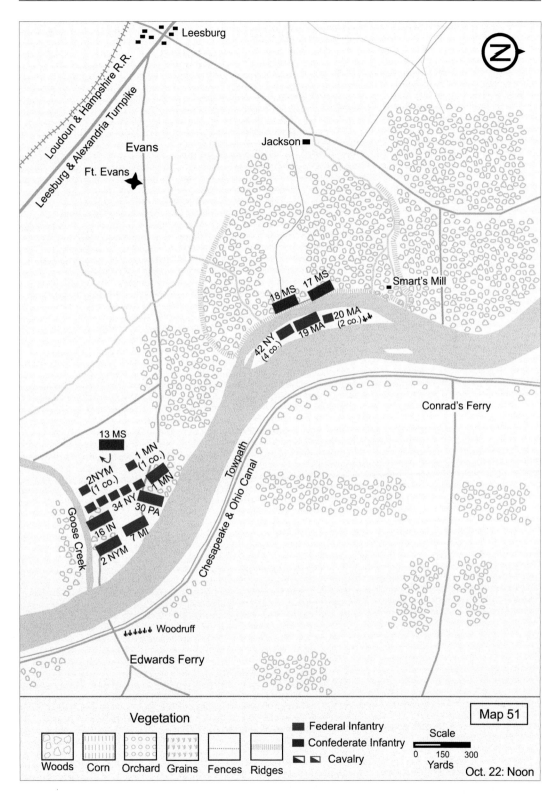

Leesburg

Loudoun & Hampshire R.R.

Leesburg & Alexandria Turnpike

Evans

Ft. Evans

Jackson ■

18 MS   17 MS

Smart's Mill

42 NY
(4 co.)
19 MA   20 MA
(2 co.)

Conrad's Ferry

13 MS

1 MN
(1 co.)

2NYM
(1 co.)
1 MN
34 NY   30 PA

16 IN   7 MI

2 NYM

Goose Creek

Towpath

Chesapeake & Ohio Canal

Woodruff

Edwards Ferry

Vegetation

Woods   Corn   Orchard   Grains   Fences   Ridges

■ Federal Infantry
■ Confederate Infantry
◣ ◢ Cavalry

Map 51

Scale

0   150   300
Yards

Oct. 22: Noon

Appendix 1

First Bull Run (Manassas) Order of Battle and Losses

Army of Northeastern Virginia
Brigadier Gen. Irvin McDowell

First Division: Brig. Gen. Daniel Tyler

First Brigade: Col. Erasmus Keyes

2nd Maine: 13 killed, 24 wounded, 118 missing
1st Connecticut: 8 wounded, 9 missing
2nd Connecticut: 2 killed, 5 wounded, 9 missing
3rd Connecticut: 4 killed, 13 wounded, 18 missing

Brigade Total: 19 killed, 50 wounded, 154 missing = 223

Second Brigade: Brig. Gen. Robert Schenck

2nd New York Militia: 19 killed, 15 wounded, 36 missing
1st Ohio: 1 killed, 4 wounded, 7 missing
2nd Ohio: 1 killed, 2 wounded, 8 missing
Co. E, 2nd U.S. Artillery (6 guns) Capt. J. Carlisle: 4 wounded, 11 missing
Battery G, 1st U.S. Artillery (1 gun), Lt. Peter Hains: NA

Brigade Total: 21 killed, 25 wounded, 62 missing = 108

Third Brigade: Col. William Sherman

13th New York: 11 killed, 27 wounded, 20 missing
69th New York Militia: 38 killed, 59 wounded, 95 missing
79th New York: 32 killed, 51 wounded, 115 missing
2nd Wisconsin: 24 killed, 65 wounded, 23 missing
Co. E. 3rd U.S. Artillery (6 guns), Capt. R. Ayres: 4 killed, 2 wounded

Brigade Total: 109 killed, 204 wounded, 253 missing = 566

Fourth Brigade: Col. Israel Richardson

1st Massachusetts: 1 killed, 1 wounded
12th New York: NA
2nd Michigan: NA
3rd Michigan: NA
Co. G. 1st U.S. Artillery (2 guns), Lt. J. Edwards: NA
Co. M. U.S. Artillery (4 guns), Capt. H. Hunt: NA

Brigade Total: 1 killed, 1 wounded = 2

Second Division: Col. David Hunter

First Brigade: Col. Andrew Porter

8th New York Militia: 8 killed, 17 wounded, 13 missing
14th New York Militia: 23 killed, 48 wounded, 71 missing
27th New York: 26 killed, 44 wounded, 60 missing
U.S. Infantry Battalion (8 co.): 10 killed, 20 wounded, 53 missing
U.S. Marine Battalion: 9 killed, 19 wounded, 16 missing
U.S. Cavalry Battalion (7 co.): 13 wounded
Co. D. 5th U.S. Artillery (6 guns), Capt. Charles Griffin: 4 killed, 13 wounded, 10 missing

Brigade Total: 80 killed, 174 wounded, 223 missing = 477

Second Brigade: Col. Ambrose Burnside

2nd New Hampshire: 9 killed, 35 wounded, 63 missing
1st Rhode Island: 13 killed, 39 wounded, 39 missing
2nd Rhode Island: 23 killed, 49 wounded
71st New York: 10 killed, 40 wounded, 12 missing
Reynolds' Battery (6 guns), Capt. William Reynolds: NA
Two boat howitzers: Col. H. P. Martin: NA

Brigade Total: 55 killed, 163 wounded, 114 missing = 332

Third Division: Col. Samuel Heintzelman

First Brigade: Col. William Franklin

5th Massachusetts: 5 killed, 26 wounded, 28 missing
11th Massachusetts: 8 killed, 40 wounded, 40 missing
1st Minnesota: 42 killed, 108 wounded, 30 missing
4th Pennsylvania (not present at battle)
Co. I 1st U.S. Artillery (6 guns), Capt. J. Ricketts: 12 killed, 15 wounded

Brigade Total: 67 killed, 189 wounded, 98 missing = 354

Second Brigade: Col. Orlando Willcox

11th New York: 48 killed, 75 wounded, 65 missing
38th New York: 15 killed, 55 wounded, 58 missing
1st Michigan: 6 killed, 37 wounded, 70 missing
4th Michigan: NA
Co. D. 2nd U.S. Artillery (4 guns), Capt. R. Arnold: 2 killed, 5 wound, 4 missing

Brigade Total: 71 killed, 172 wounded, 197 missing = 440

Third Brigade: Col. Oliver Howard

3rd Maine: 5 killed, 8 wounded, 74 missing
4th Maine: 26 killed, 46 wounded, 121 missing
5th Maine: 13 killed, 40 wounded, 335 missing
2nd Vermont: 6 killed, 22 wounded, 92 missing

Brigade Total: 50 killed, 116 wounded, 622 missing = 788

Fourth Division: Brig. Gen. Theodore Runyon (not engaged)

1st New Jersey Militia
2nd New Jersey Militia
3rd New Jersey Militia
4th New Jersey Militia
1st New Jersey
2nd New Jersey
3rd New Jersey
41st New York

Fifth Division: Col. Dixon Miles

First Brigade: Col. Louis Blenker

8th New York: 2 killed, 2 wounded, 7 missing
29th New York: 2 killed, 9 wounded, 25 missing
39th New York: 2 killed, 5 wounded, 54 missing
27th Pennsylvania: NA
Co. A, 2nd U.S. Artillery (4 guns), Capt. J. Tidball: NA
Brookwood's (Varian's) New York Battery (6 guns), Capt. C. Brookwood: NA

Brigade Total: 6 killed, 16 wounded, 86 missing = 108

Second Brigade: Col. Thomas Davies

16th New York: 1 wounded, 1 missing
18th New York: NA
31st New York: 1 wounded, 1 missing
32nd New York: NA
Co. G 2nd U.S. Artillery (4 guns), Lt. O. Greene: NA

Brigade Total: 2 wounded, 2 missing = 4

Army of the Potomac
Brig. Gen. P. G. T. Beauregard

First Brigade: Brig. Gen. Milledge Bonham

11th North Carolina: NA
2nd South Carolina: 6 killed, 43 wounded
3rd South Carolina: NA
7th South Carolina: NA
8th South Carolina: 5 killed, 23 wounded
8th Louisiana: NA
30th Virginia Cavalry
Alexandria Art. (4 guns) Capt. D. Kemper:
1st Co., Richmond Howitzers (4 guns), Capt. J. Shields: NA

Brigade Total: 11 killed, 66 wounded = 77

Second Brigade: Brig. Gen. Richard Ewell (not engaged)

5th Alabama
6th Alabama
6th Louisiana
Cavalry Battalion: Col. J. G. Jenifer
Washington Artillery (4 guns) Capt. T. Rosser

Third Brigade: Brig. Gen. David Jones

17th Mississippi: 2 killed, 10 wounded
18th Mississippi: 9 killed, 29 wounded
5th South Carolina: 3 killed, 23 wounded
30th Virginia Cavalry (one co.): NA
Washington Artillery (2 guns), Capt. M. Miller: NA

Brigade Total: 14 killed, 62 wounded = 76

Fourth Brigade: Brig. Gen. James Longstreet

5th North Carolina: 1 killed, 3 wounded
1st Virginia: 6 wounded
11th Virginia: NA
17th Virginia: 1 killed, 3 wounded
24th Virginia: NA
30th Virginia Cavalry (one co.), Capt. E. Whitehead: NA
Washington Artillery (2 guns), Lt. J. Garnett: NA

Brigade Total: 2 killed, 12 wounded = 14

Fifth Brigade: Col. P. Cocke

8th Virginia: 6 killed, 23 wounded
18th Virginia: 6 killed, 13 wounded
19th Virginia: 1 killed, 4 wounded, 1 missing
28th Virginia: 9 wounded
49th Virginia Battalion: 10 killed, 30 wounded
Cavalry Co., Capt. John Langhorne: NA
Loudoun Artillery (4 guns), Capt. A. Rogers: 3 wounded
Lynchburg Artillery (4 guns), Capt. H. Latham: 1 wounded

Brigade Total: 23 killed, 83 wounded, 2 missing = 108

Sixth Brigade: Col. Jubal Early

7th Louisiana: 3 killed, 20 wounded
13th Mississippi: 6 wounded
7th Virginia: 9 killed, 38 wounded
Washington Artillery (5 guns), Lt. C. Squires: NA

Brigade Total: 12 killed, 64 wounded = 76

Seventh Brigade: Col. Nathan Evans

1st Louisiana Battalion: 8 killed, 38 wounded, 2 missing
4th South Carolina: 11 killed, 79 wounded, 6 missing
Alexander's Troop (30th Virginia): NA
Terry's Troop (30th Virginia): NA
Latham's Artillery (2 guns), Lt. George Davidson and Lt. Clark Leftwich: NA

Brigade Total: 19 killed, 117 wounded, 8 missing = 144

Reserve Brigade: Brig. Gen. Theophilus Holmes (not engaged)

1st Arkansas
2nd Tennessee
Purcell Artillery (6 guns), Capt. L. Walker

Hampton's Legion: Col. Wade Hampton: 19 killed, 100 wounded, 2 missing = 121

Camp Pickens Battery: Capt. Sterrett: NA

Army of the Shenandoah
Gen. Joseph Johnston

First Brigade: Brig. Gen. Thomas Jackson (w)

2nd Virginia: 18 killed, 72 wounded
4th Virginia: 31 killed, 100 wounded
5th Virginia: 6 killed, 47 wounded
27th Virginia: 19 killed, 122 wounded
33rd Virginia: 45 killed, 101 wounded
Rockbridge Artillery (4 guns), Col. William Pendleton: NA

Brigade Total: 119 killed, 442 wounded = 561

Second Brigade: Col. Francis Bartow (k)

7th Georgia: 19 killed, 134 wounded
8th Georgia: 41 killed, 159 wounded
Wise Artillery (4 guns) Capt. E. Alburtis/Lt. John Pelham

Brigade Total: 60 killed, 293 wounded = 353

Third Brigade: Brig. Gen. Barnard Bee (mw)

4th Alabama: 40 killed, 156 wounded
2nd Mississippi: 25 killed, 81 wounded, 1 missing
11th Mississippi (2 co.): 7 killed, 21 wounded
6th North Carolina: 23 killed, 50 wounded
Staunton Artillery (4 guns) Capt. J. Imboden: NA

Brigade Total: 95 killed, 308 wounded, 1 missing = 404

Fourth Brigade: Brig. Gen. Edmund Smith

1st Maryland Battalion: 1 killed, 5 wounded
3rd Tennessee: 1 killed, 3 wounded
10th Virginia: 6 killed, 10 wounded
Newtown Artillery (4 guns), Capt. George Groves/Lt. R. Beckham: NA

Brigade Total: 8 killed, 18 wounded = 26

Not Brigaded

1st VA Cavalry, Col. J.E.B. Stuart: 1 killed, 1 wounded
Thomas Artillery (Stanard's Battery, 4 guns) Capt. P. B. Stanard: NA

Appendix 2

Ball's Bluff Order of Battle and Losses

Federal Forces

Stone's Division: Brig. Gen. Charles Stone

First Brigade: Brig. Gen. Frederick Lander

19th Massachusetts: NA
20th Massachusetts: 35 killed, 44 wounded, 115 missing
1st Minnesota Sharpshooters: NA
7th Michigan: NA

Second Brigade: Brig. Gen. Willis Gorman

1st Minnesota: NA
2nd New York State Militia: NA
34th New York: NA

Third Brigade: Col. Edward Baker

1st California: 25 killed, 40 wounded, 214 missing = 279

Unassigned

15th Massachusetts: 35 killed, 65 wounded, 128 missing = 228
42nd New York: 24 killed, 131 wounded, 20 missing = 175

Artillery

Battery I, 1st U.S. Artillery: 1 wounded
Battery B, 1st Rhode Island Artillery: 5 wounded, 4 missing
Battery K, 9th New York State: 1 wounded

Total: 119 killed, 169 wounded, 581 missing = 869

Confederate Forces

Seventh Brigade: Col. Nathan Evans

13th Mississippi: 4 killed, 2 wounded, 1 missing
17th Mississippi: 2 killed, 9 wounded
18th Mississippi: 22 killed, 63 wounded
8th Virginia: 8 killed, 43 wounded, 1 missing

Brigade Total: 36 killed, 117 wounded, 2 missing = 155

Notes

Map 1

1. United States War Department, *The War of the Rebellion: A Compilation of the Official Records of the Union and Confederate Armies.* 128 volumes (Washington: U.S. Government Printing Office, 1880-1901), vol. 27, part 3, 858-859, hereinafter *OR*.

2. *OR* 2, 726; *OR* 51, pt. 1, 396, 399, 406; John Hennessy, *The First Battle of Manassas* (Lynchburg, VA: H. E. Howard, 1989), 130-132.

3. *OR* 2, 943-44; William C. Davis, *Battle at Bull Run* (New York: Doubleday, 1977), 59.

4. Davis, *Battle at Bull Run*, 20; Russel H. Beatie, *Army of the Potomac: Birth of Command* (New York: DaCapo, 2002), 169-70.

5. Beatie, *Birth of Command*, 217-18.

Map 2

1. Davis, *Battle at Bull Run*, 63.

2. *OR* 2, 124-130.

3. *OR* 2, 265, 934-35; Joseph E. Johnston, Narrative of Military Operations, Directed, During the Late War Between the States (New York: D. Appleton and Co., 1874), 19, 24-25; Beatie, *Birth of Command*, 176-77; Davis, *Battle at Bull Run*, 45-46.

4. U.S. Committee on the Conduct of the War (Washington: Government Printing Office, 1863), 36-37, 55, 62, hereafter *JCCW*; Davis, *Battle at Bull Run*, 74-75. Modern scholarship on the importance of holding Joe Johnston's army in the Shenandoah Valley is evolving. McDowell assumed Johnston would be held in the Valley, but he also anticipated that the Confederates would bring up about 10,000 more men from other locations in the South. McDowell expected to face about 35,000 Confederates. Even though Johnston's men reached the battlefield on July 21, McDowell still confronted about 35,000 enemy. The idea that McDowell's plan was contingent upon holding Johnston in the Valley is thus not quite true. The conclusion that his plan was therefore foiled by Johnston's arrival is also not quite true.

Map 3

1. *OR* 2, 691, 715; 51, pt. 1, 397-98; Davis, *Battle at Bull Run*, 79-81; Beatie, *Birth of Command*, 175.

2. Beatie, *Birth of Command*, 175; *OR* 51, pt. 1, 397-98; *OR* 2, 187.

3. James I. Robertson, *Stonewall Jackson* (New York: Macmillan, 1997), 245-46, 247-249.

4. Johnston, *Narrative*, 27-30; *OR* 2, 735; Davis, 84-85, 86.

Map 4

1. R. H. Beatie, Jr., *Road to Manassas* (New York: Cooper Square Publishers, 1961), 84-85, *OR* 2, 157, 158, 161-2, 179-85; 967, 969; Johnston, *Narrative*, 30-31; Beatie, *Birth of Command*, 222-227.

2. Beatie, *Road to Manassas*, 104-105; Robert Patterson, *A Narrative of the Campaign in the Valley of the Shenandoah* in 1861 (Philadelphia: Sherman and Co. Printers, 1865), 57-58; U.S. Committee on the Conduct of the War, 163-64, 191, 229-31; *OR* vol. 2, 165-68, 171, 172; Beatie, *Birth of Command*, 241-42.

3. *OR* 2, 478; Johnston, *Narrative*, 33-4; Davis, *Battle at Bull Run*, 134-35.

4. D. B. Conrad, "History of the First Battle of Manassas and Organization of the Stonewall Brigade," *Southern Historical Society Papers*, XIX (191), 87; Davis, *Battle at Bull Run*, 134-38.

Map 5

1. *OR* 2, 302-05; Davis, *Battle at Bull Run*, 90; Beatie, *Birth of Command*, 250-253.

General Runyon's Fourth Division was left behind to guard the approaches to Alexandria, and although counted in McDowell's total aggregate force, was not available during the battle. James B. Fry, "McDowell's Advance to Bull Run," *Battles and Leaders of the Civil War* (New York: Thomas Yoseloff, 1956), Vol. 1, 176.

2. *OR* 2, 304, 447, 449; Davis, *Battle at Bull Run*, 98-100.

3. Beatie, *Birth of Command*, 255.

4. *OR* 2, 304, 309; Beatie, *Birth of Command*, 253-55.

5. Beatie, *Birth of Command*, 257-58; *OR* 2, 307. The fighting at Blackburn's Ford was already underway during McDowell's personal reconnaissance, and so it did not influence his decision to switch his plan and attack the Confederate left.

Map 6

1. Alfred Roman, *The Military Operations of General Beauregard in the War Between the States* (New York: Harper and Brothers, 1884), vol. 1, 89; Rose

Greenhow, *My Imprisonment and the First Year of Abolition Rule at Washington* (London: Richard Bentley, 1863), 16; General Orders No. 120, July 16, 1861; Davis, *Battle at Bull Run*, 103, 110.

2. Davis, *Battle at Bull Run*, 103.

3. OR 2, 565, 469-70, 487.

4. OR 2, 478; Davis, *Battle at Bull Run*, 133-36.

Map 7

1. OR 2, 310-11; Davis, *Battle at Bull Run*, 112-13; John Hennessy, *The First Battle of Manassas* (Lynchburg, Va: H. E. Howard, Inc., 1989), 12.

2. OR 2, 310, 313; Hennessy, *The First Battle of Manassas*, 13.

3. OR 2, 461, 463-64; Charles T. Loehr, *Of the Old First Virginia Infantry Regiment* (Richmond: Wm. Ellis Jones, 1884), 9; Hennessy, *The First Battle of Manassas*, 15. Longstreet's men had constructed a crude breastwork of logs, rails, and dirt on the south bank of Bull Run. His orders to the commanders of the two guns were "retire the moment it was ascertained that our pieces were commanded by those of the enemy." (Jeffry D. Wert, *General James Longstreet* (New York: Simon and Schuster, 1993), 67; OR 2, 461.

4. Hennessy, *The First Battle of Manassas,* 16-7; OR 2, 311-13; James Longstreet, *From Manassas to Appomattox* (Bloomington, IN: Indiana University Press, 1960), 38-9.

Map 8

1. *JCCW*, 162, 199; Warren H. Cudworth, *History of the First Regiment [Massachusetts] Infantry* (Boston: Walker, Fuller, and Co., 1866), 43.

2. OR 2, 311; Davis, *Battle at Bull Run*, 117-18; R. L. Murray, *The Greatest Battle of the Age: New Yorkers at First Bull Run* (Walcott, NY: Benedum Books, 2002), 51.

3. Hennessy, *The First Battle of Manassas*, 20-21; Davis, *Battle at Bull Run*, 119.

4. OR 2, 462, 464; Longstreet, *From Manassas to Appomattox*, 39; Jubal Early, *Lieutenant General Jubal A. Early* (Philadelphia: Lippincott, 1912), 7-8. According to Lt. C. Squires of the Washington Artillery, five guns rolled after Early's troops, but only two deployed behind Blackburn's Ford; another section deployed nearby. OR 2, 267-68.

Map 9

1. OR 2, 313; Cudworth, *History of the First Massachusetts*, 35; Davis, *Battle at Bull Run*, 119-21; Murray, *The Greatest Battle of the Age*, 51-53. One New York soldier later wrote, "Our regiment had the old muskets and were in miserable condition; about three in five were in condition for firing. Our cartridges were of different sizes. . . . The men had no confidence in their pieces, which was one of the reasons why they [had] problems standing and fighting later in the engagement." Murray, *The Greatest Battle of the Age*, 50-51.

2. Ed Bearss, *First Manassas Battlefield Map Study* (Lynchburg: H. E. Howard, Inc., nd), 3; OR 2, 443, 462; Longstreet, *Manassas to Appomattox*, 39; Davis, *Battle at Bull Run*, 129.

3. OR 2, 311, 313; Murray, *The Greatest Battle of the Age*, 55-57; Davis, *Battle at Bull Run*, 121-2.

4. Early, *Early*, 8; OR 2, 313, 464. Longstreet helped position the 7th Virginia. So anxious were these green troops to open fire on the enemy that they forgot that Longstreet was still in front of them. He survived by throwing himself off of his horse onto the ground (Wert, *General James Longstreet*, 70-71).

5. Davis, *Battle at Bull Run*, 124, 130; OR 2, 311, 314; Loehr, *First Virginia*, 10.

Map 10

1. Davis, *Battle at Bull Run*, 136-40; Robertson, *Stonewall Jackson*, 256.

2. Davis, *Battle at Bull Run*, 141-42. Beauregard's 23,000-man army was composed of seven brigades of infantry, three unbrigaded infantry regiments, a regiment and three battalions of cavalry, and six artillery batteries with a total of twenty-seven guns. Johnston brought an additional 8,340 men organized into four infantry brigades, two unbrigaded infantry regiments, one cavalry regiment, and five batteries sporting twenty guns. General McDowell's army consisted of four infantry divisions with eleven brigades and nine unbrigaded regiments, ten artillery batteries, of forty-nine guns. He was light on cavalry—only seven companies. Fry, "McDowell's Advance to Bull Run," 171-72.

3. OR 2, 330-331; *JCCW*, 39.

4. OR 2, 745.

5. *JCCW*, 39. Regarding numbers and McDowell's expectations, see note 4, Map 2.

6. OR 2, 479-80.

Map 11

1. *OR* 2, 318. A large number of curious civilians thronged the camps, including Secretary of War, Simon Cameron (Fry, "McDowell's Advance to Bull Run," 183).

2. *OR* 2, 348, 353, 357; Hennessy, *The First Battle of Manassas*, 37-9.

It took Schenck's men an hour to cover the one-half mile route to Cub Run. Ethan S. Rafuse, *A Single Grand Victory* (Wilmington, DE: SR Books, 2002), 120.

3. Jesse W. Reid, *History of the Fourth Regiment* of S. C. Volunteers (Greenville, SC: Shannon and Co., 1892), 23-24; Letter from J. W. Reid, July 23, 1861 (copy in the 4th South Carolina folder, Manassas National Military Park, hereafter MNMP); *OR* 2, 558-60. A Federal officer characterized Tyler's advance as "slow and feeble" and hypothesized that he was still affected by the Blackburn Ford skirmish of a couple of days before. Fry, "McDowell's Advance to Bull Run," 179, 184.

4. *OR* 2, 488-89.

Map 12

1. G. T. Beauregard, "First Battle of Bull Run," *Battles and Leaders of the Civil War* (New York: Thomas Yoseloff, 1956), Vol. 1, 205; Hennessy, *The First Battle of Manassas*, 42-43; *OR* 2, 543, 544-45. Since the rear of this Union flanking column (Howard) had not left the turnpike, Evans faced only the leading elements of this column, fewer than one-half of the 15,000 troops.

Both Jones and Longstreet received their orders at 7:00 a.m. that morning, but Ewell never received his directive to cross, despite being ready to take the offensive. *OR* 2, 537.

2. *JCCW*, 30, 160-61; Beatie, *Birth of Command*, 286-87; E. P. Alexander, "The Battle of Bull Run," *Scribner's Magazine*, vol. XLI (1907), 87-88; Hennessy, *The First Battle of Manassas*, 44-46; Bearss, *First Manassas Battlefield Map Study*, 13; Fry, "McDowell's Advance to Bull Run," 184; *OR* 2, 559. A Federal officer called Evans' actions "one of the best pieces of soldiership on either side during the campaign, but it seems to have received no special commendation from his superiors. Fry, "McDowell's Advance to Bull Run," 185. It took Hunter's column about seven and a half hours (2:00 a.m. to 9:30 a.m.) to reach its destination, and as a result the men were already tired when the action began. JoAnna M.

McDonald, *We Shall Meet Again* (New York: Oxford University Press, 1999), 48.

3. Robert Hunt Rhodes, *All For the Union* (New York: Orion Books, 1991), 26; Account, 71st New York folder, MNMP.

4. Hennessy, *The First Battle of Manassas*, 47; B.B. Brezeale, "Company J, 4th South Carolina Infantry at the First Battle of Manassas" (Manassas: Manassas Journal Publishing Company, 1912), 6. The Louisianans fired about five volleys before the South Carolinians joined them (Hennessy, *The First Battle of Manassas*, 53). The two guns were part of Captain H. G. Latham's Lynchburg Artillery. Lieutenant Davidson retained command of the piece on the right; Lieutenant Clark Leftwich commanded the one on the left, on Buck Hill (*OR* 2, 489, 490).

5. Rhodes, *All for the Union*, 26; Hennessey, *The First Battle of Manassas*, 50; McDonald, *We Shall Meet Again*, 50. As the Federal infantry approached Sudley Ford they encountered civilians on their way to church. Augustus Woodbury, *The Second Rhode Island Regiment: A Narrative of Military Operations* (Providence: Valpay, Angell, and Company, 1875), 31-32.

Map 13

1. Hennessey, *The First Battle of Manassas*, 50-51; *The Reunion of the Palmetto Riflemen* (Greenville, SC: Hoyt & Keys, Printers, 1886), 13-14. Slocum was taken to the Matthews' barn, and then to a field hospital at the Sudley Church on a door that the men removed from its hinges. He died after the battle. Woodbury, *The Second Rhode Island Regiment*, 34.

2. Terry Jones, *Lee's Tigers* (Baton Rouge, LA: Louisiana State University Press, 1987), 51; *OR* 2, 561. There was also a patch of woods between the two units. "Movements of the 4th South Carolina Volunteers at the Battle of First Manassas," 4th South Carolina Folder, MNMP.

3. Hennessey, *The First Battle of Manassas*, 53-54; Woodbury, *The Second Rhode Island Regiment*, 32-33; Augustus Woodbury, *A Narrative of the Campaign of the First Rhode Island Regiment in the Spring and Summer of 1861* (Providence: Knowles, Anthony, and Co. Printers, 1862), 92.

4. *OR* 2, 487; Beauregard, "First Battle of Bull Run," 206-207; R. T. Coles, "The First Manassas Campaign" (Alabama Department of Archives and History); Hennessey, *The First Battle of Manassas*, 48; Lewis H. Metcalfe, "So Eager Were We All," *American Heritage*, vol. 16 (June 1965), 35; John D. Imboden, "Incidents of the First Bull Run," *Battles and Leaders of the Civil War* (New York: Thomas

Yoseloff, 1956), Vol. 1, 232-3. Two companies of the 11th Mississippi were present, attached to the 2nd Mississippi. Another Georgian wrote, "[Nothing] can try the courage of men . . . [as] to be in such a position as to not be able to see the enemy, and yet to know that you are being shot at." Battle of First Manassas: Letter of Captain Robert Grant (copy in the 8th Georgia folder, MNMP).

Map 14

1. *Providence Evening Post,* July 25, 1861.

2. *OR* 2, 559; Hennessey, *The First Battle of Manassas,* 54-55; *Providence Evening Post,* July 25, 1861; Rhodes, *All for the Union,* 37. According to Woodbury, the officers of the 1st Rhode Island mistook the Louisianans for Federal soldiers, causing them to yell, "Throw up your muskets, boys . . . for God's sake, don't fire on our own men!" Woodbury, *A Narrative of the Campaign of the First Rhode Island Regiment in the Spring and Summer of 1861,* 98.

3. Coles, "The First Manassas Campaign," Hennessey, *The First Battle of Manassas,* 55.

The left of Jones' line was protected by a cornfield. Coles, "The First Manassas Campaign."

4. Beauregard, "First Battle of Bull Run," 207-08. The 7th Georgia did not advance to Matthews Hill; it was held in a reserve position in the turnpike in front of the Robinson House. Rafuse, *A Single Grand Victory,* 132, estimated that the Confederates on Matthews Hill numbered about 2,800.

Map 15

1. Lt. Col. Henry Persons, Jr., "7th Georgia at First Manassas" (copy in 7th Georgia file, MNMP); John Reed's Journal (copy in the 8th Georgia folder, MNMP).

2. Bearss, *First Manassas Battlefield Map Study,* 27-28; *OR* 2, 489-90; Beauregard, "The First Battle of Bull Run," B. & L., vol. 1, 207; Warren Wilkinson and Steven E. Woodworth, *A Scythe of Fire* (New York: Morrow, 2002), 70; B. T. Lowe, "Written in 1861," (copy in the 7th Georgia folder, MNMP); Reed's Journal; Davis, *Battle at Bull Run,* 176.

3. OR 2, 346, 383, 384, 387, 388, 392, 391-92, 394; Woodbury, *A Narrative of the Campaign of the First Rhode Island Regiment in the Spring and Summer of 1861,* 95-96; Martin A. Haynes, *History of the Second Regiment New Hampshire Volunteers*

(Manchester, NH: Charles F. Livingston, Printer, 1865), 20.

4. *OR* 2, 403, 405-06, 408, 411, 416.

5. Hennessey, *The First Battle of Manassas,* 56-7; *Providence Evening Press,* July 26, 1861.

Map 16

1. Berrien M. Zettler, *War Stories and School-Day Incidents: For the Children* (New York: Neale Publishing Company, 1912), 66; *Providence Evening Post,* July 26, 1861.

2. Robert G. Carter, *Four Brothers in Blue OR Sunshine and Shadows of the War of the Rebellion* (Austin: University of Texas, 1913); 13; "Reminiscences of Bull Run," *National Tribune,* January 25, 1907; Hennessey, *The First Battle of Manassas,* 58, 60; "Captain V. P. Sisson Tells Vividly of Close Calls." *Atlanta Journal,* February 2, 1901. It appears that a large number of recruits filled the ranks of the "Regulars," which made this unit little better than the average volunteer regiment. Hennessey, *The First Battle of Manassas,* 58.

3. James Hamilton Couper account, copy in the 8th Georgia folder, MNMP.

Map 17

1. Hennessey, *The First Battle of Manassas,* 60; Bearss, *First Manassas Battlefield Map Study,* 27-35; "Fowler's 1st Bull Run Report." *Brooklyn Eagle,* March 17, 1901 (courtesy of Jim McLean). Both James Ricketts and Charles Griffin moved to the infantry, ending the war as major generals in command of divisions in the Army of the Potomac. Ezra J. Warner, *Generals in Blue* (Baton Rouge, LA: LSU Press, 1964) 190-91, 403-04.

2. Zettler, *War Stories and School-Day Incidents,* 67; Hennessey, *The First Battle of Manassas,* 60; Davis, *Battle at Bull Run,* 185-86. The time of Colonel Jones' actual mortal wounding is the subject of much debate. Some believe he fell earlier in the fight. He ultimately died on September 3, 1861. McDonald, *We Shall Meet Again,* 61. Although the Southerners on Matthews Hill were ultimately defeated, the ninety or so minutes they battled the Federal flank movement bought valuable time for reinforcements to be dispatched to the sector. Rafuse, *A Single Grand Victory,* 139.

3. Mary Boykin Chestnut. *A Diary from Dixie* (New York: Houghton Mifflin, 1949), 69.

Sherman's and Keyes' brigades skirted the Stone Bridge because it was said to be mined and to avoid a direct clash with its unknown number of defenders.

4. William Todd, *The Seventy-ninth Highlanders New York Volunteers in the War of the Rebellion* (Albany, NY: Brandow, Barton and Co., 1886), 34; Hennessey, *The First Battle of Manassas*, 61-2.

Map 18

1. Hennessey, *The First Battle of Manassas*, 63-64; Joseph E. Johnston, "Responsibilities of First Bull Run." *Battles and Leaders of the Civil War*, vol. 1, 247. Although outranked, Beauregard convinced Johnston to assume overall command of the two forces while he controlled the units on the battlefield. Beauregard, "First Battle of Bull Run," 202, 226. Beauregard's orders were often contradictory and confusing on July 21.

2. John Coxe, "The Battle of First Manassas," *Confederate Veteran*, vol. 23, 25; Hennessey, *The First Battle of Manassas*, 65-66; John Reed's Journal; Persons, "7th Georgia at First Manassas," 13. It is unclear who was ordering Hampton around the field. Neither Johnston nor Beauregard had arrived on the scene, and Bee was too preoccupied on Matthews Hill to know that Hampton had even arrived. Hampton's Legion was a mixed unit made up of infantry, cavalry, and artillery that Hampton financed and formed himself. Regarding the Federal artillery: Documentation supports Griffin's advance 200 yards down the hill from his first position after Imboden's withdrawal, but Ricketts does not seem to have advanced until ordered to Henry Hill around 1:30 p.m.

3. OR 2, 394; Murray, *The Greatest Battle of the Age*, 65, 66; Hennessey, *The First Battle of Manassas*, 66.

Map 19

1. OR 2, 388-89; Captain James Conner to mother, July 25, 1861, copy in the Hampton Legion folder, MNMP; Hennessey, *The First Battle of Manassas*, 66-67; McDonald, *We Shall Meet Again*, 78; Murray, *The Greatest Battle of the Age*, 70-71; C. B. Fairchild, *History of the 27th Regiment NY Vols.* (Binghamton, NY: n.p., 1888), 12-13.

2. *JCCW*, 214-15; John D. Imboden, "Incidents of the First Bull Run," *Battles and Leaders of the Civil War* (New York: Thomas Yoseloff, 1956), vol. 1, 233-34; Coxe, "The Battle of First Manassas," 26; *JCCW*, 215. The newly arriving Southern artillery would have to

have been Imboden's three remaining guns returning to the field along with two guns of the Thomas Artillery deploying with Jackson's brigade.

Lieutenant Colonel E. B. Fowler of the 14th Brooklyn wrote about this part of the engagement: "When we arrived opposite the woods on the right side of that road [Warrenton Turnpike] we received a severe and continued fire of musketry from a force in ambush in the woods, whom we could not see. Our men returned partially the fire and retired behind the fence and reformed." (*Brooklyn Eagle*, March 17, 1901).

3. Hennessey, *The First Battle of Manassas*, 68; James Conner to mother, July 24, 1861; Coxe, "The Battle of First Manassas," 26. One South Carolina private wrote of the retreat, "By this time we didn't care much as to what happened . . . our throats were choked with powder, and we were burning up with thirst." Coxe, "The Battle of First Manassas," 26.

Map 20

1. Hennessey, *The First Battle of Manassas*, 69-70; "John Newton Lyle, 4th Virginia," copy in the 4th Virginia folder, MNMP; Imboden, "Incidents of the First Bull Run," 233-34; Robertson, *Stonewall Jackson*, 260. As Jackson's men emerged from the woods ringing Henry Hill, they immediately were engulfed by the remnants of Bee's and Bartow's commands. One of Imboden's cannon had to be left behind when a Federal shell broke its axle.

2. Robertson, *Stonewall Jackson*, 262.

3. OR 2, 481; Robertson, Stonewall Jackson, 262; R. M. Johnston, *Bull Run: Its Strategy and Tactics* (Boston: Houghton, Mifflin, and Co., 1913), 206. The arriving Southern guns included (eventually) two guns from the Loudoun Artillery, five guns from the Washington Artillery, and four of the Wise Artillery under Lt. Pelham. According to Jim Burgess, Museum Specialist at Manassas National Battlefield Park, four guns of the Rockbridge Artillery (Pendleton) arrived after Imboden withdrew his three pieces, and after the guns of the Washington Artillery and Loudoun Artillery had arrived. Although the Confederates had easy access to twenty cannon, it seems likely that no more than thirteen were in position at any given time on Henry Hill because of the difficulty finding space along the line. David Detzer, *Donnybrook: The Battle of Bull Run, 1861* (Harcourt, 2004), 336.

Jackson's men lay at the edge of the woods for almost three hours awaiting the renewed Federal push, much of the time trying hard not to be hit by the ever-present Federal artillery shells. The 4th Virginia lost about twenty-seven men during this period. Robertson, *Stonewall Jackson*, 262-63.

4. Hennessey, *The First Battle of Manassas*, 71; Brezeale, *First Battle of Manassas*, 7.

When Johnston encountered General Bee, the latter had tears rolling down his face as he exclaimed, "My command is scattered and I am alone." Johnston quickly consoled his subordinate and told him. "The day is not lost yet." Symonds, Craig L. *Joseph E. Johnston* (New York: W. W. Norton and Co., 1994), 119-20.

Map 21

1. *JCCW*, 214. Rafuse, in *A Single Grand Victory*, 144, hypothesized that McDowell waited two hours to launch his attack on Henry Hill because he wanted to await reinforcements, was reluctant to cause a Southern bloodbath (which could prevent the South from capitulating after the battle), and was mentally and physically exhausted from the morning's excitement.

2. *OR* 2, 346, 349, 353. The forward movement by Captain Reynolds was not coordinated with Keyes' advance. It is also important to keep in mind that Tyler and Keyes never joined forces and at this point were operating independently of all other Union troops on the field.

3. Hennessey, *The First Battle of Manassas*, 74-5; *OR* 2, 353, 566-67; "The Fifth Virginia Regiment in the Battle of Manassas," *Richmond Dispatch*, August 16, 1861; William H. Shaw "Account of First Bull Run" (Connecticut Historical Society). Note that the balance of Evans', Bee's, and Bartow's commands were too scattered at this point to be effective.

According to his report, Colonel Kenton Harper's 5th Virginia was to hold its ground until the enemy appeared at the brow of the hill, about fifty yards away from his line. Only then was he to open fire. However, the front was clogged with the survivors of Bee's, Bartow's, and Evans' brigades, so he advanced his regiment, only to return again to his designated position. He advanced a second time, but this time encountered Keyes' men, and "after a brief contest I again retired to my first position, and subsequently fell back through the skirt of woods in my rear." Report of 5th Virginia (copy in the 5th Virginia folder, MNMP).

4. *OR* 2, 353; Imboden, "Incidents of the First Bull Run," 238; B. F. Smart to father, July 23, 1861, copy in the 2nd Maine folder, MNMP.

After retreating to the base of Henry Hill, Abiather Knowles and Henry Wheeler trekked back up the hill to bring down several of their wounded comrades. For this act they were later awarded the Medal of Honor. Rafuse, *A Single Grand Victory*, 154.

It is unlikely a musket ball struck Jackson because there were no Union troops within range at that time. According to Captain Imboden, Jackson's wound became infected after the battle.

Map 22

1. *JCCW*, 149, 168, 172; *OR* 2, 347; Hennessey, *The First Battle of Manassas*, 77-78; Lewis Metcalf, "So Eager Were We All," *American Heritage*, June 1965, 37. Ricketts' guns sliced through the 1st Minnesota during its trek to Henry Hill. This split off two companies to the right that fought the rest of the battle independent of the regiment. Richard Moe, *The Last Full Measure* (New York: Henry Holt & Company, 1993), 48.

Griffin knew the Zouaves would not adequately support his exposed guns. "Yes they will," Barry replied, and "at any rate it is General McDowell's order to go there." "I will go," Griffin responded, "but mark my words, they will not support us." *JCCW*, PP. 168-169. Griffin's and Ricketts' rifled cannon easily reached the Confederate artillery deployed on Henry Hill. The same was not true for the latter, as their smooth-bores could not find the Federal range. They were effective against the closer enemy infantry, however.

The 11th New York, *OR* the "Fire Zouaves," was a very colorful unit. Most of the men stripped off their jackets as they prepared for action, exposing their red blouses. It was also a large unit, exceeding 1,000 in size, but it was not in a condition to effectively fight. This can be seen in the following portion of a letter written by a member of the unit: "The fact is that we were whipped before we reached the field, after so long a march, without anything to eat, and nothing to drink but water so thick that it would scarcely drop [from puddles], you may believe that we were not in a very good condition to fight." R. L. Murray, *They Fought Like Tigers* (Walcott, NY: Benedum Books, 2005), 57, 59.

2. *JCCW*, 169, 219, 243.

3. *JCCW*, 143, 216, 219, 243; George W. Baylor, *Bull Run to Bull Run or Four Years in the Army of Northern Virginia* (Washington DC: Zenger Publishing Co., 1900), 20. The cannon fire of Ricketts' and Griffin's eleven guns terrified Jackson's men. Jackson merely rode along the line,

oblivious to his personal safety. When Captain Imboden later asked how he remained so calm under these harsh conditions, Jackson replied, "My religious belief teaches me to feel as safe in battle as in bed. God has fixed the time for my death." Imboden, "Incidents of the First Bull Run," 234.

4. Hennessey, *The First Battle of Manassas*, 80-81; *JCCW*, 216; OR 2, 392, 408, 483; Murray, *They Fought Like Tigers*, 60-61, 70. Colonel Willcox's full quote about the 11th New York was: "The ground was slightly rising before us, and the enemy opened a heavy but not destructive fire as we reached the crest. The zouaves returned the fire, but immediately fell back, bewildered and broken." OR 2, 408.

The commander of the Marines, Major John G. Reynolds, tried to explain the behavior of his men this way: "The battalion . . . took a position indicated by the general [McDowell], but was unable to hold it, owing to the heavy fire which was opened upon them. They broke three several [sic] times, but as frequently formed, and urged back to their position, where finally a general rout took place, in which the marines participated." OR 2, 392.

5. OR 2, 405, 483; Hennessey, *The First Battle of Manassas*, 81. The 11th New York had been formerly commanded by Colonel Elmer Farnsworth, who attracted national attention when he was killed hauling down a Confederate flag in Alexandria.

According to R. L. Murray, only two companies on the right of the 11th New York were in the process of retreating when charged by Stuart's horsemen. According to the Federal perspective, they repulsed Stuart with heavy losses, which was not true. Murray, *They Fought Like Tigers*, 61-65. Murray suggested that defeat was all but certain, given the condition of the men, their inexperience, and noted the regiment's large size made it almost unmanageable. Consider: the average Federal regiment at Gettysburg numbered 330 men; the 11th New York at First Bull Run had about 1,100 men in the ranks. Murray, *They Fought Like Tigers*, 67.

Map 23

1. OR 2, 475, 552, 561; Hennessey, *The First Battle of Manassas*, 83.
See Hennessey, *The First Battle of Manassas*, 152, for an analysis of the four eye-witness accounts of Bee's remarks.

2. Hennessey, *The First Battle of Manassas*, 83; OR 2, 414; Lowell Reidenbaugh, *27th Virginia* (Lynchburg, VA: H. E. Howard, Inc., 1993), 14. According to Lieutenant E. B. Fowler of the 14th Brooklyn, "A mounted officer from Griffin's battery then appealed to us to protect that battery, saying that if we did not give them our aid the battery would be lost. We then formed in rear of the battery." *Brooklyn Eagle*, March 17, 1901.

3. *JCCW*, 219, 220; OR 2, 394.

4. OR 2, 552; Lowell Reidenbaugh, *33rd Virginia* (Lynchburg, VA: H. E. Howard, Inc., 1987), 8. The first attack on Griffin's two isolated guns is confusing and there is much debate about the identity of the attackers. John Hennessey, *The First Battle of Manassas*, 84-85, Ethan Rafuse, *A Single Grand Victory*, 166-67, and others believe that three companies of 49th Virginia, a company of Nathan Evans' 4th South Carolina, and two more companies from the 11th Mississippi of Barnard Bee's brigade joined in the attack. However, Park Museum Specialist James Burgess and Detzer, in *Donnybrook*, 368-369, believe only the 33rd Virginia made the first charge, and were joined a short time later by the other units. I subscribe to the latter view, and the main text reflects that point.

5. *JCCW*, 143-5, 169.

6. *JCCW*, 243; OR 2, 552; Fry, "McDowell's Advance to Bull Run," 189; Rafuse, *A Single Grand Victory*, 166; "Diary of a Soldier of the Stonewall Brigade," *Shenandoah Herald*, January 8, 1909; Hennessey, *The First Battle of Manassas*, 84-85.

Map 24

1. *Brooklyn Eagle*, March 17, 1906; *JCCW*, 147; *Richmond Times Dispatch*, June 4, 1905; George Baylor, *Bull Run to Bull Run*, 22; James I. Robertson, *The Stonewall Brigade* (Baton Rouge, LA: LSU Press, 1963), 41.

2. Hennessey, *The First Battle of Manassas*, 97; OR 2, 482; *Brooklyn Daily Eagle*, July 31, 1861; Dennis E. Frye, *Second Virginia* (Lynchburg, VA: H. E. Howard, Inc., 1984), 15.

3. OR 2, 552.

4. Detzer, *Donnybrook*, p. 384.

Map 25

1. *Brooklyn Eagle*, March 17, 1906; Hennessey, *The First Battle of Manassas*, 97; John A. Wells, "14th Brooklyn Militia Chasseurs at Bull Run, July 21, 1861" (copy in the 14th Brooklyn folder, MNMP); Lyle, 4th Virginia. James Wadsworth was a volunteer on McDowell's staff. He would rise to

division command and die in the Wilderness fighting in May 1864. Sifakis, *Who Was Who in the Civil War* (New York: Facts on File, 1988), 681-2.

2. Hennessey, *The First Battle of Manassas*, 97-8; McDonald, *We Shall Meet Again*, 113; *Brooklyn Eagle*, March 17, 1906; J. B. Caddall, "The Pulaski Guards, Company C, 4th Virginia Infantry at the First Battle of Manassas, July 21, 1861." *SHSP*, vol. XXXII, 176.

3. *OR* 2, 552; William Smith, "Reminiscences of the First Battle of Manassas," *SHSP*, Vol. X, 439-40; Clark, *NC Regiments*, vol. 1, 294, 344; vol. 5, 582.

Map 26

1. John Warwick Daniel, "A Charge at First Manassas," *SHSP*, Vol. 39 (1914), 345; "The Liberty Hall Volunteers at First Manassas." Rockbridge County News, February 2, 1911. A section of Reynolds' battery under Lt. J. Albert Monroe dropped trail behind to open fire on the Virginians and South Carolinians arrayed near the Henry house, but Monroe wrote that his arrival on Henry Hill coincided with the loss of Ricketts and Griffin's guns and that he quickly evacuated that position without firing a shot.

2. Walter Clark, ed., *Histories of Several Regiments and Battalions from North Carolina* (Wilmington, NC: Broadfoot Publishing Company, 1991), vol. 1, 344-45, vol. 5, 583-84. Hereafter, *NC Regiments*; Hennessey, *The First Battle of Manassas*, 98-99; Moe, *The Last Full Measure*, 50-51. Colonel Fisher purportedly fell at the approximate location of the flagpole in front of the current visitor center (Hennessey, *The First Battle of Manassas*, 153), but a walk on the field does not seem to support this conclusion. Red shirts worn by the 11th New York and 1st Minnesota could explain why members of the 6th North Carolina, if they received fire from either Federal unit, believed it was coming from the similarly attired 4th Alabama.

A note on "Zouaves" at First Bull Run: There is a lot of confusion in Confederate reports when they reference "Zouaves." The 11th New York were Zouaves, but were not dressed like Zouaves; the 14th were not Zouaves, though one might describe their uniforms as Zouave—even though they were in fact chasseur uniforms. The fact that both units fought in the same area doesn't help clarify matters. Further complicating things is the fact that the 11th New York and 1st Minnesota both wore red shirts, as did parts of the 4th Alabama. In a word, sorting it

all out is difficult and will likely never be fully understood.

3. *OR* 2, 411-2.

Map 27

1. *OR* 2, 409, 412; Lowell Reidenbaugh, *27th Virginia*, 16. An old marker on the battlefield behind Ricketts' guns suggests that the 7th Georgia did assist in defending the pieces.

2. C. A. Fonerden, *A Brief History of the Military Career of Carpenter's Battery* (New Market, VA: Henkel and Co., 1911), 12-13.

3. Hennessey, *The First Battle of Manassas*, 100; Alfred S. Roe, *The Fifth Regiment, Massachusetts Volunteer Infantry in its Three Years of Duty* (Boston: Fifth Regiment Volunteers Association, 1911), 81; *OR* 2, 406.

Map 28

1. Roe, *The Fifth Regiment Massachusetts*, 81-82; Henry N. Blake, *Three Years in the Army of the Potomac* (Boston: Lee and Shepard, 1865), 21; *OR* 2, 406, 482.

2. *OR* 2, 406.

3. *OR* 2, 494; James Conner to mother, July 24, 1861; Hennessey, *The First Battle of Manassas*, 101; John N. Opie, *A Rebel Cavalryman with Lee, Stuart, and Jackson* (Chicago: W. B. Conkey, 1899), 32; Gustavus B Hutchinson, *A Narrative of the Formation and Services of the Eleventh Massachusetts Volunteers, from April 15, 1861, to July 14, 1865* (Boston: Alfred Mudge and Son, 1893), 24. As the 5th Virginia reached the guns, its lieutenant colonel, William Harmon, recognized Captain Ricketts lying alongside of one of them. Rushing up to him, he asked, "Why, Ricketts is this you?" The two men, who had fought together in the Mexican War, shook hands, and then Harmon had to leave as he had unwounded Yankees to fight. McDonald, *We Shall Meet Again*, 127-28.

Map 29

1. *Savannah Republican*, August 1, 1861; Hennessey, *The First Battle of Manassas*, 101; Imboden, "Incidents of the First Bull Run," 237; *Brooklyn Eagle*, March 17, 1906; Jack D. Welsh, *Medical Histories of Confederate Generals* (Kent, OH: Kent State University Press, 1995), 20; Lowe, "Written in 1861," 15; Richard Watson York, "The 'Old Third' Brigade, and the Death of General Bee" *Our Living and Our Dead*, vol. xx, 561-5. Colonel Kenton Harper's report of his 5th Virginia

states: "At this junction a considerable number of our troops of different commands had rallied on my left and formed perpendicularly to my line who were seemingly inactive. I dispatched my adjutant to inform them of my purpose and invite their co-operation which was promptly given." These were the men of the 4th Alabama, 7th Georgia, and 2nd Mississippi. Report of 5th Virginia (copy in the 5th Virginia folder, MNMP).

According to McDonald, Bee may only have had twenty men with him as he advanced against the massed enemy in his front. McDonald, *We Shall Meet Again*, 128. All of the Confederate artillery on Henry Hill was withdrawing at this time. There were other versions of Bee's last words, but all seemed to differ in their final phrase. The exact time of Bee's mortal wounding is in dispute.

Bartow's horse was shot, throwing him to the ground. Seeing the 7th Georgia's flagbearer fall, Bartow rushed over, picked up the flag and led his Georgians forward and was mortally wounded as he yelled, "On my boys, we will die rather than yield or retreat." William B. Styple, ed., *Writing and Fighting the Confederate War* (Kearney, NJ: Belle Grove Publishing Company, 2002), 22, 36-37.

2. Hennessey, *The First Battle of Manassas*, 102.

3. Charles C. Brown to sister, July 29, 1861 (copy in the 13th New York folder, Manassas Military Park); Hennessey, *The First Battle of Manassas*, 102-03.

Map 30

1. George Otis, *The Second Wisconsin Infantry* (Dayton, OH: Morningside Publishing, 1984), 35; Murray, *They Fought Like Tigers*, 80; OR 2, 369-70; Rafuse, *A Single Grand Victory*, 176-7; Hennessey, *The First Battle of Manassas*, 102; Roe, *The Fifth Regiment Massachusetts*, 81-82; OR 2, 369-70. The left wing, composed of four companies, took on the Hampton Legion; the right wing battled the 5th Virginia.

2. William Todd, *The Seventy-Ninth Highlanders: New York Volunteers in the War of Rebellion, 1861-1865* (Albany: Press of Brandow, Barton and Co., 1886), 37-38; Terry A. Johnston, Jr., *Him on the One Side and Me on the Other* (Columbia, SC: University of South Carolina Press, 1999), 32-33.OR 2, 70; Hennessey, *The First Battle of Manassas*, 103-4; Rafuse, *A Single Grand Victory*, 177-8. Detzer, *Donnybrook*, p. 384; Cudworth,

First Regiment, 42; Davis, *The Battle at Bull Run*, 218.

Map 31

1. OR 2, 414, 547; J. Albert Monroe, "The Rhode Island Artillery at the First Battle of Bull Run." *Personal Narratives of Rhode Island Soldiers and Sailors Historical Society*, No. 2 (1878), 21.

2. OR 2, 414; Murray, *The Greatest Battle of the Age*, 101; D. P. Conyngham, *The Irish Brigade and its Campaigns* (Boston: Patrick Donahoe, 1869), 43; McDonald, *We Shall Meet Again*, 144.

Anti-Irish sentiment raged through the country and army at this time. In his report, Captain James Kelly of the 69th New York wrote bitterly: "The Sixty ninth had good reason to complain that whilst regiments of other divisions were permitted to have baggage and provision wagons immediately in the rear, the regiment I have the honor to command was peremptorily denied any facilities of the sort. The consequence was that the Sixty-ninth arrived on the field of action greatly fatigued and harassed, and but for their high sense of duty and military spirit would not have been adequate to the terrible duties of the day." OR 2, 371-2.

3. OR 2, 545, 547; McDonald, *We Shall Meet Again*, 144.

Map 32

1. Rafuse, *A Single Grand Victory*, 180.

2. OR 2, 546-47, 567; James I. Robertson, *18th Virginia Infantry* (Lynchburg: H. E. Howard, Inc., 1984), 6.

3. Robert E. Withers, *Autobiography of an Octogenarian* (Roanoke, VA: Stone Printing, 1907), 149; Josias R. King, "The Battle of Bull Run: A Confederate Victory Obtained but Not Achieved." *Glimpses of the Nation's Struggle*, vol. 6 (Minneapolis: Aug. Davis, Publisher), 506.

According to Captain James Conner, Hampton's Legion was involved in this charge. "[We] then charged up the hill, and drove the Yankees out of the house and garden [Henry's]. . . . Advancing, and leaving the house behind us, we kept forcing them back. They broke and scattered as Kershaw"s regiment came up." James Conner to mother, July 24, 1861.

4. OR 2, 414, 547-48; *New York Times*, July 26, 1861; *Brooklyn Eagle*, March 17, 1901; Hennessey, *The First Battle of Manassas*, 110; Davis, *Battle at Bull Run*, 226.

5. Hennessey, *The First Battle of Manassas*, 109; OR 2, 332, 747.

Map 33

1. OR 2, 418, 423; Oliver O. Howard, *Autobiography of Oliver Otis Howard* (New York: The Baker and Taylor Co., 1908), vol. 1, 158; Paul Zeller, *The Second Vermont Volunteer Infantry Regiment, 1861-1865* (Jefferson, NC: McFarland Press, 2002), 29. The poker analogy is particularly apt in describing Schenck, since he wrote (literally) the book on draw poker: *The Game Of Draw Poker* (1889).

2. OR 2, 522-23, 530-31. Smith assumed command at Piedmont. The time of the brigade's arrival on the battlefield is uncertain. Detzer, in his recent book *Donnybrook*, 395, has it reaching the Lewis (Portici) house about 3:45 p.m., while the reports of Joe Johnston and P. G. T. Beauregard (OR 2, 476, 496) place its arrival at 3:00 p.m.

3. McHenry Howard, *Recollections of a Maryland Confederate Soldier* (Baltimore: Williams and Wilkins Company, 1914), 36, 38; Terrence V. Murphy, *10th Virginia* (Lynchburg, VA: H. E. Howard, Inc., 1989), 8. The arrival of Elzey's and Early's brigades caused Beauregard some anxiety as he did not initially know the identity of the troops kicking up the clouds of dust in the Confederate rear. He feared that they were Federal troops and the day could be lost.

According to George Booth, "Colonel Elzey much resented the command of the brigade passing to General Smith." George Wilson Booth, *A Maryland Boy in Lee's Army* (Lincoln, NE: University of Nebraska Press, 2000), 15.

4. Howard, *Autobiography of Oliver Otis Howard*, vol. 1, 159; George W. Bicknell, *History of the Fifth Regiment Maine Volunteers* (Portland, ME: Hall L. Davis, 1871), 30; Rafuse, *A Single Grand Victory*, 186-87. According to a soldier the men in the 1st Maryland "blazed out in a succession of volleys, of a character so destructive as to throw the foe in our front into disorder then retreat." Another noted, "And as one man belched forth the leaden messengers of death—The Column of our enemy stunned by the blow, reeled, and staggered like a drunken man." Booth, *A Maryland Boy in Lee's Army*, 16-17; Robert J. Driver, *The First and Second Maryland Infantry, C.S.A.* (Willow Bend Books, 2003), 27.

5. Hennessey, *The First Battle of Manassas*, 113; Howard, *Autobiography of Oliver Otis Howard*, vol. 1, 159.

Map 34

1. Bicknell, *History of the Fifth Regiment Maine*, 30-31; Gerald S. Henig, ed., "Give My Love to All; The Civil War Letters of George S. Rollins,"*Civil War Times Illustrated* (November, 1972), 24; Zeller, *The Second Vermont Volunteer Infantry Regiment*, 32-33.

2. Hennessey, *The First Battle of Manassas*, 114-15.

3. Howard, *Recollections of a Maryland Confederate Soldier*, 38-39; Murphy, *Tenth Virginia*, 9.

4. Henig, "Give My Love to All; The Civil War Letters of George S. Rollins," 24; Bicknell, *History of the Fifth Regiment Maine*, 31.

5. Bearss, *First Manassas Map Study*, 89, 92.

6. Hennessey, *The First Battle of Manassas*, 115-16; Fry, *McDowell's Advance to Bull Run*, vol. 1, 191.

Map 35

1. OR 2, 374.

2. OR 2, 374, 429. Davies' men broke camp at about 2:30 that morning.

3. OR 2, 518, 521, 543; Bearss, *First Manassas Battlefield Map Study*, 10.

4. OR 2, 374, 429. Dixon Miles was relieved of command by General McDowell during the retreat after Colonel Israel Richardson accused Miles of being drunk. A court of inquiry confirmed the accusation.

5. OR 2, 522, 530, 535.

6. OR 2, 430, 537-38, 540, 541, 542; Col. W. S. Nye, "Action North of Bull Run," *Civil War Times Illustrated*, vol. IV (April 1965), 48-49; George A. Gibbs, "With a Mississippi Private in a Little Known Part of the Battle of First Bull Run and at Ball's Bluff," *Civil War Times Illustrated*, vol. IV (April 1965), 44-5.

Map 36

1. Todd, *The Seventy-ninth Highlanders New York Volunteers*, 42; OR 2, 390, 416; Howard, *Autobiography of Oliver Otis Howard*, 162; James B. Fry, *McDowell and Tyler in the Campaign of Bull Run* (New York: Van Nostrand, 1884), 191; George J. Hundley, "Reminiscences of the First and Last Days of the War," *SHSP*, vol. 23, 304.

2. OR 2, 483, 551; Early, *Autobiographical Sketch*, 26. Note that Sykes' was one of three reports of squares formed by Union troops that afternoon. The other two were the 69th NY during the retreat, and the 12th New York of Israel Richardson's brigade.

3. Hennessey, *The First Battle of Manassas*, 118; Alfred Ely, *The Journal of Alfred Ely, A Prisoner of War in Richmond* (New York: D. Appleton and Company, 1862), 16. Hennessey, *The First Battle of Manassas*, 156.

4. Peter C. Haines, "The First Gun at Bull Run." *Cosmopolitan Magazine*, vol. 51 (1911), 396; *OR* 2, 534; Beauregard, "The First Battle of Bull Run," 215; *OR* 2, 543-4.

5. *JCCW*, 24-28; *OR* 2, 375-76.

First Bull Run (Manassas) Summation

1. *OR* 2, 327, 328, 477.

2. Hennessey, *The First Battle of Manassas*, 124-26, 156; McDonald, *We Shall Meet Again*, 176-78. Donald G. Mitchell, *Daniel Tyler: A Memorial Volume Containing His Autobiography and War Record* (New Haven: Tuttle, Morehouse, and Taylor: 1883), 62-3; *OR* 2, 321; Rafuse, *A Single Grand Victory*, 196-8.

3. McDonald, *We Shall Meet Again*, 176-78; Stewart Sifakis, *Who Was Who In the Civil War*, 414-15; *OR* 2, 438-39.

4. Styple, ed., *Writing and Fighting from the Army of Northern Virginia*, 29, 36-37. McPherson died of his wounds a year later, after he fought in the Second Battle of Manassas.

August/September 1861

Map 37

1. Beatie, *Birth of Command*, 356-7; J. Harrison Mills, *Chronicles of the Twenty-First Regiment of New York State Volunteers* (Buffalo: 21st reg't Veteran Association of Buffalo, 1887), 93-5.

2. *OR* 2, 753, 754-5; Beatie, *Birth of Command*, 357-8.

3. Freeman, *Lee's Lieutenants*, vol. 1, 77-80.

4. *OR* 2, 753; Beatie, *Birth of Command*, 360-62.

Map 38

1. Wert, *The Sword of Lincoln*, 32-37.

2. *OR* 5, 32.

3. *OR* 5, 881; Russel H. Beatie. *Army of the Potomac: McClellan Takes Command* (New York: DaCapo, 2004), 29. Map after Beatie, *Army of the Potomac: McClellan Takes Command*, 29.

4. *OR* 5, 15-17; Beatie, *Army of the Potomac: McClellan Takes Command*, 177-189.

5. *OR* 5, 909, 913-4.

Map 39

1. Bradley M. Gottfried, Bradley M., "Baldy's 'Excursions.'" *Civil War Times Illustrated*, volume XL, 4 (August 2001), 49; *OR* 5, 169. Map after Beatie, *Army of the Potomac: McClellan Takes Command*, 6.

2. One of Griffin's guns was placed on the west side of the road leading to Leesburg Pike to the north; a second along the road leading from Vienna; a third along the road leading to Falls Church; a fourth was held in reserve. *OR* 5, 169-70.

3. *OR* 5, 183.

4. *OR* 5, 173, 183.

5. *OR* 5, 171.

6. *OR* 5, 168, 171.

7. *OR* 5, 168.

Ball's Bluff

Map 40

1. Beatie, *Army of the Potomac: McClellan Takes Command*, 11.

2. Beatie, *Army of the Potomac: McClellan Takes Command*, 44.

3. *OR* 5, 50, George B. McClellan, "The Peninsular Campaign" *Battles and Leaders of the Civil War*, vol. 2, 161; Beatie, *Birth of Command*, 469-481. Stone's division was called a "Corps of Observation" because of its critical role in watching for a Confederate incursion from the direction of Leesburg.

On August 18, 1861, McClellan telegrammed, "General Banks today confirms the belief that the enemy intends crossing the Potomac in your vicinity and moving on to Baltimore or Washington." Stone knew better, noting that only two Mississippi regiments were across the river, but he would accept additional men if McClellan wanted to send them. *OR* 5, 567-8.

4. *OR* 5, 347.

5. George McClellan, *McClellan's Own Story: The War for the Unions* (New York: Easton Press, 1886), 181; Beatie, *Army of the Potomac: McClellan Takes Command*, 43; *JCCW*, 508.

6. *OR* 5, 290; William F. Howard, *The Battle of Ball's Bluff* (Lynchburg: H. E. Howard, Inc., 1994), 6, 9.

Map 41

1. James A. Morgan, *A Little Short of Boats: The Fights at Ball's Bluff and Edwards Ferry* (Cincinnati: Ironclad Publishing, 2004), 26-7; *OR* 5, 349.

2. *JCCW*, 448; *OR* 5, 290, 293; Moe, *The Last Full Measure*, 86; Morgan, *A Little Short of Boats*, 29. Stone retained the 42nd New York and the 15th Massachusetts until Philbrick's men returned from their scouting mission (*OR* 5, 293).

3. *JCCW*, 277, 403; *OR* 5, 293-4; Morgan, *A Little Short of Boats*, 29-34. Stone wanted the expedition to depart immediately, but Colonel Devens could not be found. He was apparently at a church service. Stone probably knew the bluff was a safe place to land, as he had been sending reconnaissance parties into this region for several weeks. Howard, *The Battle of Ball's Bluff*, 10, 12.

4. Kim Bernard Holien, *Battle at Ball's Bluff* (Alexandria, VA: Rapidan Press, 1985), 27; *OR* 5, 294, 308, 318, 349; Morgan, *A Little Short of Boats*, 36.

Map 42

1. *OR* 5, 308-9; Howard, *The Battle of Ball's Bluff*, 13, 16. *JCCW*, 405.

2. *OR* 5, 294-5, 335; Morgan, *A Little Short of Boats*, 45-46. A member of the 1st Minnesota recalled the action somewhat differently: the regiment was roused from his camp at 1:30 a.m. on October 21 and marched to Edward's Ferry, accompanied by the 82nd New York. At daybreak, the entire regiment crossed the Potomac, but only two companies were thrown forward with Mix's cavalry. R. I. Holcombe, *History of the First Regiment Minnesota Volunteer Infantry, 1861-1865* (Stillwater: Easton & Masterson, 1916), 75-6. Major Mix claimed that members of the 18th Mississippi fired on his men. *OR* 5, 33.

3. *OR* 5, 309, 363-4. Although Devens' after-battle reported that initial contact was made at 7:00 a.m., he later determined it to be closer to 8:00 a.m. Duff's men had superior arms than Devens' soldiers—rifled muskets accurate at many hundreds of yards, while the Federals sported ancient smoothbore Austrian muskets, which were awkward to handle and accurate only during close-in fighting. Morgan, *A Little Short of Boats*, 50-51; Holien, *Battle at Ball's Bluff*, 31.

Map 43

1. *OR* 5, 309; Holien, *Battle at Ball's Bluff*, 33-4; Howard, *The Battle of Ball's Bluff*, 23.

2. *OR* 5, 303; Bradley M. Gottfried, *Stopping Pickett: The History of the Philadelphia Brigade*

(Shippensburg: White Mane Publishing Co., 1999), 2. Evans' Brigade served as a small outpost guarding the Southern left flank. It was tasked with watching the fords and ferries over the Potomac, lest the Yanks make a quick dash toward Richmond (Howard, *The Battle of Ball's Bluff*, 3).

3. *OR* 5, 349.

4. *OR* 5, 310, 349, 368-9. According to Evans' report, he determined the need to reinforce his small force with the 8th Virginia. However, the author of the 8th Virginia history indicated that Jenifer had requested the additional troops. Jenifer's report is silent on this issue. *OR* 5, 343, 369; John Divine, *8th Virginia* (Lynchburg: H. E. Howard, 1983), 4.

5. *OR* 5, 367, 369.

Map 44

1. The 8th Virginia was so small because many of its men were ill and a company had been detached. *OR* 5, 367.

2. Devine, *8th Virginia Infantry*, 4; Andrew E. Ford, *The Story of the Fifteenth Regiment Massachusetts Volunteer Infantry* (Clinton: W. J. Coulter, 1898), 78-9.

3. *OR* 5, 310; Holien, *Battle at Ball's Bluff*, 48.

4. *OR* 5, 297, 320; Byron Farwell, *Ball's Bluff* (McLean, VA: EPM, 1990), 80-81; Morgan, *A Little Short of Boats*, 94-95; Holien, *Battle at Ball's Bluff*, 48. *JCCW*, 230.

5. Morgan, *A Little Short of Boats*, 100-1. Baker purportedly told Devens, "I congratulate you upon the splendid manner in which your regiment has behaved this morning." *JCCW*, 408.

6. Morgan, *A Little Short of Boats*, 101-2; *JCCW*, 308.

7. *OR* 5, 349, 354, 365. The 13th Mississippi was positioned on the right side of Edward's Ferry Road, and along with one battery, was able to hold Gorman's brigade in check. *OR* 5, 354.

Map 45

1. *JCCW*, 478.

2. *OR* 5, 319; Isaac J. Wistar, *Autobiography of Isaac Jones Wistar* (Philadelphia: Wistar Institute of Anatomy and Biology, 1937), 364-5.

3. *OR* 5, 320; Holien, *Battle at Ball's Bluff*, 55.

4. *OR* 5, 312. The 19th Massachusetts did not cross the river, so it did not participate in the battle.

5. *OR* 5, 349, 365; Holien, *Battle at Ball's Bluff*, 56.

6. Morgan, *A Little Short of Boats*, 104-5. Baker apparently only sent one communication to Stone. He wrote at 1:30 p.m., "I acknowledge your order

of 11:50, announcing their force at 4,000. I have lifted large boat out of the canal onto the river. I shall, as soon as I feel strong enough, advance steadily, guarding my flanks carefully. I will communicate with you often…" *OR* 51, pt. 1, 502.

As an example of the confusion, one of McClellan's messages referred to the town of Darnsville. He meant Darnstown, Maryland, where Banks' division was stationed, but Stone took it to mean Dranesville, Virginia, which he believed to be occupied by McCall's men. This resulted in his continued belief that the latter would help protect Stone's left flank, when in fact McCall's men were already pulling back.

Map 46

1. *OR* 5, 321.
2. Gottfried, *Stopping Pickett*, 32; Isaac J. Wistar, *Autobiography*, 365; Elijah V. White, *History of the Battle of Ball's Bluff* (Leesburg: The Washington Print, nd), 10; R. A. Shotwell, "The Battle of Ball's Bluff," *The Philadelphia Weekly Times*, April 6, 1878. Three months before to the day, Evans had gambled in a similar fashion. Leaving a small force to contain a full Federal division at the Stone Bridge at the First Battle of Manassas, Evans rushed the rest of his men to blunt an enemy movement around his flank.
3. *JCCW*, 79.
4. Morgan, *A Little Short of Boats*, 127-8.
5. Morgan, *A Little Short of Boats*, 130-1; Howard, *The Battle of Ball's Bluff*, 40.

Map 47

1. *OR* 5, 349.
2. White, *History of Ball's Bluff*, 11; Morgan, *A Little Short of Boats*, 132.
3. *OR* 5, 365; Morgan, *A Little Short of Boats*, 133-4.
4. Morgan, *A Little Short of Boats*, 134-5.

Map 48

1. *OR* 5, 365.
2. Lamar Fontaine, *My Life and My Lectures* (New York: Neale Publishing Company, 1908), 84-85; Wistar, *Autobiography*, 365.
3. *OR* 5, 322.
4. *OR* 51, 47-48.
5. *OR* 5, 367; Robert G. Scott, ed. *Fallen Leaves* (Kent: Kent State University Press, 1991), 62.
6. Morgan, *A Little Short of Boats*, 143-4.

7. Gregory Acken, *Inside the Army of the Potomac* (Chambersburg: Stackpole, 1998), 34.

Map 49

1. *OR* 5, 310.
2. White, *History of the Battle of Ball's Bluff*, 14; *OR* 5, 311; Morgan, *A Little Short of Boats*, 152-3. It appears that Lieutenant Wildman may have been drunk, hence his unusual behavior.
3. *OR* 5, 322; *JCCW*, 410.
4. Francis W. Palrey, *Memoir of William Francis Bartlett* (Boston: Houghton, Osgood & Co., 1878), 26; Scott, *Fallen Leaves*, 62-63.

Map 50

1. Morgan, *A Little Short of Boats*, 160-1; Calvin Vance, "My First Battle." *Confederate Veteran* 34 (1926), 139.
2. *OR* 5, 319, 358; *OR* 51, 48; Gottfried, *Stopping Pickett*, 36; Ford, *The Story of the Fifteenth Regiment Massachusetts*, 88-89.
3. Gottfried, *Stopping Pickett*, 36-37; James W. Silver, *A Life for the Confederacy* (Jackson, TN: McCowat-Mercer Press, 1959), 70; Francis W. Palfray, *Memoir of William Francis Bartlett*, 25-26.

Map 51

1. Howard, *The Battle of Ball's Bluff*, 87-88.
2. *OR* 5, 350; Gibbs, "With a Mississippi Private in a Little Known Part of the Battle of First Bull Run and at Ball's Bluff," 47.
3. Morgan, *A Little Short of Boats*, 73.
4. *OR* 51, pt. 1, 502; *JCCW*, 487.
5. *OR* 5, 316-7; vol. 51, pt. 1, 500.
6. *OR* 51, pt. 1, 500; vol. 5, 336-7.
7. *OR* 5, 333, 355; *JCCW*, 497.
8. *OR* 5, 330-2.

Bibliography

Official Documents

U.S. Congress. Joint Committee on the Conduct of the War. Washington, 1863.
U.S. War Department. War of the Rebellion: Official Records of the Union and Confederate Armies. Washington, 1880-1901. 128 Volumes.

Firsthand Accounts and Secondary Sources

Acken, Gregory. *Inside the Army of the Potomac*. Chambersburg: Stackpole Pub. Co., 1998.
Alexander, E. P. "The Battle of Bull Run," *Scribner's Magazine*, vol. XLI (1907), 80-94.
Baylor, George W. *Bull Run to Bull Run or Four Years in the Army of Northern Virginia*. Zenger Pub. Co., 1900.
Bearss, Ed. *First Manassas Battlefield Map Study*. H. E. Howard, Inc., nd.
Beatie, Jr., R. H. *Road to Manassas*. Cooper Square Publishers, 1961.
———. *Army of the Potomac: Birth of Command*. DaCapo, 2002.
———. *Army of the Potomac: McClellan Takes Command*. DaCapo, 2004.
Beauregard, G. T. "First Battle of Bull Run," *Battles and Leaders of the Civil War*. Thomas Yoseloff, 1956, Vol. 1, 196-227.
Bicknell, George W. *History of the Fifth Regiment Maine Volunteers*. Hall L. Davis, 1871.
Blake, Henry N. *Three Years in the Army of the Potomac*. Lee and Shepard, 1865.
Booth, George Wilson. *A Maryland Boy in Lee's Army*. University of Nebraska Press, 2000.
Brezeale, B.B. "Company J, 4th South Carolina Infantry at the First Battle of Manassas." Manassas Journal Pub. Co., 1912.
"Captain V. P. Sisson Tells Vividly of Close Calls." *Atlanta Journal*, February 2, 1901.
Caddall, J. B. "The Pulaski Guards, Company C, 4th Virginia Infantry at the First Battle of Manassas, July 21, 1861." *SHSP*, vol. XXXII (1904), 174-178.
Carter, Robert G. *Four Brothers in Blue Or Sunshine and Shadows of the War of the Rebellion*. University of Texas, 1913.
Chestnut, Mary Boykin. *A Diary from Dixie*. Houghton Mifflin, 1949.
Clark, Walter, ed. *Histories of Several Regiments and Battalions from North Carolina*. 5 vols. Broadfoot Pub. Co., 1991.
Conrad, D. B. "History of the First Battle of Manassas and Organization of the Stonewall Brigade," *Southern Historical Society Papers*, XIX (1891), 82-94.
Conyngham, D. P. *The Irish Brigade and its Campaigns*. Patrick Donahoe, 1869.
Coxe, John. "The Battle of First Manassas," *Confederate Veteran*, vol. 23, 24-26.
Cudworth, Warren H. *History of the First Regiment [Massachusetts] Infantry*. Walker, Fuller, and Co., 1866.
Daniel, John Warwick. "A Charge at First Manassas," *SHSP*, Vol. 39 (1914), 345-46.
Davis, William C. *Battle at Bull Run*. New York: Doubleday, 1977.
Detzer, David, *Donnybrook: The Battle of Bull Run, 1861*. Harcourt, Inc., 2004.
"Diary of a Soldier of the Stonewall Brigade, *Shenandoah Herald,* January 8, 1909.
Divine, John. *8th Virginia*. H. E.Howard, 1983.
Driver, Robert J. *The First and Second Maryland Infantry, C.S.A.* Willow Bend Books, 2003.
Early, Jubal. *Lieutenant General Jubal A. Early*. Lippincott, 1912.
Ely, Alfred. *The Journal of Alfred Ely, A Prisoner of War in Richmond*. D. Appleton and Co., 1862.
Fairchild, B. *History of the 27th Regiment NY Vols*. n.p., 1888.
Farwell, Byron. *Ball's Bluff*. EPM, 1990.
Fonerden, C. A. *A Brief History of the Military Career of Carpenter's Battery*. Henkel and Co., 1911.

Fontaine, Lamar. *My Life and My Lectures.* Neale Pub. Co., 1908.

Ford, Andrew E. *The Story of the Fifteenth Regiment Massachusetts Volunteer Infantry.* W. J. Coulter, 1898.

Fry, James B. *McDowell and Tyler in the Campaign of Bull Run.* Van Nostrand, 1884.

Fry, James B. "McDowell's Advance to Bull Run," *Battles and Leaders of the Civil War.* Thomas Yoseloff, 1956, Vol. 1, 167-93.

Frye, Dennis E. *Second Virginia.* Lynchburg. H. E. Howard, Inc., 1984.

Gibbs, George A. "With a Mississippi Private in a Little Known Part of the Battle of First Bull Run and at Ball's Bluff," *Civil War Times Illustrated*, vol. IV (April 1965), 42-47.

Gottfried, Bradley M. *Stopping Pickett: The History of the Philadelphia Brigade.* White Mane, 1999.

———. "Baldy's 'Excursions.'" *Civil War Times Illustrated,* volume XL, 4 (August 2001), 49-56.

Greenhow, Rose. *My Imprisonment and the First Year of Abolition Rule at Washington.* Bentley, 1863.

Haines, Peter C. "The First Gun at Bull Run." *Cosmopolitan Magazine*, vol. 51 (1911), 388-400.

Haynes, Martin A. *History of the Second Regiment New Hampshire Volunteers.* Charles F. Livingston, Printer, 1865.

Henig, ed., Gerald S. "Give My Love to All; The Civil War Letters of George S. Rollins," *Civil War Times Illustrated* (November 1972), 16-28.

Hennessy, John. *The First Battle of* Manassas. H. E. Howard, 1989.

Holcombe, R. I. *History of the First Regiment Minnesota Volunteer Infantry, 1861-1865.* Easton & Masterson, 1916.

Holien, Kim Bernard. *Battle at Ball's Bluff.* Rapidan Press, 1985.

Howard, McHenry. *Recollections of a Maryland Confederate Soldier.* Williams and Wilkins Co., 1914.

Howard, Oliver O. *Autobiography of Oliver Otis Howard.* The Baker and Taylor Co. 1908.

Howard, William F. *The Battle of Ball's Bluff.* H. E. Howard, Inc., 1994.

Hundley, George J. "Reminiscences of the First and Last Days of the War," *SHSP*, vol. 23, 294-313.

Hutchinson, Gustavus B. *A Narrative of the Formation and Services of the Eleventh Massachusetts Volunteers, from April 15, 1861, to July 14, 1865.* Alfred Mudge and Son, 1893.

Imboden, John D. "Incidents of the First Bull Run," *Battles and Leaders of the Civil War.* Thomas Yoseloff, 1956, vol. 1, 229-39.

Johnston, Terry A., Jr., *Him on the One Side and Me on the Other.* Univ. of South Carolina Press, 1999.

Johnston, J. E. "Responsibilities of First Bull Run." *Battles and Leaders of the Civil War*, vol. 1, 240-60.

———. Narrative of Military Operations, Directed, During the Late War Between the States. D. Appleton and Co., 1874.

Johnston, R. M. *Bull Run: Its Strategy and Tactics.* Houghton, Mifflin, and Co., 1913.

Jones, Terry. *Lee's Tigers.* Louisiana State University Press, 1987.

King, Josias R. "The Battle of Bull Run: A Confederate Victory Obtained but Not Achieved." *Glimpses of the Nation's Struggle*, vol. 6. Davis, Publisher, 497-510.

Loehr, Charles T. *Of the Old First Virginia Infantry Regiment.* Wm. Ellis Jones, 1884.

Longstreet, James. *From Manassas to Appomattox.* Indiana University Press, 1960.

McClellan, George B. "The Peninsular Campaign" *Battles and Leaders of the Civil War*, vol. 2, 160-187.

———. *McClellan's Own Story: The War for the Unions.* Easton Press, 1886.

McDonald, JoAnna M. *We Shall Meet Again.* Oxford University Press, 1999.

Metcalfe, Lewis H. "So Eager Were We All," *American Heritage*, vol. 16 (June 1965), 32-41.

Mills, J. Harrison. *Chronicles of the Twenty-First Regiment of New York State Volunteers*, Buffalo: 21st Reg't Veteran Association of Buffalo, 1887.

Mitchell, Donald G. *Daniel Tyler: A Memorial Volume Containing His Autobiography and War Record.* Tuttle, Morehouse, and Taylor: 1883.

Moe, Richard. *The Last Full Measure.* Henry Holt & Co., 1993.

Monroe, J. Albert. "The Rhode Island Artillery at the First Battle of Bull Run." *Personal Narratives of Rhode Island Soldiers and Sailors Historical Society*, No. 2. Providence: 1878.

Morgan, James A. *A Little Short of Boats: The Fights at Ball's Bluff and Edwards Ferry.* Ironclad Pub., 2004.

Murphy, Terrence V. *10th Virginia.* H. E. Howard, Inc., 1989.

Murray, R. L. *The Greatest Battle of the Age: New Yorkers at First Bull Run.* Benedum Books, 2002.

———. *They Fought Like Tigers.* Benedum Books, 2005.

Nye, W. S. "Action North of Bull Run." *Civil War Times Illustrated,* vol. IV (April 1965), 48-49.

Opie, John N. *A Rebel Cavalryman with Lee, Stuart, and Jackson.* W. B. Conkey, 1899.

Otis, George. *The Second Wisconsin Infantry.* Morningside Pub., 1984.

Palrey, Francis W. *Memoir of William Francis Bartlett.* Houghton, Osgood & Co., 1878.

Patterson, Robert. *A Narrative of the Campaign in the Valley of the Shenandoah in 1861.* Sherman and Co. Printers, 1865.

Rafuse, Ethan S. *A Single Grand Victory.* SR Books, 2002.

Reid, Jesse W. *History of the Fourth Regiment of S. C. Volunteers.* Shannon and Co., 1892.

Reidenbaugh, Lowell. *33rd Virginia.* H. E. Howard, Inc., 1987.

———. *27th Virginia.* H. E. Howard, Inc., 1993.

Rhodes, Robert Hunt. *All For the Union.* Orion Books, 1991.

Robertson, James I. *The Stonewall Brigade.* LSU Press, 1963.

———. *18th Virginia Infantry.* H. E. Howard, Inc., 1984.

———. *Stonewall Jackson.* Macmillan, 1997.

Roe, Alfred S. *The Fifth Regiment Massachusetts Volunteer Infantry in its Three Years of Duty.* Fifth Regiment Veteran Association, 1911.

Roman, Alfred. *The Military Operations of General Beauregard in the War Between the States.* Harper and Brothers, 1884. 2 vols.

Scott, Robert G., ed. *Fallen Leaves.* Kent State University Press, 1991.

Shotwell, R. A. "The Battle of Ball's Bluff," *The Philadelphia Weekly Times,* April 6, 1878.

Sifakis, Stewart, *Who Was Who In the Civil War.* Facts on File, 1988.

Silver, James W. *A Life for the Confederacy.* McCowat-Mercer Press, 1959.

Smith, William. "Reminiscences of the First Battle of Manassas," *SHSP,* Vol. X (1882), 433-44.

Styple, William B. ed. *Writing and Fighting the Confederate War.* Belle Grove Pub. Co., 2002.

———. ed. *Writing and Fighting from the Army of Northern Virginia.* Belle Plain Pub. Co., 2003.

Symonds, Craig L. *Joseph E. Johnston.* W. W. Norton and Co., 1994.

"The Fifth Virginia Regiment in the Battle of Manassas," *Richmond Dispatch,* August 16, 1861.

"The Liberty Hall Volunteers at First Manassas." *Rockbridge County News,* February 2, 1911.

The Reunion of the Palmetto Riflemen. Hoyt & Keys, Printers, 1886.

Todd, William. *The Seventy-ninth Highlanders New York Volunteers in the War of the Rebellion.* Brandow, Barton and Co., 1886.

Vance, Calvin. "My First Battle." *Confederate Veteran* 34 (1926), 139.

Warner, Ezra J. *Generals in Blue.* LSU Press, 1964.

Welsh, Jack D. *Medical Histories of Confederate Generals.* Kent State University Press, 1995.

Wert, Jeffry D. *General James Longstreet.* Simon and Schuster, 1993.

White, Elijah V. *History of the Battle of Ball's Bluff.* The Washington Print, nd.

Wilkinson, Warren and Steven E. Woodworth, *A Scythe of Fire.* Morrow, 2002.

Wistar, Isaac J. *Autobiography of Isaac Jones Wistar.* Wistar Institute of Anatomy and Biology, 1937.

Withers, Robert E. *Autobiography of an Octogenarian.* Stone Printing, 1907.

Woodbury, Augustus. *A Narrative of the Campaign of the First Rhode Island Regiment in the Spring and Summer of 1861.* Knowles, Anthony, and Co. Printers, 1862.

———. *The Second Rhode Island Regiment: A Narrative of Military Operations.* Valpay, Angell, and Co., 1875.

York, Richard Watson. "The 'Old Third' Brigade, and the Death of General Bee" *Our Living and Our Dead,* vol. xx , 561-5.

Zeller, Paul. *The Second Vermont Volunteer Infantry Regiment, 1861-1865.* McFarland Press, 2002.

Zetler, Berrien M. *War Stories and School-Day Incidents for the Children.* Neale Pub. Co., 1912.

Index